LatinX Voices

LatinX Voices: Hispanics in Media in the U.S. is the first undergraduate textbook to provide an overview of Hispanic/LatinX Media in the U.S., with chapters written by top scholars and professionals, giving readers an understanding of how the LatinX audience has transformed media in the United States. Editors Katidia Barbara Coronado and Erica Rodríguez Kight cover this evolving industry with years of professional and research experience, as well as years of teaching broadcast media courses in the classroom. Students will discover unique perspectives on topics related to Latin American areas of interest. With chapters from professionals who have left their mark in print, radio, television, film, and new media, this volume brings together expert voices in Hispanic/LatinX media from across the U.S., and explains the impact of this population on the media industry today.

Katidia Barbara Coronado, M.A., is a journalist and associate instructor of broadcast journalism, radio-television, and Hispanic media. Her area of specialization is in broadcast journalism with a focus on Hispanic media. She currently teaches news writing as well as on-air delivery. As part of her commitment to educating the next generation of journalists, she launched the university's first Spanish-language product, Knightly Latino, which offers students an outlet to cover issues of interest to the Latino community in both English and Spanish.

Erica Rodríguez Kight, Ph.D., teaches courses in journalism, radio-television and Hispanic media at the University of Central Florida Nicholson School of Communication. She is also part of the UCF NSC Hispanic Media Initiative. Kight previously worked as a newspaper reporter, TV news assignment editor, and TV news reporter. As a journalist, she won several awards, including recognitions from Florida Associated Press Broadcasters, the Society of Professional Journalists, and the Florida Emergency Preparedness Association.

LatinX Voices

Hispanics in Media in the U.S.

Edited by
Katidia Barbara Coronado
Erica Rodríguez Kight

 Routledge
Taylor & Francis Group

NEW YORK AND LONDON

First published 2019
by Routledge
711 Third Avenue, New York, NY 10017

and by Routledge
2 Park Square, Milton Park, Abingdon, Oxon, OX14 4RN

Routledge is an imprint of the Taylor & Francis Group, an informa business

© 2019 Taylor & Francis

The right of Katidia Barbara Coronado and Erica Rodríguez Kight, to be identified as the author of the editorial material, and of the authors for their individual chapters, has been asserted in accordance with sections 77 and 78 of the Copyright, Designs and Patents Act 1988.

Library of Congress Cataloging in Publication Data
A catalog record for this book has been requested

ISBN: 978-1-138-24021-6 (hbk)
ISBN: 978-1-138-24030-8 (pbk)
ISBN: 978-1-315-28413-2 (ebk)

Typeset in Bembo
by Florence Production Ltd, Stoodleigh, Devon, UK

Cover image credits:
Background image: ARENA Creative/Shutterstock.com
Top row: Rosa Flores; Courtesy of Univision Network (Jose Zamora); Courtesy of Telemundo Network; Photo Courtesy of Gilda Mirós
Bottom row: Nancy Alvarez; Photo Courtesy of WFTV Channel 9; *Recovering the US Hispanic Literary Heritage*, Arte Publico Press

Contents

Preface

Mr. Rogers, Chespirito, Celia Cruz, and Ropa Vieja.

All of this formed part of my childhood growing up in our humble apartment in Queens, New York, in the 1980s. Media and culture have always held a very important place in my heart, and it is with great pride and appreciation that I am happy to bring some of these experiences that mark our America to future generations.

My mother was born in Camajuani, Cuba, a small town a few hours away from Havana, and my father was born in Guayaquil, Ecuador. In our house, my brother, sister, and I spoke Spanish and watched mostly Spanish-language television. Today, I know that exposure to language and culture is one of the greatest gifts my parents could have given us. It is my hope that this textbook will open doors and hearts as well as provide an understanding of where we are, and more importantly how United States Hispanic/LatinX media continues to evolve and how we can all contribute.

Finally, it would be impossible to include everyone who impacted Hispanic/LatinX media in the U.S., because there are so many exemplary professionals who have left their mark. It is my hope to continue to add to the list of influencers and that we have an opportunity to add infinite names to the future editions of this book.

Cordialmente,

Katidia Barbara Coronado, M.A.

A Labour of Love, Responsibility, and Pride.

Compiling the materials, testimonies, and images for this textbook has been an emotional experience for me. I remember being a little girl in Philadelphia, Pennsylvania, watching children's programming like *The Flintstones*, *Captain Kangaroo*, and *She-Ra Princess of Power*.

I loved She-Ra so much that I dressed up as her two Halloweens in a row (minus the flowing blonde hair).

But there was another character on children's television back in the 1980s that I didn't realize I connected with on a much deeper level until I was an adult. In 2015, at the University of Central Florida in Orlando, Sonia Manzano spoke at our annual Diversity Breakfast. Manzano was 'Maria' on Sesame Street —and, as she addressed the crowd, I suddenly realized how much this woman had impacted my life.

I remembered watching her when I was a little girl and thinking she reminded me of my mom. As a Cuban-American child in the 1980s, I didn't have many characters to look up to on television who looked like me or shared the same culture as me. There were very few positive representations of Latinos on children's programs at the time, and Manzano's character filled that void.

Today, my son has so many more options. He watches *Handy Manny*, *Elena of Avalor*, and even *Mickey Mouse Clubhouse* en español. We're also starting to see a change for the better in films. The 2017 animated film *Coco* was absolutely beautiful and so true to Mexican culture and tradition. I believe this increase in options is a direct result of all the hard work, dedication, and perseverance of all the Hispanic and LatinX people working in media over the years.

Being able to piece together a textbook about so many of the great accomplishments of so many amazing people is truly an honor. We have attempted to cover as many facets of media as possible in this text. Through the process, we discovered that it's impossible to include every individual or every example of Hispanics' contributions to media in the U.S. That is a good problem to have. I hope this text shows that this is just the beginning, we all have so much more work to do, and we have so many more stories to tell— as academics, students, and as media professionals.

Best,

Erica Rodríguez Kight, Ph.D.

Acknowledgments

Developing this textbook from an idea to a reality took several years and hundreds of hours of research and collaboration. We would like to thank all of the contributors who took time to write chapters, share their experiences, and provide important pieces of history, such as newspaper clippings and photographs. This publication would not be possible without their dedication and support. We would also like to thank the following organizations for contributing to this important project: University of Central Florida Nicholson School of Communication, National Association of Hispanic Journalists, National Hispanic Media Coalition, Univision Network, NBC/Universal, Telemundo Network, *La Gaceta*, WFTV Channel 9, and CNN. To our research assistants Kelly Merrill and Sofia Salazar for their work and contributions to this text. To our friends and families, who patiently supported our efforts and absence during this long process. To our parents and grandparents, whose hard work as immigrant families in this country made it possible for us to have this opportunity and a shot at the American dream.

About the Editors

Katidia Barbara Coronado, M.A.

Editor

Katidia Barbara Coronado, M.A., is a journalist and associate instructor of broadcast journalism, radio-television, and Hispanic Media. After working in both English- and Spanish-language media for more than 13 years, NSC appointed her to the position of instructor in 2011. She currently teaches news writing as well as on-air delivery. As part of her commitment to educating the next generation of journalists, she launched the university's first Spanish-language course, Knightly Latino, which offers students an outlet to cover issues of interest to the Latino community in both English and Spanish. She has also helped pave the way with the School's Hispanic Media Initiative, which includes the first Hispanic/Latino Media Certificate to help introduce students to work on air and behind the scenes in a multicultural environment. Coronado is

Katidia Barbara Coronado, M.A.

Photo courtesy of University of Central Florida

also a NATPE fellow. She continues to work as a bilingual freelance reporter, which helps her bring real-world experience into the classroom. During her free time, she enjoys spending time with her family and traveling.

Erica Rodríguez Kight, Ph.D.

Editor

Erica Rodríguez Kight, Ph.D., is a lecturer in journalism, radio-TV, and Hispanic media at the University of Central Florida Nicholson School of Communication. She is also part of the UCF NSC Hispanic Media Initiative. Kight previously worked as a newspaper reporter, TV news assignment editor, and TV news reporter. Kight completed her undergraduate studies in English Literature at Florida State University and later earned graduate degrees in Mass Communication from the University of Florida. As a journalist, she won several awards for her work, including recognition from Florida AP Broadcasters, the Society of Professional Journalists, and the Florida Emergency Preparedness Association. In her free time, Kight enjoys traveling, home improvement projects, planning parties, and spending time with her family.

Erica Rodríguez Kight, Ph.D.

Photo courtesy of University of Central Florida

Ana G. Hidalgo, M.A.

Assistant Editor

Ana Hidalgo, M.A., is a recent graduate of the Nicholson School of Communication at the University of Central Florida. Hidalgo earned a master's degree in Communication with a concentration in Mass Communication and a graduate certificate in Corporate Communication. She also earned a bachelor's degree in Radio-Television from UCF. As a teaching and research assistant, Hidalgo collaborated with the NSC's Hispanic Media Initiative to develop efforts to better serve the Hispanic community. Her research interests include corporate social responsibility, crisis/risk communication, environmental communication, and minority studies. During her free time, she enjoys traveling the world and spending time with her family and friends.

Ana G. Hidalgo, M.A.

Photo courtesy of Ana Hidalgo

Foreword

John Leguizamo

I am so honored to be asked to write the foreword for this textbook. I feel that this is an essential time for us LatinX Americans to be reflecting on our history and contributions. We have been written out of much of this country's narrative, and I think the most important place to begin the work of setting the historical record straight is with textbooks like this one.

That is what drove me to write my new play *Latin History for Morons*. I was helping my son—then an 8th grader—with a history assignment for school. When I looked through his textbook, I was shocked. There was no mention of LatinX American contributions. No mention of LatinX artists, scientists, philosophers, or veterans. (Little known fact: LatinX Americans have served in every single American

John Leguizamo
Photo courtesy of Timothy Greenfield-Sanders

war, starting with the American Revolution.) That information was never in textbooks when I was growing up, and the problem persists to this day. So I had to go find it myself, because white Anglo-Saxon protestants populated these lands and decided long ago to build a wall around our history. And, by the way, I mean no offense to anyone who is a descendant of the "founding fathers," "pioneers," and good American heroes. You're not responsible for your forefathers' actions. All I'm saying is that white Americans don't have a monopoly on goodness and greatness. This country is made from the contributions of peoples of all colors and creeds, but we need our historical narrative and our textbooks to reflect that.

I am excited about this book, because LatinX people have contributed so much to this country, and it is time to start telling that story. We are the largest minority group in the United States, and we've been here since the very beginning.

The media industry in this country reaches everyone, invisibly shaping the way we think of ourselves and our relation to others. This is a powerful force that can do a lot of good, but it can also perpetuate stereotypes and old beliefs that we need to shed. People tend to assume that the media is a mirror, reflecting back the world as it is. But we all need to question the objectiveness of that reflection—especially us LatinX people and other minority groups—because just like a lot of media products, there is plenty of selective editing and "photoshopping" used to portray a certain image that is often far from the truth.

I am excited about this project to revisit LatinX voices in the media, and to give them the spotlight they deserve. Our voices have always been here, and textbooks like this help ensure these voices from the past can be fully heard—and that the voices in the future can be even louder.

Unit 1

Immigration and the Emergence of Hispanic Periodicals in the U.S.

1   Waves of Migration

A Brief History of the Hispanic/ LatinX Presence in the U.S.

Fernando I. Rivera, Ph.D.

Associate Professor of Sociology,
University of Central Florida

Immigration to the U.S. is one of the fundamental features of the history of this country. Waves of migration from different regions of the world, including Asia, Europe, Latin America, the Caribbean, and others, have transformed and shaped the social fabric of the U.S. These waves of migration were the result of wars, labor shortage, political revolutions, social, and economic upheaval, among other things. The decision to migrate is a combination of what immigration scholars call push-pull factors. **Push factors** refer to social and economic conditions that push groups of people to migrate in response to events such as wars, economic downfalls, and degrading environmental conditions. **Pull factors** refer to those conditions that incentivize people to migrate to places where there is a need for labor, or a better quality of life, among other favorable social and economic conditions.

The immigration of Hispanics and Latinos to the U.S. is vital to the rapid growth of this sector of the population. A recent report by the U.S Census Bureau indicates that Hispanics represented 17.6% or 56.6 million of the U.S. population as of July 1, 2015. Mexicans represented 63.4% of the Hispanic population, followed by Puerto Ricans (9.5%), Salvadorans (3.8%), Cubans (3.7%), Dominicans (3.3%), and Guatemalans (2.4%). The rest were from other Central and South American countries or were of another Hispanic origin. As a group, Hispanics are the largest minority group in the U.S.[1] Around 65% of all Hispanics live in California (15 million), Texas (10.4 million), Florida (4.8 million), New York (3.7 million), and Illinois (2.2 million).[2] Over the years, key historical and public policy events have impacted the immigration of Latinos from their homelands to the U.S.

Migration Over the Years

Mexicans

An important event in the history of the U.S.–Mexican relations was the **Treaty of Guadalupe Hidalgo**, which ended the Mexican–American war that lasted from 1846 to 1848. The treaty gave the U.S. Mexican territories of what are now Arizona, California, Colorado, Nevada, New Mexico, Utah, and Wyoming. It also established the Río Grande as the border between Mexico and the U.S.[3] The phrase *"no cruzamos la frontera, la frontera nos cruzó,"* or "we did not cross the border, the border crossed us," refers to the outcome of this treaty and the sometimes-thorny issue of immigration between the U.S. and Mexican borders.

There were other important historical events that impacted several push-pull factors in the decision of Mexicans to migrate to the U.S. In the late 1800s and early 1900s there was a push to build railroads and expand agricultural markers from the southwest to regions in the Midwest and East of the U.S. This expansion work was done primarily by Asian immigrants. During that time period, a nativist and exclusionary vision of immigrants in the U.S. led to legislation such as the 1882 **Chinese Exclusion Act**, which prohibited labor from Chinese immigrants and reduced migration from southern and eastern Europe. Employers in the southwest looked to Mexico to satisfy their labor needs. Along with the 1910 Mexican Revolution, which created dire economic and social conditions in Mexico, the influx of Mexican immigrants flourished.

Figure 1.1 Mexican-American migrant woman, harvesting tomatoes in the Santa Clara Valley, California, November 1938.

Everett Historica/Shutterstock

Throughout the 1900s, there were other federal government restrictions to curb immigration, particularly from Europe and Asia. In 1917, the Immigration Act restricted entry to the U.S. for those deemed undesirable, including persons dependent on public services, radicals, and Asians. Consequently, the 1924 **National Origins Acts** established immigration quotas from Europe and Asia and the creation of the Border Patrol. As before, these restrictions created a labor shortage that was filled primarily by Mexican immigrants.[4]

Conditions changed during the Great Depression of the late 1920s and early 1930s. The dire economic conditions in the U.S. revived past anti-immigrant sentiments, and there was a call for a mass deportation of Mexican immigrants from U.S. soil. Migration halted as a result of these conditions but resumed again as World War II created yet another need for labor. From 1948 to 1964, the **Bracero program** allowed Mexicans to come to the U.S. as temporary guest workers to do farm work. Approximately 4.5 million Mexican citizens participated in the program, primarily in Texas and California. The need for labor was so high that those who were not able to participate in the program decided to enter the U.S. illegally. There were also incentives for employers to hire undocumented, non-Bracero workers as they could be paid less and their undocumented legal status left them with no rights.[5] This is a pattern still seen today. The program established a working class that the farming industry continues to rely upon for their agricultural needs that is subject to much debate in the ongoing immigration reform talks.

The Immigration Act of 1965, also known as the **Hart–Celler Act**, eliminated some of the per-country quotas established in previous years. This allowed immigrants from Europe, Asia, and Africa to come to the U.S. but also put restrictions on the number of visas granted to people from Western Hemisphere countries, including Mexico. This restriction on legal immigration, combined with the dire economic conditions in Mexico and the end of the Bracero program, pushed the flow of Mexican migration, often illegal, to the U.S. Other pieces of legislation included the 1978 Select Commission on Immigration and Refugee Policy (SCRIP), Immigration Reform and Control Act of 1986, the North American Free Trade Agreement (NAFTA) in 1994, and the 2012 Consideration of Deferred Action for Childhood Arrivals.[6] These were aimed at curbing illegal migration, regulating the status of undocumented immigrants, and establishing economic ties.

Although recent analyses of U.S. Census population data showed that the number of Latino immigrants stalled around 2010, there was a resurgence of anti-immigrant sentiment aimed primarily at Mexican undocumented immigrants.[7] This sentiment was exhibited in the campaign of U.S. President Donald J. Trump, who promised to build a wall on the U.S.–Mexico border. The promise of building a wall became a campaign slogan and a top priority for the Trump administration.[8] This is, yet again, another cycle of push-pull factors that affect migration to the U.S.

Puerto Ricans

The formal relation between Puerto Rico and the U.S. began as a result of the Spanish–American war. Puerto Rico, a colony of Spain, became a U.S. territory as part of the conditions set by the Treaty of Paris in 1898. Certain events during the period from 1898 to 1930 gave Puerto Ricans different pull/push factors to migrate to the mainland U.S. During World War I, there was active recruitment of Puerto Ricans to the U.S. military. In 1917, as part of the **Jones-Shafroth Act**, Puerto Ricans were granted U.S. citizenship, allowing free movement between Puerto Rico and the mainland U.S. During this period, there were high levels of migration to Hawaii to fill the labor demand for sugar workers, and to New York to fill employment opportunities in manufacturing and services due to the decline of immigration from Europe in the 1920s.[9] The period between the Great Depression in the 1930s and World War II in the 1940s marked another time of economic and political uncertainty for Puerto Rico. Puerto Ricans were again recruited to join the armed forces fighting in World War II.

The end of the war marked the beginning of the "Great Migration" period from 1945 to 1964. Migration to the U.S. mainland peaked as a result of the economic strategy put forth by the federal and Puerto Rican governments after the island became a **commonwealth** of the U.S. in 1952. There was a push to transform Puerto Rico's economy from rural to industrial. **Operation Bootstrap** was put in place to industrialize Puerto Rico. The operation displaced thousands of rural workers to urban areas. In addition, the Puerto

Figure 1.2 Puerto Rican and American flags serve as a reminder of the Jones-Shafroth Act.

Oculo/Shutterstock

Rican Farm Labor Program was established in 1947 to facilitate the migration of Puerto Rican workers to travel to the mainland. In the 1960s, an annual average of 17,600 workers participated in the program.[10]

The years between 1965 and 1980 were known as the **revolving door period**, in which Puerto Ricans migrated back to the island as New York experienced a financial crisis while wages increased in Puerto Rico. After the 1980s, the economic conditions of the island began to decline, and migration to the mainland resumed. From 2000 to 2015, Puerto Rico experienced a 9% population decline, as the island experienced one of the worst economic crises that led to a mass exodus of Puerto Ricans to the mainland, particularly to the state of Florida.[11] On September 20, 2017, Hurricane Maria made landfall in Puerto Rico as a Category 4 storm causing severe damage to the island, resulting in a total collapse of the electric grid. Recovery from the storm was expected to take years and has resulted in a massive exodus of Puerto Ricans to the mainland U.S. Estimates suggests that between 114,000 and 213,000 Puerto Ricans will leave the island annually as a result of the hurricane. Florida is estimated to be the principal destination for this exodus.[12]

Cubans

After the Spanish–American War, Cuba became an independent country in 1902. The independence was limited by the 1901 **Platt Amendment**. This amendment stipulated the conditions of withdrawal of U.S. troops from Cuba, restricted Cuban authority to negotiate treaties and conduct land transfers to non-U.S. countries, and it gave the U.S. rights to the naval base in Guantanamo Bay. The amendment expired in 1934. Fulgencio Batista ruled the island for 17 years, from 1933 to 1958 (except between 1944 and 1952). The first half of the twentieth century was dominated by American entertainment and gambling industries that provided a local service economy and few incentives for Cubans to migrate to the U.S. Some agricultural workers left the island for higher-wage jobs in the U.S., including tobacco factories in Tampa, Florida.[13]

The population growth of Cubans in the U.S. was accelerated as a result of Fidel Castro's revolution in 1959. The U.S. welcomed Cubans fleeing the Castro regime to its shores. The **Cuban Refugee Program** provided financial, medical, and employment assistance to Cuban immigrants. Further legislation, such as the **Cuban Adjustment Act** of 1966, allowed Cuban migrants to qualify for U.S. residency after living in the country for a year. The **Operation Peter Pan** program, also known as Operación Pedro Pan, was established as a collaboration between the U.S. Department of State and Catholic Charities of Miami to grant visa waivers for children to come to the U.S. and later be reunited with their parents and family members. Between 1960 and 1962, an estimated 14,000 unaccompanied children from ages 4 to 16 years old participated in the program. Also during this time, the U.S. government established an **embargo** that restricted economic ties with the Castro regime, which had aligned itself with the Soviet Union.

Other programs and policies allowed the entry of Cubans to the U.S. For instance, the 1965 to 1973 Freedom Flight program transported more than 260,000 Cubans to the U.S. Also, in a period of five months in 1980, more than 125,000 Cubans migrated to the U.S. from the Port of Mariel in Cuba during the Mariel Boatlift.[14] Fourteen years later, during what was known as the Rafter Crisis, Cubans migrated to the U.S. in small boats and rafts. In the summer of 1994, more than 30,000 Cubans arrived on U.S. soil. Tensions between the U.S. and Cuban governments have continued to shape immigration policies. Although diplomatic ties with Cuba were restored by U.S. President Barack Obama in 2014, which was coined as the Cuban Thaw. U.S. President Donald Trump rolled back some of those changes in 2017.[15]

Covering Cuban Immigration: A Journalist's Perspective

by Eliott Rodríguez
News Anchor, WFOR CBS 4 News in Miami, Florida

The Mariel Boatlift and the Cuban Rafter Crisis were two of the biggest news stories in Miami's history. I covered both events and saw first-hand how the sudden, massive migrations—125,000 during the Mariel Boatlift and 30,000 during the Rafter Crisis—challenged every aspect of life in Miami, impacting housing, employment, crime, and race relations.

In the spring of 1980, I was a cub reporter at WTVJ-TV in Miami, Florida, when the first boats sailed into Key West from the Port of Mariel. "There is no news in the newsroom," was the mantra of the station's assistant news director Ruth Sperling. So off we went to Key West to cover the story.

The boats from Mariel arrived daily at the Truman Annex Naval Air Station in Key West. That's where I saw refugees with dazed looks on their faces pull into port aboard dangerously overcrowded boats. My Spanish-speaking skills came in handy. Reporters were allowed to speak to the refugees but only briefly as they were escorted onto buses for the trip to processing sites in Miami.

The "Marielitos" were housed in tent cities set up under expressway overpasses, football stadium parking lots, and public parks. If you saw the movie *Scarface* you know what the camps were like. They were overcrowded with military-style cots, outdoor shower facilities, and government surplus food rations. Most of the interviews I did in the tent cities centered on the refugees' desire to get out. The city officials I interviewed seemed overwhelmed, demanding that the federal government do more to help them deal with the crisis.

Figure 1.3 News anchor Eliott Rodríguez and videographer Lenny Yeoman in Havana, Cuba, covering a flotilla of humanitarian aid from Florida in 1993.

Photo courtesy of Eliott Rodríguez

Many of the stories I covered focused on crimes committed by criminals who arrived in Miami during Mariel. Again, shades of *Scarface* come to mind as I think back on the crime wave that hit post-Mariel Miami. Covering one murder case, I can still remember the stone-cold look on the face of the Mariel criminal as he was sentenced to death for killing a young woman who worked at a Miami Burger King.

Fourteen years after the Mariel Boatlift, I found myself back in Key West covering another mass migration from Cuba. The 1994 Rafter Crisis started out as a repeat of Mariel. When the first rafts and makeshift vessels arrived in Key West, I was sent to cover the story as family members drove to Key West after hearing news from Cuba that loved ones had left the island.

This time, however, the Coast Guard appeared more prepared. They interdicted thousands of refugees at sea and transferred them to the Guantanamo Bay Naval Base. They were held for months while the U.S. negotiated a migration agreement with the Cuban government that resulted in the "wet-foot, dry-foot" policy. The refugees from Guantanamo were eventually released, most of them, like the Marielitos, settling in the Miami area.

Nearly four decades have passed since Mariel and nearly three decades since the Rafter Crisis. In 2016, President Barack Obama ended the controversial wet-foot, dry-foot program that allowed Cubans who arrived illegally to stay in the U.S. The change resulted in a dramatic drop in the number of Cubans fleeing the island on rafts and makeshift boats, many losing their lives in the treacherous waters of the Straits of Florida. We may never see an exodus of humanity from Cuba like these events ever again—although Cuba is always full of surprises.

Central Americans

Immigrants from Central America—Guatemala, El Salvador, Honduras, Nicaragua, Costa Rica, Panama, and Belize—are another large segment of the Hispanic/LatinX population in the U.S. Significant immigration to the U.S. during the 1970s and 1980s was due to political upheaval in El Salvador and Guatemala, and the Sandinista Revolution in Nicaragua. Nicaraguan immigrants seeking political asylum in the U.S. had fewer obstacles in obtaining such permits than asylum seekers from El Salvador and Guatemala. Both governments were sympathetic to U.S. interests, while the U.S. backed the opposition group fighting against the Sandinista government in Nicaragua. Eventually, Salvadorans and Guatemalans were allowed to reapply for political asylum as a result of family reunification legal decisions. To this day, economic and political upheaval continue to push Central Americans to seek better opportunities in the U.S.[16]

Dominicans

Immigration from the Dominican Republic has been marked by four distinctive migration waves. The first wave of immigration, between 1930 and 1960, was mostly upper-class Dominicans. The second wave, between 1961 and 1965, was a result of the U.S. invasion of the Dominican Republic after the assassination of dictator Rafael Leónidas Trujillo on May 30, 1961. Most of the migration from this period was from elites and political supporters of Trujillo. After the invasion, political upheaval and economic conditions were factors for the other waves of migration.[17] Dominicans have concentrated in the Northeast region, with almost half living in the state of New York.[18]

Continued Growth and Impact

As the largest minority group in the U.S., Hispanic/LatinX people have had a significant impact on U.S. society. Latino immigrants have enriched U.S. culture with significant contributions to music, food, literature, and art. They are responsible for growth in rural areas experiencing population loss in the Midwest and the South. They continue to influence the political landscape because of their political mobilization and activism. Immigration has resulted in different blurring of language and identity boundaries.[19] It is not uncommon to navigate between Spanish and English in a conversation, and international identities continue to be acknowledged and celebrated, including Hispanic Heritage Month, the Puerto Rican Day Parade, and other traditional celebrations such as Mexico's *Día de los Muertos* (Day of the Dead), among others.

Still, significant challenges remain for Latinos as a result of their immigration history and experiences. As a group, Latinos have higher poverty rates and lower income levels than non-Hispanic Whites.[20] Meanwhile, the experience of all Latinos in the U.S. is not the same. Voluntary immigrants escaping political upheaval or seeking economic opportunity may have a different experience from those immigrants incorporated through warfare. For example, studies show people from various countries as having different health issues or levels of education.

Looking Ahead

More than half of the population growth in the U.S. between 2010 and 2014 was due to Latinos. While the rapid Latino population growth has stalled due to decreased immigration, the current growth is due to Latino births in the U.S. (see Figure 1.4).[21]

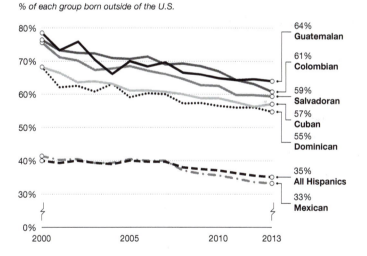

Note: Immigrants' includes those born outside the U.S. or its territories (e.g. Puerto Rico) to non-U.S. citizen parents. People in group quarters such as college dormitories or institutions are not included in figures for 2001 to 2005. Changes in the wording of the Hispanic origin question in the 2000 decennial census may have led to an undercount of some Hispanic origin groups. For more, see http://www.pewhispanic.org/2002/05/09/counting-the-other-hispanics/

Source: Pew Research Center tabulations of 2000 census (5% IPUMS) and 2001–2013 American Community Surveys (1% IPUMS)

PEW RESEARCH CENTER

Figure 1.4 Immigrant share falls among largest Hispanic origin groups since 2000.

Pew Research Center

Not foreseeing any other immigration changes, projections of future Latino population growth indicate that by 2060 Hispanics will make up 31% of the overall U.S. population.[22] This continuous growth will only accelerate the impact that Hispanic and Latino immigrants are having in the U.S. Addressing the challenges of legal status, poverty, and integration should be top policy priorities to resolve. It would also be shortsighted not to see Hispanic/LatinX immigrants and the Hispanic population as valuable assets to the economic and social future of the U.S.

Vocabulary Words

Bracero Program
Chinese Exclusion Act
Commonwealth
Cuban Adjustment Act
Cuban Refugee Program
Cuban Thaw
Embargo
Hart-Celler Act
Jones-Shafroth Act

National Origins Act
Operation Bootstrap
Operation Peter Pan
Platt Amendment
Pull Factors
Push Factors
Revolving Door Period
Treaty of Guadalupe Hidalgo

Points to Remember

- As of July 1, 2015, the U.S. Census Bureau reported that Latinos account for 17.6% or 56.6 million of the U.S. population, with Mexicans being the largest group, 63.4%. Latinos are the largest minority group in the U.S.
- The Treaty of Guadalupe Hidalgo, Chinese Exclusion Act, Bracero program, Hart-Celler Act, and Jones-Shafroth Act are a few crucial pieces of legislation that have shaped and affected Hispanic immigration to the U.S.
- Immigration of Latinos to the U.S. has enriched the country's music, food, literature, and art. Furthermore, they are increasingly influencing the U.S. political environment and removing language and social barriers.
- Not all Latinos share the same experiences. Different circumstances have pushed them to voluntarily and involuntarily migrate to the U.S., such as political disorder in their home countries, warfare, or economic necessity.
- Even though Latino immigration has stalled, this population continues to grow due to births in the U.S. Projections show that, by 2060, Hispanics will make up 31% of the U.S. population.

Names to Remember

Barack Obama
Donald Trump
Fidel Castro

Fulgencio Batista
Rafael Leónidas Trujillo

Practice Questions

1   Throughout its history, the U.S. has been a prime destination for migration from many nations around the world. What caused these waves of migration? Also, name and explain the factors that contributed to these migration movements.

2   How did the period of strict federal government immigration regulations in the 1900s, particularly on immigrants from Europe and Asia, positively impact Mexican immigrants? What historical period halted it and revived anti-immigrant sentiments? Explain in detail.

3   After World War II, what was the name of the period that increased migration from Puerto Rico to the U.S.? What strategy did the Federal and Puerto Rican governments intend to apply to shape the future of the island?

4   In response to Fidel Castro's control of Cuba, the U.S. government implemented several programs that increased migration from this nation. Name two programs that facilitated Cuban migration and how it benefited them.

5   While the U.S. has developed several programs that have promoted immigration from Hispanic nations, what are some challenges that they have faced? What group has been particularly affected by the Latino health paradox? Explain in detail.

Activity

Organization Research: In a group or individually, search the web for organizations that have aided Latino immigrants in the U.S. While you conduct research, make sure to include who founded the organization, what Hispanic group(s) they are committed to help, what their mission statement is, and what they have accomplished.

Timeline

1846: Beginning of Mexican–American war.
1848: End of Mexican–American war.
1882: The **Chinese Exclusion Act** established that Chinese immigrants were prohibited from labor.
1898: Puerto Rico becomes a U.S territory under the conditions set by the Treaty of Paris.
1910: Mexican Revolution.
1917: Puerto Ricans are granted U.S. citizenship under the **Jones-Shafroth Act**.

1924: The National Origins Act implements immigration quotas from Europe and Asia, and Border Patrol is created.

1929: Beginning of the Great Depression.

1945: The Great Migration period begins and lasts until 1964.

1948: The start of the **Bracero Program**, which enabled Mexicans to work temporarily in the U.S.

1952: Puerto Rico becomes a commonwealth of the U.S.

1964: End of **Bracero Program**.

1965: **Hart-Celler Act** ruled out the per-country quotas set by the Immigration act of 1917 and permitted immigration from South and Eastern Europe, Asia, and Africa to the U.S.

1966: Cuban Adjustment Act permitted Cuban immigrants to obtain U.S. citizenship after residing in the U.S. for one year and a day.

1978: Select Commission on Immigration and Refugee Policy (SCRIP).

1986: Immigration Reform and Control Act.

1994: North American Free Trade Agreement (NAFTA).

2010: Mass migration from Puerto Rico to the U.S. due to massive economic crisis.

2012: Consideration of Deferred Action for Childhood Arrivals.

2014: **Cuban Thaw** by the Obama administration restores diplomatic ties between the U.S. and Cuba.

2015: Latinos accounted for 17.6% of the U.S. population, becoming the largest minority group.

Additional Resources

Aranda, Elizabeth M., Sallie Hughes, and Elena Sabogal. *Making a Life in Multiethnic Miami: Immigration and the Rise of a Global City.* (Lynne Rienner, 2014).

Duany, Jorge. *Puerto Rico: What Everyone Needs to Know.* (Oxford University Press, 2017).

Sáenz, Rogelio, and María Cristina Morales. *Latinos in the United States: Diversity and Change.* (John Wiley & Sons, 2015).

About the Author

Fernando I. Rivera, Ph.D., is an Associate Professor of Sociology at the University of Central Florida. His published work has investigated how different mechanisms are related to health and mental health outcomes with a particular emphasis on Latino populations. Several publications have investigated

Fernando I. Rivera

Photo courtesy of University of Central Florida

the Puerto Rican diaspora in Florida. He earned his M.A. and Ph.D. in Sociology from the University of Nebraska-Lincoln and his B.A. degree in Sociology from the University of Puerto Rico-Mayagüez. He also completed a National Institute of Mental Health-sponsored post-doctoral fellowship at the Institute for Health, Health Care Policy, and Aging Research at Rutgers University.

Notes

1 U.S. Census Bureau, "FFF: Hispanic Heritage Month 2016," October 12, 2016, www.census.gov/newsroom/facts-for-features/2016/cb16-ff16.html.

2 Renee Stepler and Mark Hugo Lopez, "U.S. Latino Population Growth and Dispersion Has Slowed Since Onset of the Great Recession," *Pew Research Center*, September 8, 2016, www.pewhispanic.org/2016/09/08/latino-population-growth-and-dispersion-has-slowed-since-the-onset-of-the-great-recession.

3 Julian Samora and Patricia Vandel Simon, *A History of the Mexican-American People* (Notre Dame, IN: University of Notre Dame Press, 1993).

4 Timothy J. Henderson, *Beyond Borders: A History of Mexican Migration to the United States* (Malden, MA: John Wiley & Sons, 2011).

5 Richard B. Craig, *The Bracero Program: Interest Groups and Foreign Policy* (Austin, TX: University of Texas Press, 2014).

6 U.S. Citizenship and Immigration Services, "Consideration of Deferred Action for Childhood Arrivals (DACA)," www.uscis.gov/humanitarian/consideration-deferred-action-childhood-arrivals-daca.

7 Jens M. Krogstad and Mark Hugo Lopez, "Hispanic Nativity Shift," *Pew Research Center*, April 29, 2014, www.pewhispanic.org/2014/04/29/hispanic-nativity-shift/.

8 Associated Press, "Trump Wants to Build 30-Foot-High Wall at Mexican border," *CNBC*, March 16, 2017, www.cnbc.com/2017/03/19/trump-wants-to-build-30-foot-high-wall-at-mexican-border.html.

9 Edna Acosta-Belén and Carlos Enrique Santiago, *Puerto Ricans in the United States: A Contemporary Portrait* (Boulder, CO: Lynne Rienner, 2006).

10 Jorge Duany, "Puerto Rico, Migration 1968 to Present," in Ness, Immanuel, *The Encyclopedia of Global Human Migration* (Hoboken, NJ: Wiley-Blackwell, 2013).

11 Jens M. Krogstad, "Historic Population Losses Continue Across Puerto Rico," *Pew Research Center*, 2016, www.pewresearch.org/fact-tank/2016/03/24/historic-population-losses-continue-across-puerto-rico/.

12 Edwin Meléndez and Jennifer Hinojosa, "Estimates of Post-Hurricane Maria Exodus from Puerto Rico," *Center for Puerto Rican Studies Research Brief*, 2017, https://centropr.hunter.cuny.edu/sites/default/files/RB2017-01-POST-MARIA%20EXODUS_V3.pdf.

13 Norma Fuentes-Mayorga, "Caribbean, Spanish Migration, 19th Century to Present," *The Encyclopedia of Global Human Migration* 2 (Hoboken, NJ: Wiley-Blackwell, 2013): 878–886.

14 Felix R. Masud-Piloto, "Cuba: Migration to United States, 1957 to present," in Ness, Immanuel, *The Encyclopedia of Global Human Migration* 3 (Hoboken, NJ: Wiley-Blackwell, 2013): 1134–1138.

15 Michael Shifter, "The US-Cuba Thaw and Hemispheric Relations," *Current History* 115, no. 778 (2016): 75.

16 Nora Hamilton, "Central America: Migration 1960s to Present," *The Encyclopedia of Global Human Migration* 2 (Hoboken, NJ: Wiley-Blackwell, 2013): 902–907.

17 Norma Fuentes-Mayorga, "Caribbean, Spanish Migration, 19th Century to Present," *The Encyclopedia of Global Human Migration* 2 (Hoboken, NJ: Wiley-Blackwell, 2013): 878–886.

18 Gustavo López, "Hispanics of Dominican Origin in the United States, 2013," *Pew Research Center*, 2015, www.pewhispanic.org/2015/09/15/hispanics-of-dominican-origin-in-the-united-states-2013/.

19 Rogelio Sáenz, *Latinos and the Changing Face of America* (New York: Russell Sage Foundation, 2004).

20 Alberto Davila, Marie T. Mora, and Alma D. Hales, "Income, Earnings, and Poverty: A Portrait of Inequality Among Latinos/as in the United States," in Rodríguez, Havidan, Rogelio Sáenz, and Cecilia Menjívar, *Latinas/os in the United States: Changing the face of America* (New York: Springer, 2008): 181–195.

21 Pew Research Center. "Immigrant Share Falls Among Largest Hispanic Origin Groups Since 2000," *Pew Research Center Hispanic Trends*, September 11, 2015, www.pewhispanic.org/2015/09/15/the-impact-of-slowing-immigration-foreign-born-share-falls-among-14-largest-us-hispanic-origin-groups/ph_2015-09-15_hispanic-origins-01–2/.

22 Jens M. Krogstad, "A View of the Future through Kindergarten Demographics," *Pew Research Center*, July 8, 2014, www.pewresearch.org/fact-tank/2014/07/08/a-view-of-the-future-through-kindergarten-demographics/.

2 Paving the Way

Hispanic Newspapers in the U.S. before World War II

Nicolás Kanellos, Ph.D.

Brown Foundation Professor of Hispanic Studies,
University of Houston

This chapter is adapted from the book *Hispanic Periodicals in the U.S., Origins to 1960: A Brief History and Comprehensive Bibliography*, co-written by Nicolás Kanellos and Helvetia Martell.

Throughout the last few centuries, Hispanic communities from coast to coast have supported newspapers of varying sizes and missions—running the gamut from the eight-page weekly, written in Spanish or bilingually, to the highly entrepreneurial large-city daily, written exclusively in Spanish. Since the founding in New Orleans in 1808 of *El Misisipí*, probably the first Spanish-language newspaper published in the United States, the Hispanic press has had to serve functions hardly ever envisioned in Mexico City, Madrid, or Havana. Besides supplying basic news of the homeland and of the Hispanic world in general, advertising local businesses, and informing the community about relevant current affairs and politics of the U.S., Hispanic **periodicals** additionally have had to offer alternative information services that present their own communities' views of news and events.

At times, this information has had to take on a contestatory and challenging posture vis-à-vis the English-language news organizations and U.S. official government and cultural institutions. Furthermore, the newspapers have had to take the lead in the effort to preserve Hispanic language and cultural identity in the face of the threat of annihilation by Anglo-Saxon culture and the English language. Most of the Hispanic press, whether a small weekly or a large-city daily, has had to assume a leadership role in cultural, if not political, resistance—and, beyond that, in the battle to protect the very real economic and political interests of the local Hispanic community, whether envisioned as a community, an internal colony, or a racial-minority ghetto.

In many cases during the last two centuries, the local Hispanic press has often provided leadership in solidifying the community, protecting it and furthering its cultural survival. Not always as a means of furthering their own commercial interests and financial profit, Hispanic newspapers have historically assumed roles that have been associated with patriotic and **mutual aid societies**. Such efforts—often alongside churches and other groups—include sponsoring patriotic and cultural celebrations, as well as organizing the community for social and political action for projects like founding Spanish-language schools and community clinics, fighting segregation and discrimination, and collecting funds for relief of flood victims, refugees, and other needy or displaced persons. The pages of these newspapers have offered **editorials** and letters to the editor in support of community needs. The newspapers, in general, have had to take political stands regarding the homeland and the U.S. They have offered their pages to the playing out of the dramas that envelope their special communities.

Historically, the newspapers have functioned as purveyors of education, high culture, and entertainment. During the nineteenth century and the first half of the twentieth century, they became the principal publishers of literature by including poetry, literary prose, and even serialized novels in their pages. As a function of cultural preservation and elevating the level of education of the community, the newspapers provided this fare, which often was drawn from local writers as well as reprinted from works by writers in the homeland and throughout the Hispanic world. As an extension of the latter interest, many newspapers founded publishing houses, and even bookstores, to further distribute Hispanic intellectual and artistic thought.

The Nineteenth Century

The Southwest

Even before the Mexican–American War (1846–1848), Hispanic newspapers, in what became the Southwest of the U.S., were already carrying on and promoting political activities, as has been pointed out by scholar Luis Leal in "The Spanish Language Press: Function and Use." For instance, Santa Fe's *El Crepúsculo de la Libertad* (The Dawn of Liberty) headed up a campaign in 1834 for the election of representatives to the Mexican Congress, and it also served as a forum for its publisher Antonio José Martínez's defense of the civil rights and land ownership rights of the Taos Indians. After the Mexican–American War, as Leal has pointed out, the Spanish-language press defended the rights of the Mexican inhabitants in what had become the new territories of the U.S.

On the foundation laid by such newspapers as *El Crepúsculo de la Libertad*, *La Gaceta de Texas/El Mexicano* (The Texas Gazette/The Mexican), the latter founded in 1813, numerous Spanish-language newspapers were established and they began to offer an alternative to the flow of information from Anglo-American sources during the period of transition from Mexican government to U.S. rule following the war with Mexico. This was only logical, for it was

Figure 2.1 Cover of *La Crónica* published on October 1911 in Laredo, Texas.

Source: Ramón A. Gutiérrez and Genaro Padilla, *Recovering the U.S. Hispanic Literary Heritage*, Arte Público Press

their specific business plan to serve the interests of the Hispanic communities. The important commercial centers of Los Angeles and San Francisco supported dozens of periodicals during the latter half of the nineteenth century, including: Los Angeles' *La Estrella de Los Ángeles* (The Los Angeles Star), *El Clamor Público* (The Public Clamor), *La Crónica* (The Chronicle), San Francisco's *La República* (The Republic), and *La Voz del Nuevo Mundo* (The Voice of the New World). Of course, the port cities were not the only populations that supported Spanish-language newspapers. Hispanic journalism also flourished in the inland towns and villages, especially in New Mexico, where virtually every sizable town had its own weekly by the 1890s, including Bernalillo, Las Cruces, Mora, Santa Fe, Socorro, and Las Vegas.

The Northeast

Although the Spanish-language newspapers in the Southwest often took up the defense of their communities, this was not as pressing an issue as Hispanic American independence movements were for the newspapers serving Hispanic immigrants in Philadelphia and New York during the same time period. In New York, the Spaniards, Cubans, Mexicans, and other Hispanic immigrants founded periodicals that provided more for the typical interests of immigrants: news from the homeland, coverage of local Hispanic affairs and business, and also the preservation and enrichment of the Spanish language and Hispanic culture in the alien environment.

The earliest newspapers on record were Philadelphia's Cuban revolutionary newspaper, *El Habanero* (1823, The Havana News) and New York's *Mensajero Semanal* (1828–1831, The Weekly Messenger), *El Mercurio de Nueva York* (1828–1833, The New York Mercury), *La Crónica* (1850, The Chronicle), and *La Voz de América* (1860s, The Voice of America). It was not until the end of the nineteenth century that the periodicals began to multiply in New York, undoubtedly responding to increased Hispanic immigration and the political fervor that developed in the Cuban and Puerto Rican communities that were promoting independence from Spain for their homelands. In this regard, the most noteworthy institution was the Cuban newspaper *Patria* (1892–1898, Homeland), in whose pages essays were published by the leading Cuban and Puerto Rican patriots. Newspapers like *Patria* served not only as forums for revolutionary ideas, but were actually tools of organization and propaganda around which many of the expatriate conspirators rallied. The most widely circulated Hispanic weekly in New York during that time was *Las Novedades* (1893–1918, The News), whose theatre, music, and literary critic was the famed Dominican writer Pedro Henriquez Ureña. Other periodicals publishing at this time were *El Porvenir* (The Future) and *Revista Popular* (The People's Magazine).

The Twentieth Century

At the beginning of the twentieth century, a record number of immigrants from Cuba, Mexico, Puerto Rico, and Spain entered the U.S., seeking refuge from political violence in their home countries or simply looking for better economic conditions in which to raise families. Spanish-language periodical literature immediately flourished throughout the Southwest, Midwest, New York, and Tampa to serve the needs of these immigrants and political refugees.

The Southwest

In the Southwest, educated political refugees of the Mexican Revolution played a key role in publishing. From their educationally privileged and/or upper-class, expatriate perspectives, these intellectuals and entrepreneurs created and promoted the idea of a Mexican community in exile, or a "*México de afuera*," in which the culture and politics of Mexico could be duplicated until Mexico's internal politics allowed for the expatriates' return. The "*México de afuera*" campaign was markedly nationalistic and militated to preserve Mexican identity in the U.S.

Among the most powerful of the political, business, and intellectual figures in expressing the **"*México de afuera*" ideology** was Ignacio E. Lozano, founder and operator of the two most powerful and well-distributed daily newspapers: *La Prensa* (The Press) and *La Opinión* (The Opinion). Lozano settled in San Antonio in 1908, founded *La Prensa* in 1913, and in 1926 established *La Opinión* in Los Angeles. He brought to Hispanic journalism in the U.S. a professionalism and business acumen that resulted in longevity for his two newspapers. Indeed, *La Opinión* is still published today.

Lozano's sound journalistic policies and emphasis on professionalism were reflected in his hiring of well-trained journalists, starting at the top with his appointment of Teodoro Torres to edit *La Prensa*. The ideas of men like Torres, known as "the father of Mexican journalism," reached thousands, not only in San Antonio, but throughout the Southwest and Midwest as well as interior Mexico, through a vast distribution system that included newsstand sales, home

Figure 2.2 Ignacio E. Lozano, founder of *La Prensa* and *La Opinión*.

Gutiérrez and Padilla, *Recovering the U.S. Hispanic Literary Heritage*, Arte Público Press

delivery, and mail. *La Prensa* also set up a network of correspondents throughout the U.S. who were able to regularly issue reports on the current events and cultural activities of the Mexican community in exile and other Hispanics in such faraway places as Detroit, Chicago, and even New York.

Lozano and many of his prominent political writers became leaders of the diverse Mexican and Mexican-American communities they served in the U.S., precisely because they were able to dominate print media. Businessmen such as Lozano captured an isolated and specialized market. They shaped and cultivated their market for cultural products and print media as efficiently as other businessmen did for material goods, Mexican foods, and specialized immigrant services. The Mexican community truly benefited in that these businessmen did provide needed goods, information, and services that were

Figure 2.3 La Voz de la Mujer *newspaper was founded in El Paso, Texas.*

Gutiérrez and Padilla, *Recovering the U.S. Hispanic Literary Heritage*, Arte Público Press

often denied by the larger society through official and open segregation. And, of course, the writers, artists, and intellectuals provided the high culture and entertainment in the native language for the Mexican community that was not offered by **Anglo-American society**.

In the editorial offices of *La Prensa, La Opinión,* and *El Heraldo de México* (The Mexican Herald), some of the most talented writers from Mexico, Spain, and Latin America earned their living as reporters, columnists, and critics, including such writers as Miguel Arce, Esteban Escalante, Gabriel Navarro, and Daniel Venegas. These, and many others, used the newspapers as a stable source of employment and as a base from which they could launch their literary publications in book form or write plays and revues for the flourishing dramatic stages. Various newspaper companies established publishing houses and marketed

Figure 2.4 Teresa Villarreal, active revolutionary and feminist organizer.

Gutiérrez and Padilla, *Recovering the U.S. Hispanic Literary Heritage,* Arte Público Press

the books of these authors and others. The *Casa Editorial Lozano*, affiliated with San Antonio's *La Prensa*, not only advertised the books in the family's two newspapers to be sold via direct mail, but also operated a bookstore in San Antonio, as did *El Heraldo de México* in Los Angeles.

Despite the overwhelmingly male administration and editorship of the newspapers, there is an extensive record of feminist writings in Southwestern newspapers. Among the first manifestations of this are the editorials and publications of teachers such as Sara Estela Ramírez (1881–1910) and Leonor Villegas de Magnón (1876–1955) in Laredo's *La Crónica* and in Ramírez's own periodicals, *Aurora* and *La Corregidora*. There was also El Paso's short-lived newspaper, *La voz de la mujer* (1907), and newspapers founded by revolutionaries Andrea and Teresa Villarreal, sisters from San Antonio. An important woman columnist, poet, and novelist was San Antonio's María Luisa Garza, who used the pen name of Loreley in her columns. It seems that working-class cultural and anarchist movements successfully created a space for women's leadership, as well, as exemplified by Colombian anarchist publisher and writer Blanca de Moncaleano, especially in her editorship of *Pluma Roja* (1913–1915) in Los Angeles as part of the Ricardo Flores Magón revolutionary group.

Much of this journalistic and literary activity in the Southwest came to an abrupt end with the Great Depression and the **repatriation**, both forced and voluntary, of Mexican immigrants. A large segment of the society Mexicans had created in the Southwest disappeared over a period of some ten years, beginning in 1930. With the economic distress brought on by the Great Depression and the depopulated Mexican communities, numerous periodicals and publishing ventures failed. It was not until the 1960s that small weeklies would began to flourish again in Mexican-American communities.

New York

In New York, the period from 1880 to 1930 was one of increased Hispanic immigration and of intense interaction among various Hispanic nationality groups. While Spaniards and Cubans made up the majority of New York's Hispanic community, this period saw increased migration of Puerto Ricans facilitated by the Jones-Shafroth Act of 1917, which declared Puerto Ricans to be U.S. citizens. From the 1930s to the 1950s, Puerto Rican migration to New York assumed the proportions of a **diaspora**, as economic conditions worsened on the island and the U.S. suffered labor shortages in manufacturing during World War II. Also in the 1930s, a new wave of refugees from the Spanish Civil War was drawn to New York's Hispanic community.

At the turn of the twentieth century, Spanish and Cuban journalists dominated the Spanish-language print media in New York. The first decade of the century saw the founding of *La Prensa* (The Press), a daily whose heritage continues today in *El Diario–La Prensa* (The Daily–The Press) born of the fusion of *La Prensa* with *El Diario de Nueva York* (The New York Daily) in 1963.

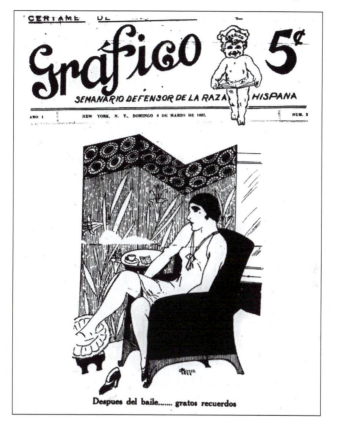

Figure 2.5 Gráfico, periodical founded in 1927 in New York City to reach and defend Hispanic community concerns.

Gutiérrez and Padilla, *Recovering the U.S. Hispanic Literary Heritage*, Arte Público Press

Among the various specialized weeklies that appeared in New York between 1910 and 1940, one merits special attention: *Gráfico* (The Graphic). What was notable about the newspaper, aside from its intent to live up to its title by including numerous photos and illustrations, was that in its early years it was an openly declared "amateur" enterprise written and directed by writers and artists. Many of them were involved in the Hispanic professional stage in Manhattan and Brooklyn.

The founders of *Gráfico* felt that they could better defend community interests, especially those of **Spanish Harlem**, as amateurs, because the professional Spanish-language newspapers, which depended greatly on advertising, could not deal with controversial social and political issues. *Gráfico* was founded in 1927 under the editorship of Alberto O'Farrill, an important playwright and comic actor of the *teatro bufo cubano* (Cuban blackface, musical farces). As such,

Gráfico was replete with theatre and entertainment news, as well as poems, short stories, and essays by the leading Hispanic writers in the city. As in the Southwest, these writers labored to unify the Hispanic community—a difficult task because of the various Hispanic national and racial groups there. While in the Southwest the immigrant writers and entrepreneurs promoted "*México de afuera,*" in New York they often articulated a "*Trópico en Manhattan*" (a Tropics or Caribbean culture in Manhattan). In the pages of *Gráfico*, one finds expressions of an intense Hispanic nationalism. The need to defend the civil rights and culture of the Hispanic community was continually voiced in such declarations as, "[we] will come forward to defend our rights, our lives and homes whenever they will be at stake" (July 31, 1937).

The Hispanic community in New York saw itself at this point as the most recent of immigrant groups bent on establishing a permanent place for itself on the ladder of economic opportunity. Hispanics in New York were there to stay; they were not just awaiting the end of the Mexican Revolution before

Figure 2.6 Alberto O'Farrill, founder of *Gráfico*.

Gutiérrez and Padilla, *Recovering the U.S. Hispanic Literary Heritage*, Arte Público Press

returning home, as was the case with expatriate Mexicans in the Southwest. The plea for the protection of their civil rights was common in editorials, especially since after 1917 Puerto Ricans were U.S. citizens and entitled to constitutional rights.

The ideology of exile among Mexicans in the Southwest left no room for citizenship nor was it interested in promoting a Mexican addition to the American stew. Instead, it promoted a return to Mexico, the American experience posited as temporary. But citizenship and pluralism did not translate to **assimilation** for the Puerto Ricans. Once they were automatically citizens, the pressure to assimilate was lessened. With the advent of the Great Depression, New York did not experience the massive repatriation of Hispanics that occurred in the Southwest. Instead, the opposite was true. Hard economic times brought even more Puerto Ricans to the city, a trend that would intensify during World War II as northeastern manufacturing and service industries experienced labor shortages.

Tampa

The history of Spanish-language newspapers in Tampa diverges somewhat from that of the periodicals in Hispanic communities in other parts of the U.S. At the end of the nineteenth century, the Tampa area became home to a large segment of Cuba's cigar manufacturing industry. Various cigar companies engineered this move to avoid the hostilities of the Cuban wars for independence from Spain, to relocate closer to their principal market in the U.S., to avoid excise taxes, and to skirt labor unions. In 1886, factories were built in the mosquito-infested swamps just east of Tampa in what became Ybor City, which was named after the principal cigar manufacturer, Rafael Ybor. The owners were not able to escape the labor unrest that characterized the industry in Cuba and only partially escaped the repercussions of the wars of independence, which were followed upon by the U.S. war with Spain in 1898.

The Tampa-Ybor City Hispanic community was divided by ethnicity, nationality, and class. The owners and managers of the cigar industry were mostly conservative Spaniards, who sympathized with European colonial power. The cigar workers were mostly Cuban, Asturian, and other working-class Spaniards. Ethnic and racial divisions in this group were reflected in the establishment of various mutual aid societies: the Centro Español (Spanish Center), the Centro Asturiano (Asturian Center), the Círculo Cubano (Cuban Circle), and the Sociedad Martí-Maceo (José Martí-Antonio Maceo Society, named after the revolutionary leaders), the latter being a center for Afro-Cubans who were not welcome in the other clubs and who experienced discrimination from Anglos and white Hispanics in the Jim Crow South.

These class, racial, and ethnic divisions were reflected in the periodical literature. Among the periodicals that served the interests of the owners of the cigar factories was *La Revista* (The Magazine), directed by Rafael M. Ybor, the son of the owner of the largest and most important factory. Several periodicals

Figure 2.7 Patria, Cuban origin newspaper that advocated for the independence from Spain for Cuba and Puerto Rico.

Gutiérrez and Padilla, *Recovering the U.S. Hispanic Literary Heritage*, Arte Público Press

served the interests of the workers and unions: *El Esclavo* (The Slave), *Federación* (Federation), *Federal* (Federal), *El Internacional* (The International), and *Boletín Obrero* (Workers' Bulletin). Some of the ethnic societies also issued periodicals, such as the bi-weekly review of the Círculo Cubano: *El Cubano* (The Cuban). The Afro-Cubans were given very little coverage in any of the Tampa newspapers. There were other periodicals that promoted ethnic unity in the Hispanic community. Out of these efforts came such publications as *Tampa/Ilustrado* (Tampa Illustrated) and *La Gaceta* (The Gazette), whose unifying effort was "Latin," rather than Hispanic, by even including Tampa's Italian community. *La Gaceta* continued publishing in trilingual format—English, Spanish, and Italian—well into the 1980s and beyond.

Vocabulary Words

Anglo-American Society
Assimilation
Diaspora
Editorial
"*México de afuera*" Ideology

Mutual Aid Societies
Periodicals
Repatriation
Spanish Harlem

Points to Remember

- In 1808, *El Misisipí* was established in New Orleans and it was probably the first Spanish-language newspaper published in the U.S.
- Since the nineteenth century, newspapers have been dedicated to preserving and representing Hispanic communities. Class, racial, and ethnic divisions were reflected in periodical literature.
- In New York, Spanish, Cuban, Mexican, and other Hispanic immigrants covered news on issues that affected them locally, as well as international affairs, news about their home countries, and topics that strengthened the Hispanic community.
- A breaking number of immigrants came from Cuba, Mexico, Puerto Rico, and Spain at the beginning of the twentieth century, escaping political violence in their home countries.
- The Great Depression hampered journalistic and literary activities in the Southwest, causing numerous periodicals and publishing ventures that served Hispanic communities to close. The rebirth of periodicals in Mexican-American communities did not begin until the 1960s.

Names to Remember

Andrea and Teresa Villarreal, sisters
Antonio Martínez
Blanca de Moncaleano
Daniel Venegas
Esteban Escalante
Gabriel Navarro
Ignacio E. Lozano
Leonor Villegas de Magnón
Luis Leal
María Luisa Garza
Miguel Arce
Pedro Henriquez Ureña
Rafael M. Ybor
Sara Estela Ramírez

Practice Questions

1 Aside from fulfilling commercial interests and financial profits, what kind of role has the press taken in order to serve the Hispanic community? What have they been trying to preserve?

2 During the nineteenth century, what major historical event incited Spanish-language periodicals to protect the rights of Mexican inhabitants in the U.S? Name a few newspapers that contributed to this movement and what they were attempting to defend.

3 How did Spanish-language periodicals differ in the Southwest from the Northeast? In what major cities in the Northeast were most newspapers founded? Provide the names of a few newspapers.

4 The early twentieth century was an era marked by an increased number of Hispanics migrating to the U.S. What historical figure promoted the "*México de afuera*" ideology and what were some of his major contributions to journalism in the U.S.?

5 According to what was the Hispanic community divided in Tampa and how did it affect the content of its periodicals? What periodical intended to be more inclusive of the communities that resided in the Tampa area? Until what year did it operate?

Activity

Periodical Research: Find a local newspaper in the area where you reside that targets the Hispanic/LatinX community. Next, research the person(s) who founded it, the year in which it was established, and how often it publishes. Read three to five articles recently published by the periodical and determine the dominant issues that they address. Think about what you read and decide whether they had similarities in their coverage. Are they targeting a specific demographic?

Timeline

1808: Founding of *El Misisipi*—first language newspaper published in the U.S.

1813: *La Gaceta de Texas/El Mexicano* newspaper was founded (other Spanish-language newspapers were established around this time too).

1820s–1860s: Several of the earliest newspapers were established in the northeast, including *El Habanero* (*1823*), *Mensajero Semanal* (*1828*), *El Mercurio de Nueva York* (*1828–1833*), *La Crónica* (*1850*), and *La Voz de América* (*1860s*).

1834: Political activity promotions. Hispanics run for congress, civil rights, and land ownership.

1846–1848: Mexican–American War.

1880–1930: Extensive Hispanic immigration in New York.

1886: Many Cuban cigar manufacturing companies were built in Tampa to avoid duty fees, be closer to their main market (U.S.), and avoid conflict brought by Cuba's yearning for independence from Spain.

1890s: Journalism significantly developed in inland towns and villages (New Mexico). Most sizable towns had their own weekly newspapers.

1892–1898: *La Patria*, highly inspiring newspaper written by leading Cuban and Puerto Rican patriots.

Early 1900s: Extensive record of feminist writers in Southwestern newspapers, including Sara Estela Ramírez, Leonor Villegas de Magnón, Andrea and Teresa Villarreal, María Luisa Garza, and Blanca de Moncaleano.

1913: Revolutionary Ignacio E. Lozano founded one of two powerful newspapers, *La Prensa* in San Antonio.

1917: Jones-Shafroth Act allowed Puerto Ricans to have U.S. citizenship, which was signed by President Woodrow Wilson.

1926: Lozano established *La Opinión*, which is still published today.

1927: Theater and entertainment newspaper *Gráfico* was established.

1929: The Great Depression, which lasted for about ten years, ended with many Mexican-American journalists returning to their home country.

1930s: Large Puerto Rican immigration and exodus of refugees from the Spanish Civil War to Hispanic communities in New York.

1960s: Weekly newspapers began to reappear in Mexican-American communities.

Additional Resources

Nicolás Kanellos and Helvetia Martell, *Hispanic Periodicals in the United States: A Brief History and Comprehensive Bibliography* (Houston, TX: Arte Público Press, 2000).

Francine Medeiros, "La Opinión: A Mexican Exile Newspaper: A Content Analysis of its First Years, 1926–1929," *Aztlán: A Journal of Chicano Studies* 11, (1980): 65–87.

About the Author

Nicolás Kanellos holds a Ph.D. in Spanish and Portuguese and an M.A. in Romance languages from the University of Texas. He has received many notable awards for his publications, including the 1996 Denali Press Award of the American Library Association, the 1998 American Book Award, and the 1988 Hispanic Heritage Award for Literature. Kanellos has also

Nicolás Kanellos

Photo courtesy of Nicolás Kanellos

been the recipient of the PEN Southwest Award for Non-Fiction for his most recent book, *Hispanic Immigrant Literature: El Sueño del Retorno* (2011). Currently, he is a professor at the University of Houston in the Department of Hispanic Studies, where he teaches Hispanic Literature and Theater of the United States. He is also a founding member of the biggest non-profit literature publisher in the U.S., Arte Público Press, and Director of a major national research program, Recovering the U.S. Hispanic Heritage.

Bibliography

Richard A. García, "Class, Consciousness and Ideology—The Mexican Community of San Antonio, Texas 1930–1940," *Aztlán: A Journal of Chicano Studies* 8, (1977): 23–69.

Félix Gutiérrez, "Spanish Language Media in America: Background, Resources, History," *Journalism History* 4, (1977): 34–41.

Ramón A. Gutiérrez and Genaro Padilla, *Recovering the U.S. Hispanic Heritage* (Houston, TX: Arte Público Press, 1993).

Nicolás Kanellos and Helvetia Martell, *Hispanic Periodicals in the United States: A Brief History and Comprehensive Bibliography* (Houston, TX: Arte Público Press, 2000).

Luis Leal, "The Spanish Language Press: Function and Use," *The Americas Review* 17, (1989): 157–162.

Francine Medeiros, "La Opinión: A Mexican Exile Newspaper: A Content Analysis of its First Years, 1926–1929," *Aztlán: A Journal of Chicano Studies* 11, (1980): 65–87.

University of Houston, "Nicolas Kanellos, Ph.D.," Hispanic Studies, www.uh.edu/class/spanish/faculty/kanellos_n/.

3   *Extra! Extra!* Bold, Vibrant, and Punchy

Hispanic Newspapers in the U.S. Since World War II, From Print to the Digital Age

Rick Brunson, M.A.

Associate Instructor of Journalism,
University of Central Florida

Twenty-one-year-old Roland Manteiga was working at his father's newspaper, *La Gaceta*, in Tampa, Florida, on December 7, 1941, the day Japanese forces bombarded the U.S. naval base at Pearl Harbor in Hawaii almost 5,000 miles away—plunging America into World War II. A second-generation Cuban-American, Manteiga had worked at the Spanish-language daily newspaper since he was ten, delivering its punchy style of journalism to the streets and homes of the Latino enclaves of West Tampa and Ybor City. Ink, politics, and a passion for the printed word were in young Roland's DNA. His father, Victoriano, who immigrated to the U.S. from Cuba in 1913, became a *lector* the second day he arrived in Tampa, reading newspapers and novels to the Latino *torcedores* and *tabaqueros*, highly skilled tobacco workers, as they plied their craft on the shop floor of Tampa's cigar factories.

Victoriano left the cigar industry and launched his own newspaper, *La Gaceta*, in 1922 to serve the growing Latino population of Tampa. It was a family business and, by the time World War II broke out, Victoriano's son, Roland, had risen from delivery boy to circulation manager of the paper. But duty to his country and his heritage called. Roland left his job at the newspaper and immediately volunteered with about sixty other Tampa Latinos who joined the Army, went to boot camp together and shipped off overseas. He served in the Pacific theater in key battles at Guadalcanal, New Caledonia, and Luzon in the Philippines where he was injured. "He found himself carrying a .50-caliber machine gun on point because the Japanese always shot at the guy carrying the .50-cal—and Latins always got that assignment," recalled Roland's son, Patrick.[1]

Like the other estimated 400,000 Hispanic men and women who served in the U.S. Armed Forces during World War II, Roland Manteiga was doing

Figure 3.1 Roland Manteiga (1920–1998), second-generation Cuban-American and the pioneering editor and publisher of *La Gaceta*, America's oldest trilingual newspaper.

Photo courtesy of *La Gaceta*

more than fighting fascists on a foreign field. He was fighting discrimination at home and broadening the definition of what it meant to be an "American." As historian Lorena Oropeza writes,

> At the heart of the modern Latino experience has been the quest for first-class citizenship. Within this broader framework, military service provides unassailable proof that Latinos are Americans who have been proud to serve, fight, and die for their country, the U.S.[2]

When the war ended, Manteiga put down his .50-caliber, returned home to his newspaper job in Tampa, picked up his typewriter, and began to rat-tat-tat out words instead of bullets, aiming to be a voice for the city's Latino community and a champion of its political and economic interests. In the 1950s, Manteiga persuaded his father to make *La Gaceta* a trilingual weekly newspaper—offering stories in Spanish, English, and Italian to reflect Tampa's dominant cultures—and thus expanding its reach and influence. He also found new advertisers and increased the number of pages and sections.[3]

Manteiga became the paper's editor in 1961, taking over from his retiring father. Soon, his "As We Heard It Column," with its scoops, revelations, uncanny political predictions, and staunch defense of the Latino community, became must-read material for Tampa's government and business elites. Mayors, governors, and even presidential candidates—including Hubert Humphrey, Jimmy Carter, and George Bush—frequently visited Manteiga's private table at La Tropicana café, a hub for immigrants in Tampa's Ybor City, to seek his counsel and support among the state's burgeoning Hispanic population. By the time Manteiga died in 1998, *La Gaceta* had become the oldest continually published trilingual newspaper in America—a distinction it maintains to this day under Roland's son, Patrick, who serves as editor and publisher, just as his father did before him.[4]

"We understand our audience better," Patrick Manteiga says of his newspaper, which has a paid circulation of 18,000 and is distributed in ten counties across west Central Florida at retail outlets such as Wawa convenience stores. "We can give opinions that reflect the voice of the Hispanic community. I don't wear rose-colored glasses. I wear Hispanic-colored glasses. That means I don't see facts differently. But I see the effects of those facts differently because they affect my audience differently. We serve as a unique bridge. I can speak to whites about Hispanic culture and Hispanic issues and they can talk to me. That doesn't exist if we don't exist."[5]

Indeed, newspapers like *La Gaceta* have played a key role in Hispanic existence and persistence in America, as well as the preservation of Hispanics' cultural identity and the expansion of their political and economic power in the country since World War II. The colorful, collective story of Spanish-language newspapers in the modern era is one of fits and starts, as well as boldness and vibrancy, and they have served an important role in Hispanic culture in the U.S.

Migration and Circulation in the Postwar Era

In 1940, on the eve of the United States' entry into World War II, there were an estimated 1.6 million "persons of Spanish mother tongue"[6] in the country, which is how the U.S. Census Bureau counted Latinos at the time. Prior to that, the bureau counted Latinos only as "Mexicans." Many Hispanics were concentrated in major cities such as Los Angeles and New York, where they were served by newspapers published in their native language, such as Latino media entrepreneur Ignacio Lozano's *La Opinión* in L.A. and Rafael Viera y Ayala's *La Prensa* in New York.[7]

While Mexicans were the dominant Hispanic group in the country, especially in the West, Southwest, and Midwest, Puerto Ricans began to emerge and grow in numbers and influence in the East.[8] In addition to providing news and information about local, national, and international events of importance to their Spanish-speaking audiences, these newspapers served as crucial purveyors of Hispanic culture through their publication of poetry, literature, and commentary from Latino intellectuals, as well as community events and issues often ignored by Anglo newspapers. They also countered stereotypical images of Hispanics in English-language mass media and popular culture as either sombrero-wearing criminals or flamenco-dancing Latina spitfires.[9]

As World War II loomed, the number of Spanish-language newspapers in America had grown to about 400, mostly weeklies. But the economic hardships brought on by the Great Depression stalled both migration of Latinos to the U.S. and the growth of new Spanish-language publications within it.[10] That changed when Japanese bombs rained on Pearl Harbor, as the country overnight shifted into a wartime footing. The federal Bracero Program brought millions of Mexicans into the U.S. to work in an agricultural industry hit hard by wartime labor shortages. President Franklin Roosevelt's **Executive Order 8802: Prohibition of Discrimination Against Defense Industry** in 1941, banning discrimination in defense industry hiring, also opened new doors in wartime factories to Latino workers. This wartime influx swelled the Latino population, and the number of people of "Spanish surname" had doubled to 2.3 million by 1950.[11]

The postwar period brought expansion and growth in audience for Spanish-language newspapers, especially east of the Mississippi, as Mexicans, Puerto Ricans, Cubans, and other Hispanic groups migrated to cities like Chicago, New York, Miami, and Tampa. In New York City alone, eight newspapers were started after World War II, including *El Diario de Nueva York*, a daily founded in 1948. In Miami, *Diario Las Américas* was started in 1953 by Horacio Aguirre. In Chicago, *Adelanto Bienestar Cultural*, a weekly, started in 1944 to serve the growing Mexican-American population drawn to the Windy City by jobs in factories and meat-packing plants.[12] By 1959, there were at least forty-three Spanish-language newspapers in active publication in the U.S.[13]

The second half of the twentieth century brought a dramatic increase in the number of Hispanics in the United States. Between 1960 and 2000, Hispanics became the largest minority group in the U.S., growing from 3.5 million in 1960 to 35.3 million in 2000, or 12.5% of the U.S. population.[14] In the earlier part of this period, most of this explosive growth was due to immigration. Drawn by freedom and opportunity and driven to the U.S. by wars, revolutions, and economic deprivation in their home countries, people from Cuba, Guatemala, El Salvador, the Dominican Republic, and other Latin American nations joined Mexicans and Puerto Ricans—U.S. citizens who continued migrating from the island to the mainland in large numbers—to form the dominant minority in America by 2001. Most of the Hispanic population was concentrated in ten U.S. states, with four of them—California, Texas, New York, and Florida—having the largest proportion.[15]

The growth of newspapers to serve this expanding audience corresponded with migration. Traditional urban centers that had served as magnets for Hispanic immigrants, such as Chicago and New York, saw vigorous growth in newspaper publishing. Fifteen new newspapers were started in these two cities between 1960 and 1990, such as *La Raza* in Chicago, a staunch champion of Chicano rights. In the Big Apple, *La Prensa* merged with *El Diario de Nueva*

New York to become *El Diario/La Prensa*, a powerful advocate for a Hispanic community becoming more diverse with the arrival of new immigrants from the Caribbean and Central and South America. But Spanish-language newspapers also began to pop up in heartland cities such as Reno, Oklahoma City, and Kansas City. And Spanish-language newspapers emerged for the first time in Atlanta and Washington, D.C. (*El Pregonero*), reflecting the migration of Hispanics to those cities, as well. Between 1970 and 2000, the number of Spanish-language newspapers in the U.S. more than doubled from 232 to 543.[16]

The greatest newspaper growth during the postwar period occurred in Florida, blessed geographically to be a peninsular gateway to Hispanic immigrants from the Caribbean and Latin America.[17] But Florida in the 1950s, still entrenched in Old South ideas about race and ethnicity, was not always a welcoming place for Hispanics or Latino newspaper editors. When Roland Manteiga returned home to Tampa and *La Gaceta* after the war, he jumped back into the newspaper business. He took classes at the University of Tampa to broaden his journalism skills. But *La Gaceta* struggled economically during this period because many companies in Tampa reflected the prejudices of the

Figure 3.2 The front page of *La Gaceta* in 1945, the year Roland Manteiga returned home from World War II and began his innovations at what would become America's oldest trilingual newspaper, publishing news in Spanish, English, and Italian.

Photo courtesy of *La Gaceta*

era and refused to do business with Hispanic-owned enterprises, including advertising with them. Manteiga had to become resourceful.

He traveled to the state capitol in Tallahassee and advocated for and promoted what came to be known in the Florida Legislature as "The *La Gaceta* Bill," which passed in 1955. The law made it legal for state and local governments to pay for and place legal advertisements—the economic lifeblood of newspapers—in publications with a minimum of 25% content written in English. "It was about surviving as a newspaper," Patrick Manteiga said.[18]

Another challenge Roland Manteiga and other Hispanic newspapers faced was **acculturation**. The **Latin** community in Tampa began to become less cohesive after World War II. In Tampa, the term "Latin," not to be confused with the language of Latin, is often used to refer to the Italian and Hispanic community collectively. "A lot of those boys coming home from the war were English proficient, and Latins were trying not to be Latin,"[19] Patrick Manteiga said. "There was a strong effort after the war to make sure the next generation was as Anglo as possible. There was a push for the children of Latins to be as successful as possible and that meant being as white and as English-speaking as possible."[20]

Figure 3.3 Cuesta Rey Cigar Factory.
Special Collections Tampa Library University of South Florida

The Birth of a Spanish-Language Newspaper

One-on-one with Maria Padilla, Founding Editor of El Sentinel

Maria Padilla was founding editor of *El Sentinel*, the 60,000-circulation bilingual newspaper that was started by the *Orlando Sentinel* in 2001 to serve the Latino community of Central Florida. A veteran journalist and native New Yorker of proud Puerto Rican heritage, Padilla has worked as a reporter, editor, or columnist for *The Wall Street Journal*, the *Orange County Register*, the *Reno Gazette-Journal*, the *San Juan Star*, *La Prensa*, and the *Orlando Sentinel*. In 2015, Padilla started a blog called *Orlando Latino*, some of her most recent work includes being assistant editor at *Tow Times* magazine, which covers the towing industry, and being a Hispanic affairs commentator for WFTV, the ABC affiliate in Orlando, Florida. She talked in this edited Q&A with journalism professor Rick Brunson about the development of *El Sentinel* and the role it and other Spanish-language newspapers play in their communities.

Question: Tell us about how the idea for *El Sentinel* came about?
Answer: The whole push for a Spanish-language newspaper was not new at the *Sentinel* in 2001. It had previously experimented with a

Figure 3.4 Maria Padilla, veteran newspaper journalist and founding editor of *El Sentinel*.

Photo courtesy of Maria Padilla

column called "Aquí y Allá" (Here and There) and had these awkward inserts into the county sections of the paper. But after the 2000 Census [the tipping point where Hispanics became the largest minority in the United States, including Florida] they got serious. And then Tim Franklin came on board as editor and he really pushed the idea. And to be honest, I didn't want to do it [be editor of *El Sentinel*] at first because I had spent all of my life up to that point writing and reporting in English and covering all kinds of issues—some related to Latinos and some not. I was reluctant because I didn't want to be pigeonholed and not able to do other things.

Q: What happened after you accepted the job?
A: Things accelerated quickly. I accepted the job in June 2001 and we had 90 days—just three months—to launch this paper that September. We had to hire staff, and to design the graphics and look of the paper, develop production schedules, and coordinate with the advertising and marketing departments. It was very stressful, but it was the most amazing three months of my life. I had free rein and a great deal of trust from my editors.

Q: *El Sentinel* was bilingual at first. Why?
A: Yes, it had Spanish-language stories with an English summary at the end. But what we found within a couple of months, as we were out in the community and heard from readers, was that people who were Spanish-language-dominant hated that. They told us, "It's either going to be a Spanish-language newspaper or it's not." So we stopped doing that and it became just a Spanish-language paper after three months.

Q: How big was your staff in those early days?
A: It was just three. Myself as editor, coordinating assignments, editing the stories, and doing everything but putting the damn thing on the press [laughter]. Then we had a reporter, Walter Pacheco, and our designer, Lydia Enriquez, who came over from features. Eventually, as circulation grew, we added two more reporters and two copy editors, making a staff of seven by the time I left in 2004 to go to the *Orlando Sentinel* editorial board.

Q: Tell us about the circulation of the paper.
A: We did a lot of things that were new. We were a free weekly that was delivered on Saturday mornings to households in Central Florida with Spanish surnames. Everybody does that now, but it was new then. We also had to look like a newspaper people were accustomed to seeing back home in other Latin countries. We did not restrict ourselves to what

Figure 3.5 Central Florida's Spanish-language local newspaper, *El Sentinel*.
Photo courtesy of Rick Brunson

the *Orlando Sentinel* looked like. We wanted to be something else—and we were. We pushed for more color, bigger photos, shorter stories. We started as a 16-page broadsheet and then quickly grew to 40 pages, thanks to the paper's popularity with readers and advertisers. Our circulation starting out was about 24,000, but it quickly jumped, and when I left it was pushing 60,000, Another new thing we did was when we launched *El Sentinel* we also simultaneously partnered with Univision to air 2-minute segments about stories in that weekend's edition. Later, we switched to Telemundo, but it was a good example of the convergence and synergy the *Orlando Sentinel*, and its parent company, Tribune, was pushing those days.

Q: Describe *El Sentinel's* distinct editorial style.
A: Because we were a weekly with Tuesday deadlines, we couldn't cover breaking news. People had already read about it by the time our paper landed on their doorstep on Saturday. So we had to take a different approach. We wrote with a unique point of view—a Latino point of view. On any story, we would find how Latino families were being impacted and write about it from their perspective. The general newspaper is not always going to do that. But we pounded the pavement and went after

that story and that reader. That was my concept of *El Sentinel*. We're going to write the story from the point of view of the Latinos impacted by it. We could find the Latino thread to any story. We brought new voices into the paper. And with sports we stuck to those most important to our audience—the three Bs—*baloncesto, béisbol,* and *boxeo* (basketball, baseball, and boxing). We added *fútbol* later as we grew.

Q: As editor of a Spanish-language newspaper, how did you cover a Hispanic community like Central Florida's that is so diverse and has different subcultures, such as Puerto Ricans, Venezuelans, Cubans, and Colombians?

A: We took a two-pronged approach. One was staffing. Four of us were Puerto Ricans. Three were not and were from Central America. Because the Puerto Rican community is the dominant group of Hispanics in Central Florida, we decided we could not shift our eyes away from that community. But we also worked hard to strike a balance and cover events and issues of interest to Colombians, Mexicans, and other groups, whether it was a rally or a discussion forum about something going on back home. Our reporters went out and spent time in those communities to get to know them, establish relationships and cover what was important to them. That's what we did. That was the second prong of our approach. Latino reporters are not just interested in their own Latino community because when you get to the United States you understand it is Pan-Hispanic. We care about what is going on in all of the Latino communities, and it made us proud to have a good mix of stories.

Q: How did and how does *El Sentinel* continue to not only inform the Latino community but also give form, shape, and voice to the community and its identity?

A: An English-language paper tends to talk about "Latinos" in general terms. When you are a Spanish-language newspaper, you identify people and drill down to talk about them in concrete, specific ways that show what they are really like and what they really care about. Whether they are Venezuelan or Colombian or Puerto Rican. We painted a more detailed picture of who we were—more of a mosaic of people from all walks of life and all Latino cultures—and people appreciated that. I would like to think that we helped people understand and know who is here. It's not enough to know that 30% of Orange County is Latino. Who are these people? Where do they come from? Why are they here? Those are the questions we tried to answer. And I'm proud of that. It gives me great pleasure and pride that we gave voice to a whole lot of people.

However, instead of acquiescing to acculturation, Roland Manteiga creatively leveraged diversity into a strategy that both widened his audience and strengthened the political and economic power of the Latin community in Tampa. *La Gaceta* became trilingual in the 1950s, adding coverage in both English and Italian to its pages. After Manteiga became editor in 1961, a year that brought another wave of Cuban migration to Florida in the wake of Fidel Castro and his revolution's rise to power on the island, *La Gaceta's* readership swelled.[21]

In addition to reporting on international politics and events, Manteiga and *La Gaceta* started focusing intensely on the politics of Tampa, Hillsborough County, and the state of Florida, becoming a must-read for politicians and business leaders.[22] He also added a popular entertainment section in the 1970s. Readership and circulation of *La Gaceta* took off in the 1970s and 1980s as Tampa became more accepting of Latinos in government and business, and as cultural and architectural preservation began to become a priority for both Anglos and Latinos in the city. As Ybor City's rich immigrant and Latin heritage—reflected in the architecture of its cigar factories, restaurants, bakeries, and its mutual aid societies—became threatened by gentrification and the arrival of a federal interstate highway that cut through the enclave's heart, *La Gaceta* championed its preservation.

Meanwhile, down in Miami, Florida's largest English-language newspaper during this period, *The Miami Herald*, launched *El Nuevo Herald*, a Spanish-language insert, in 1976. It quickly evolved into a stand-alone newspaper that had a weekly circulation of 100,000 by the mid-1990s.[23] New Spanish-language newspapers began to pop up in cities all over the Sunshine State—such as growing tourism hubs like Orlando and even little communities like Immokalee, an agricultural town where Latino hands and backs gather much of the South Florida fruits and vegetables trucked to the rest of the nation's kitchen tables.

Anglo Expansion into the Hispanic Newspaper Market

By the 1990s, English-language newspapers and the Anglo companies that owned them had discovered Hispanics and viewed them and their growing buying power as a hot commodity. The Hispanic population in the U.S. had exploded by 53% between 1980 and 1990 to 22.4 million people. Almost one in every ten Americans was Hispanic. A higher birth rate among U.S. Hispanics than the rest of the population and a continuing influx of new arrivals from Mexico, Central, and South America and the Caribbean largely contributed to this impressive demographic growth.[24] By 2001, the nation's Hispanic population hit 35.3 million and Latinos surpassed African-Americans as the largest minority group in the United States. With this growth came a rise in education levels and household incomes, even though the median family income for Hispanics continued to significantly lag behind that of other U.S. households.[25] Nevertheless, as total newspaper circulation in the U.S. peaked in 1984 at

63.3 million and began its long slide in the face of competition from television and other electronic media, owners of Anglo newspaper companies saw potential for new readers and market growth among the nation's burgeoning Hispanic population.[26]

Starting in the late 1980s and continuing into the early 2000s, Anglo newspapers began aggressively trying to market themselves to Hispanics by offering new sections written in Spanish that were inserted into the main English-language newspaper or by starting stand-alone daily or weekly newspapers—both tabloids and broadsheets—with content exclusively in Spanish or in Spanish and English.[27] In California, the Times Mirror-owned *Los Angeles Times* launched *Nuestro Tiempo*, a monthly bilingual supplement that quickly became a weekly with a circulation of 400,000 at its peak in 1992.[28] One of the nation's largest newspaper chains, Tribune Company, owner of the flagship *Chicago Tribune*, launched the weekly *Éxito!* in Chicago and cranked out the daily *Hoy* in New York under the auspices of its Long Island *Newsday*. Building on its corporate synergy, Tribune would eventually expand the publication of *Hoy* into Chicago and Los Angeles. The A.H. Belo Company, publisher of *The Dallas Morning News*, began publication of the daily Spanish-language *Al Día* with a circulation of 80,000 in North Texas. The Washington Post Company bought its way into the Latino market by purchasing the existing *El Tiempo Latino*.[29]

Other smaller English-language papers in smaller markets around the country also got into the act. The *Garden City Telegram* in Kansas, with only a circulation of 11,000, started *La Semana*, and the 24,000-circulation *Yuma Daily Sun* in Arizona started *Baja El Sol*—all in an attempt to draw Hispanic readers.[30] The trade journal *American Journalism Review (AJR)* articulated the strategy behind these initiatives in 1999:

> The hope is that after exposure to a newspaper's non-English publication, readers will eventually gravitate to the English-language paper as they assimilate. This may be a long time coming, but at least in the meantime a newspaper's foreign-language efforts will help reflect the community it serves.[31]

As *AJR* would later report, these efforts met with mixed results. Hispanics represented only 6.7% of readers of English-language newspapers in 2001 even as they represented 13% of the country. Some Hispanics saw the creation of special Spanish-language sections or editions as "ghettoizing" coverage of the Latino community and issues of importance to them, such as immigration, education, and health care. "We do not live our life in special sections, and these sections sometimes put you in a little box," commented Raúl Ramirez, news director of KQED Public Radio in San Francisco. "It's a limited vision."[32]

Anglo-owned newspapers faced the dual challenge of either treating Hispanics as a niche audience or "**mainstreaming**" them into their coverage in the "regular" paper, as well as attracting advertisers to their Spanish-language publications. In some cases, the challenge was too much. By the early 1990s, the *Los Angeles Times* closed the money-losing *Nuestro Tiempo* and instead purchased a 50% stake in local competitor, *La Opinión*, at that time the nation's largest Spanish-language daily. The *Times* did not give up on reaching Latinos in Southern California, but it had to find other ways to go about it.[33]

In English-Language News . . .

Frances Robles

Born in New York, Frances Robles started her journalism career working for the *Plain Dealer* in Cleveland after graduating from New York University. Robles later worked for the *Miami Herald* for 19 years before the *New York Times* hired her as a correspondent. She was inducted into the National Association of Hispanic Journalists Hall of Fame, honored with a George Polk Award in Journalism, and has worked on Pulitzer Prize-winning teams. Robles is best known for her investigative work that ultimately freed several wrongly convicted prisoners. She is of Puerto Rican descent and recently covered Hurricane Maria's impact on the island.

Sources: Stanford.edu, *NY Times*, MediaMoves.com

Figure 3.6 Frances Robles
Photo courtesy of Frances Robles

For their part, the independent Spanish-language press met this new competition and incursion of Anglo-owned newspapers into their traditional market with vigor. In Miami, *Diario Lás Américas* went toe-to-toe with *El Nuevo Herald* and maintained a healthy circulation of 69,000 on weekdays and 73,000 on Sunday.[34] These papers reflected the uniqueness of their communities and their owners were local. The pages and coverage of these organic newspapers—with their bold photos, bold opinions, bold colors, and bold layouts—reflected the kinds of newspapers in substance and style that immigrants from Latin countries were accustomed to. They also were not as hidebound to U.S. journalistic notions of objectivity. At these papers, *la política y el boxeo son la misma cosa*, or "politics and boxing are the same thing." The National Association of Hispanic Publications, a trade group representing Hispanic-owned newspapers, also developed a special seal of authenticity for members to display on their pages to show that they were actually owned by Latinos.

That is not to say that the Spanish-language press remained small and provincial. In 2004, the two largest Spanish-language newspapers in the United States—*La Opinión* in Los Angeles and *El Diario/La Prensa*, its New York counterpart—joined forces to create Impremedia, a publishing powerhouse that would compete with major media companies for Latino readers in those cities, as well as other major cities such as Chicago, San Francisco, and Houston. With this merger, the Lozano family, which had founded *La Opinión* in 1926, became the most powerful Hispanic newspaper moguls in America.[35]

The New Millennium and the Digital Age

A confluence of events in the first decade of the new millennium—the recession of 2008, the advent of Apple's iPhone, and the rise of social media—sent printed newspapers, Anglo and Latino, into a tailspin as readers rushed to consume news on new digital platforms and advertisers in turn fled print to follow them. Reflecting a national trend, circulation of the three largest Spanish-language dailies—*El Nuevo Herald*, *La Opinión*, and *El Diario/La Prensa*—in just one year dipped by an average of 12%.[36]

But weeklies—always the staple and a favorite of Latino audiences—stubbornly held their own into the second decade of the new millennium and do to this day. The nation's twenty-five largest Spanish-language weeklies, with an average circulation of more than 100,000, actually grew their readership by 2% on average in 2015. Some of these weeklies enjoyed explosive growth. *The Monitor—El Extra* in the border town of McAllen, Texas, saw its circulation jump a whopping 93% year over year.[37] And its Lone Star State neighbor, Hearst Corporation's *La Voz de Houston*, expanded its circulation to 405,000 and began publishing twice weekly, offering a compelling mix of enterprise reporting on issues of importance to Latinos, sports, and entertainment news, as well as provocative commentary.[38]

Many weeklies, like Tampa's *La Gaceta*, rely on single-copy, rack, or pick-up point sales at strategic distribution points in counties, communities, and neighborhoods with heavy concentrations of Latinos. Tapping into the loyalty and cultural identity of Hispanic community are key parts of their survival strategy. They continue to persist. "In 1984, I sat down with my father and talked about how we were going to approach the internet," says *La Gaceta's* Patrick Manteiga. "We decided to wait until we could see a newspaper with a business model on the internet that worked. We're still waiting. Chasing the internet has caused newspapers to fail faster in this country more than anything else. I'm fine with not serving the people who expect us to give our product away and don't want to buy us on a regular basis."[39]

However, in the face of growing preference of all Americans—Anglo and Latino—for digital media, Spanish-language newspapers face a growing challenge. Today, Hispanics represent over 17% of the U.S. population. Six in ten of them speak English or are bilingual and are Millennials (aged 18 to 23) or younger. They have grown up with digital devices and the philosophy the internet was founded on that news and information should be free.[40] Where will these younger Hispanics get their news? Increasingly, the answer is newspaper content presented on mobile devices.

As the Pew Research Center reported in 2016,

> The story of technological adoption among Latinos has long been a unique one. While Latinos have lagged other groups in accessing the internet and having broadband at home, they have been among the most likely to own a smartphone, to live in a household without a landline phone where only a cellphone is available and to access the internet from a mobile device.[41]

Reflecting that reality, ElDiarioNY.com, ElNuevoHerald.com, and LAOpinion.com—the websites of the three largest Spanish-language daily newspapers—all report receiving at least three times as many visitors to their digital content via mobile devices than desktop computers. *El Nuevo Herald's* digital efforts are particularly noteworthy. Under the leadership of editor Myriam Márquez, *El Nuevo Herald* grew local digital traffic by 28% and video views by more than 100%.[42] Video is a key source of revenue growth for newspapers in the digital age when the subscriber base is shrinking and revenue must be captured on the advertising side. Viewers may not like those short, ten-second ads frontloaded on a news video, but they help pay the salaries of the journalists who produce the content and keep the newspaper in business.

El Nuevo Herald is also a leader on social media, with the largest number of followers on Twitter and Facebook among thirty media companies in McClatchy, the corporation that owns the paper. In 2017, Márquez launched AccesoMiami, a new digital site for business people and travelers from Latin America and Spain who are investing in or relocating to South Florida.

She also led the production of a Spanish-language news podcast, "De Todo Un Podcast." "It has never been more important to have an independent press, the pillar of a true democracy," said Márquez, a Havana-born Cuban exile who recently stepped down at *El Nuevo Herald*. "And no one understands that better than our stellar staff, many who have come to the United States fleeing the oppression of despotic governments."[43]

That spirit of today's Hispanic newspapers is also heard in the voice of young Latina reporter Tamara Mino, the Orlando, Florida, correspondent for *Mundo Hispánico*, an Atlanta-based, digital-first Spanish-language newspaper owned by Cox Media Group. Born in New York to parents who immigrated to the U.S. from Colombia and Argentina, 24-year-old Mino represents the present and future of both Hispanic demographics and American journalism. While the news stories she writes are first posted to and read by the 4 million followers of *Mundo Hispánico*'s Facebook page, her motivation is the same as the young Roland Manteiga, who returned from World War II to the pungent ink and clattering presses of Tampa's *La Gaceta* to champion the cause of the underdog and the oppressed.

Figure 3.7 Tamara Mino in Orlando, Florida, correspondent for *Mundo Hispánico*, an Atlanta-based Spanish-language digital and print newspaper operation with bureaus in 12 U.S. cities—from Los Angeles to Washington, D.C.—that publishes the latest news and videos on immigration, politics, entertainment, football, and stories that impact the Latino community.

Photo courtesy of Rick Brunson

Launching *La Voz Azteca*

by Alberto Mendoza
Executive Director for the National Association of Hispanic Journalists

In the fall of 1985, I started my sophomore year at Montgomery High School, a school located less than 7 miles from the U.S./Mexico border in south San Diego. A unique student dynamic occurred at Montgomery, the student population was made up of 65% Latinos, 30% Filipinos and 5% other. Of the Latino student percentage, nearly half were commuter students, which meant they lived in Mexico (mostly Tijuana) and crossed the border daily to attend high school. Back then, in Mexico, you had to test into the free public high school, if you didn't get in, you either had to pay to attend a private school, pay to attend a trade school, or, in our school's case, cross the border to attend high school in the U.S.

With nearly 30% of students commuting daily, the school dynamic became one in which the Filipino kids ran the school. As a student population, Latinos were the majority, but in school activities we were the minority. The Filipino students were the majority in ASB (Student Leadership), the award-winning school newspaper, the yearbook, cheerleading, sports, etc. There were some exceptions, meaning there were a few who managed to break through and land one of those leadership roles, but for the most part, we were shut out. I'm not suggesting

Figure 3.8 Alberto Mendoza, Executive Director, NAHJ
Photo courtesy of Alberto Mendoza

it was intentional; the reality was that the commuter students did not engage in our school activities. Their long daily commutes and Spanish as the primary language meant their time for other activities was minimal. I believe this also impacted the other Latino students who lived in the U.S. but were involved either because they did not not feel the support or even confidence to try out for the roles. On the other hand, the Filipino students had stronger support and networks so they easily stepped in.

While a lot of Latino students knew this was a problem, most figured it was unchangeable and the others simply didn't care.

But I did.

It was not okay for me to keep the status quo, at least not without trying to do something to promote a more balanced student engagement. I knew that this type of school involvement was also key to college admission (along with grades), so by default we were already minimizing our chances to attend a 4-year college. It was important to me to make sure the Latino students had access to these activities and especially leadership roles. So I went to the school paper administrators and asked them to include a small monthly calendar that listed school activities, meeting dates, sports tryouts, application deadlines, all of it, but in Spanish. I had hoped that, by doing so, it would encourage the commuter students who were mostly Spanish speakers and others of us who were working toward being bilingual to see this as a gesture to keep them informed and get them engaged.

They said no.

Unsatisfied with this answer, but powerless to do much about it, I decided I needed to do something drastic. For me, that meant running for Student Body Vice President, as a sophomore . . . which was unheard of since it was the juniors who usually ran to be in office their senior year. I knew the odds were against me. I wasn't popular, I had never been involved in student government or student activities, but I figured it was my only chance . . . with power maybe I could change the system from the inside. So I went for it. I was running against a very qualified student leader who was Filipino.

At first, it was a slow campaign, but then the Latino students started to get excited that one of their own was running so they started backing my campaign, cheering me on during debates, you name it, they were there . . . for a second, I thought I had a chance to win . . . but when the elections came and went, I lost. My fellow Latino students/supporters failed to show up to vote and my competitor won. In retrospect, I did not run a good campaign and I failed to have a solid platform, one that was universal to all students, not just Latino students. As I shared, there were some exceptions, such as the student who became the student body president: she was Latina and she won.

I was devastated for about a week, but deep down inside I knew I could build from this and try again the following year. Armed with experience, a new strategy, and a broader coalition of support was how I was going to win that election.

And so I did, I was elected Student Body Vice President.

And while for some that was the goal, for me it was the beginning of change . . . I believed I could leverage my leadership role to once again push for what I wanted the school paper to do the previous year . . . to do more to be inclusive and open access to all.

I remember setting up a meeting with the student newspaper advisor to discuss this and, this time, to my surprise, she eagerly said yes. But she also said, why don't we do more than a calendar, why don't you do a full page insert of stories affecting these students, written by them and for them. That seemed like a great idea to me, not really knowing what that meant, and before I knew it, I was off to recruit a team of writers, editors, photographers, you name it. It wasn't easy but in the end I was

Figure 3.9 Alberto Mendoza with the *La Voz* high school newspaper staff, targeting the Hispanic/Latino student population at Montgomery High School in South San Diego, CA.

Photo courtesy of Alberto Mendoza

able to recruit seven students and two who were already in the school paper to help us. The nine of us were going to launch a new Spanish language insert.

But what was supposed to turn into an insert, quickly turned into a four-page newspaper. It was clear that we had a lot to say and it needed its own format, so the first Spanish-language high school newspaper in California was born. I named it *La Voz Azteca*.

But the hard part was just beginning. At first some of the students in the English paper were not happy with us and felt there shouldn't be a separate paper, especially one in Spanish. "They are here to learn English," is what I heard frequently or, "then we'll have a paper in Tagalog." It got to the point where we were not allowed to share the student newsroom with them and we were only allowed to use it from 5.30–7 a.m. and from 7–9 p.m. Some of that was due to minimal capacity; their student paper had over 30 students and we only had six to eight computers, but some of it was also due to animosity.

Little by little we began to collaborate, share, and work together. Since we started late into the school year, we produced six to eight four-page newspapers and before the year was up, recruitment efforts for the next staff of *La Voz* grew to 20, then 30, and then 50.

Twenty-eight years later, *La Voz Azteca* continues to thrive, and it now has its own class in a large classroom with over 50 Macs. I've heard the class has also expanded to two periods to expand demand. They now produce digital content, award-winning stories, and, more importantly, what I had hoped for: more student engagement form Latino students. It also produced a new crop of Latino journalists that, because of their experience at *La Voz*, could now have a clear path to becoming journalists.

This last point (a new crop of Latino journalists) was one I had also hoped for, but I never knew if it had materialized. I have gone back a few times to speak to the students of *La Voz*; I did it at the 10- and 20-year anniversaries but I still did not know how many alumni became professional journalists . . . not until June 29, 2016, when at a meeting with newsroom leaders and NAHJ members, I met a *La Voz Azteca* alumni who was now working as a professional journalist, her name is Vanessa Nevarez.

I did not pursue a career in journalism. I went the route of non-profit management and community engagement, but in the mid-summer of 2015 I was hired to serve as the Executive Director of the National Association of Hispanic Journalists (NAHJ). NAHJ's mission is to diversify newsrooms by empowering Latino/Hispanic journalists to ascend to all levels of success in the field and as much as possible have newsrooms reflect the communities they serve. If it sounds similar to the reasons why I pushed for the paper 30 years prior, it is because they are. I've come full circle.

Promoting access, equality, fair representation of our communities, giving a voice to those who don't have one, and standing up for what's right. I currently support a new generation of Latino/Hispanic journalists, that has been my personal mission and it's been a part of NAHJ's work for over 30 years. To have my past and present align can only mean that this is where I was destined to be.

"I love politics, and I love covering social change," Mino says, sitting in her newsroom in downtown Orlando, her MacBook Pro cracked open as she taps out her latest dispatch. "I would never be anything else than a reporter because you get to walk in somebody else's shoes and see the world through their eyes."[44]

Those "Hispanic-colored glasses."

Vocabulary Words

Acculturation	Latin
Bracero Program	Lector
Executive Order 8802: Prohibition	Mainstream
of Discrimination Against	*Torcedores* and *Tabaqueros*
Defense Industry	

Points to Remember

- About 400,00 Hispanic men and women served in the U.S. Armed Forces during World War II.
- *La Prensa* and *La Opinión* published content in poetry, literature, and commentaries that served and reflected the Hispanic community.
- Toward the end of World War II, Spanish-language newspapers flourished to about 400 in America, especially weeklies.
- The Prohibition of Discrimination Against Defense Industry executive order signed by President Franklin Roosevelt in 1941, prohibited racial inequity and promoted employment opportunities for Latino workers.
- There was a significant increase in the Hispanic population between 1960 and 2000, making them the largest minority group in the U.S.
- Hispanics currently account for over 17% of the U.S. population. About 60% of them speak English or are bilingual and are Millennials (age 18 to 33) or younger.

Names to Remember

Ignacio Lozano
Myriam Márquez
Patrick Manteiga
Rafael Viera
Roland Manteiga

Practice Questions

1   Upon returning from serving in the armed forces in World War II, what did Roland Manteiga yearn to accomplish in *La Gaceta* newspaper? What did he propose in the 1950s that changed the direction of the newspaper?

2   With an increasing number of Hispanics migrating to the U.S. after World War II, what effect did it have on newspapers? Specify which Hispanic groups migrated in most number and to what cities.

3   In 1955, what bill did Roland Manteiga advocate for in response to the prejudices that existed in Florida? When was it passed and how did it help newspapers?

4   During what period did Anglo newspapers begin to market their content to Hispanics? What triggered this move? Give an example of a periodical that has successfully done this.

5   In this new digital age, what challenges are newspapers increasingly facing? What specific demographic is threatening the livelihood of periodicals? What approach have they adopted to counteract these issues?

Activity

Content Presentation in Online Newspapers: Explore the websites of the top three largest Spanish-language daily newspapers: ElDiarioNY.com, ElNuevo Herald.com, and LAOpinion.com. Determine and compare how they are communicating their content (video, audio, written)? Which website do you think contains content that is more interactive and appealing? Are there any differences? Or are they all presenting their information similarly? Choose the website you would most likely obtain news information from and explain why.

Timeline

1913: Victoriano Manteiga migrated from Cuba to Tampa, Florida.
1922: Newspaper *La Gaceta* is founded by Victoriano Manteiga.
1941: Pearl Harbor, America enters World War II. President Franklin Roosevelt signs the Prohibition of Discrimination executive order.
1950s: *La Gaceta* becomes a trilingual newspaper, offering content in Spanish, English, and Italian.

1955: The *La Gaceta* Bill is passed.

1959: About forty-three Spanish-language newspapers are active in the U.S.

1960: Hispanic population begins to increase exponentially.

1961: Roland Manteiga replaces his retiring father as editor of the newspaper.

1976: *The Miami Herald* launches its Spanish-language newspaper, *El Nuevo Herald*.

1998: *La Gaceta* becomes the oldest continually published trilingual newspaper in America. Manteiga dies.

2000: Spanish-language newspapers have more than doubled in number from 232 to 543 since 1970.

2001: Hispanics become the largest minority group in the U.S, accounting for 13% of the population.

2004: *La Opinión* and *El Diario/La Prensa* merged to create Impremedia, making the Lozano family the most powerful Hispanic newspaper owners in America.

2016: Sales of *El Nuevo Herald*, *La Opinión*, and *El Diario/La Prensa*, the most circulated Hispanic newspaper in the U.S., drop by about 12%. Hispanics account for over 17% of the U.S. population, with 60% of them able to speak English or being bilingual and Millennials or younger.

2017: AccessoMiami is launched by Myriam Márquez.

Additional Resources

"Hispanic and African American News Media Fact Sheet," *Pew Research Center*, August 7, 2017: www.journalism.org/fact-sheet/hispanic-and-african-american-news-media/
"More Than 200 Years of Latino Media in the United States by Félix F. Gutiérrez": www.nps.gov/heritageinitiatives/latino/latinothemestudy/media.htm
La Gaceta Newspaper: http://lagacetanewspaper.com/
America Rodríguez, *Making Latino News: Race, Language, Class* (Thousand Oaks, CA: Sage, 1999).

About the Author

Associate Instructor Rick Brunson, M.A., teaches reporting, editing, journalistic principles, and ethics, as well as magazine production in the Nicholson School's journalism program. He serves as the instructor/adviser for the NSC's award-winning magazine, *Centric*, and advises the NSC's chapter of the Radio Television Digital News Association. When he's not in the classroom, he's in the

Rick Brunson
Photo courtesy of University of Central Florida

newsroom. Brunson, who recently marked 30 years of professional experience as a working journalist, serves as the writing coach at WFTV Channel 9 Eyewitness News and works as a part-time production editor at the *Orlando Sentinel*.

Before joining the UCF faculty in 2003, Brunson worked as a reporter or editor at newspapers throughout Central Florida, including the *Sentinel*, the *Tampa Tribune*, and the *Daytona Beach News-Journal*. A proud Knight and longtime Central Florida resident, Brunson graduated from UCF in 1984 with a bachelor's degree in sociology with a minor in journalism and then earned a master's degree in American history from the University of South Florida in 1999. He lives in Orlando with his wife, Ruthe. They are the proud parents of two adult children.

Notes

1 Patrick Manteiga, interview by Rick Brunson, phone interview, June 13, 2017.
2 Lorena Oropeza, "Latinos in World War II: Fighting on Two Fronts," *National Park Service*, October 23, 2015, www.nps.gov/articles/latinoww2.htm.
3 *La Gaceta*, "Our History," http://lagacetanewspaper.com/our-history.
4 Ibid.
5 Manteiga, interview by Rick Brunson.
6 U.S. Department of Commerce, "We the American . . . Hispanics," *Bureau of the Census*, September, 1993, www.census.gov/prod/cen1990/wepeople/we-2r.pdf.
7 Ibid.
8 U.S. Department of Commerce, "We the American . . . Hispanics."
9 Felix F. Gutierrez, "More than 200 Years of Latino Media in the United States," *U.S. National Park Service*, 2013, www.nps.gov/heritageinitiatives/latino/latinothe mestudy/media.htm.
10 Robert B. Kent and Maura E. Huntz, "Spanish-Language Newspapers in the United States," *Geographical Review* 86, no. 3 (1996): 446–456.
11 U.S. Department of Commerce, "We the American . . . Hispanics."
12 Kent and Huntz, "Spanish-Language Newspapers in the United States."
13 Ibid.
14 "The Hispanic Population," *United States Census Bureau*, May, 2001, www.census.gov/prod/2001pubs/c2kbr01–3.pdf.
15 Ibid.
16 Kent and Huntz, "Spanish-Language Newspapers in the United States."
17 Ibid.
18 Manteiga, interview by Rick Brunson.
19 Ibid.
20 Ibid.
21 Gutierrez, "More than 200 Years of Latino Media in the United States."
22 *La Gaceta*, "Ronald Manteiga," 2017, http://lagacetanewspaper.com/our-history/roland-manteiga.
23 Kent and Huntz, "Spanish-Language Newspapers in the United States."
24 U.S. Department of Commerce, "We the American . . . Hispanics."
25 "The Hispanic Population," *United States Census Bureau*.
26 Pew Research Center, "Newspaper Fact Sheet," *Pew Research Center: Journalism & Media*, June 1, 2017, www.journalism.org/fact-sheet/newspapers.

27 John Morton, "Reflecting their Diverse Audiences," *American Journalism Review* 21, no. 7 (1999): 92.

28 Rosario Garriga, "The Hispanic Challenge," *American Journalism Review*, December, 2001, http://ajrarchive.org/article.asp?id=2358.

29 Morton, "Reflecting their Diverse Audiences."

30 Ibid.

31 Ibid.

32 Garriga, "The Hispanic Challenge."

33 Allen R. Meyerson, "Newspapers Cut Spanish-Language Publications," *The New York Times*, October 16, 1995, www.nytimes.com/1995/10/16/business/news papers-cut-spanish-language-publications.html.

34 Morton, "Reflecting their Diverse Audiences."

35 Abigail Goldman and Jose Cardenas, "Spanish Language Newspapers *La Opinión, El Diario* to Merge," *Los Angeles Times*, January 16, 2004, http://articles.latimes.com/2004/jan/16/business/fi-opinion16.

36 Elisa Shearer, "Hispanic News Media: Fact Sheet," *State of the News Media 2016, Pew Research Center*, June 15, 2016, www.journalism.org/2016/06/15/hispanic-media-fact-sheet/?platform=hootsuite.

37 Katerina E. Matsa, "Hispanic Media Fact Sheet," *State of the News Media 2015, Pew Research Center*, April, 2015, www.journalism.org/2015/04/29/hispanic-media-fact-sheet-2015.

38 "*La Voz de Houston* Adds Wednesday Edition, Quadruples Circulation," *Cision PR Newswire*, November 14, 2012, www.prnewswire.com/news-releases/la-voz-de-houston-adds-wednesday-edition-quadruples-circulation-179340961.html.

39 Manteiga, interview by Rick Brunson.

40 Eileen Patten, "The Nation's Latino Population is Defined by its Youth," *Pew Research Center: Hispanic Trends*, April 20, 2016, www.pewhispanic.org/2016/04/20/the-nations-latino-population-is-defined-by-its-youth.

41 Anna Brown, Gustavo Lopez and Mark Hugo Lopez, "Digital Divide Narrows for Latinos as More Spanish Speakers and Immigrants Go Online," *Pew Research Center: Hispanic Trends*, July 20, 2016, www.pewhispanic.org/2016/07/20/digital-divide-narrows-for-latinos-as-more-spanish-speakers-and-immigrants-go-online.

42 Ibid.

43 Luis F. Lopez, "Myriam Márquez Stepping Down as Head of *El Nuevo Herald*," *Miami Herald*, June 2, 2017, www.miamiherald.com/news/business/article15406 5664.html.

44 Tamara Mino, interview by Rick Brunson, personal interview, June 8, 2017.

Unit 2

Hispanic and LatinX Artists in Media

4 Hollywood's *Bronze Screen*

Hispanics and Latinos in U.S. Films

Nancy De Los Santos-Reza, M.A.

Writer, Producer, and Director for Glamorous
Tamale Productions

This chapter is adapted from the documentary film *The Bronze Screen: 100 Years of the Latino Image in Hollywood Cinema*, co-written by Nancy De Los Santos and Susan Racho.

At the beginning of the twentieth century, the motion picture was a wondrous new medium, thrilling audiences across the country and taking them to places most had neither heard of nor visited. At the time, movie-making producers were mostly East Coast businessmen who discovered they could make motion pictures in the land of sunshine, the state of California. These early filmmakers were attracted to the wide range of nearby locations that included mountains, beaches, and deserts, which made Los Angeles the ideal location for filmmaking.[1]

In addition, according to film historian Luis Reyes in *Hispanics in Hollywood: A Celebration of 100 Years in Film and Television*, East Coast filmmakers were also grateful for the distance created between them and the Edison Film Company, which controlled all of the available motion picture camera equipment on the East Coast at the time. Los Angeles represented creative and professional freedom. These early movie makers arrived in a city that just six decades earlier had been part of Mexico. Founded in 1791 by Spanish settlers, the city's name reflected its Spanish roots, "*Nuestra Señora Reina de Los Angeles*," which translates to "Our Lady Queen of Los Angeles." The city was simply known as Los Angeles. Early movie men, such as Lewis J. Selznick, Adolph Zukor, Samuel Goldwyn, and Marcus Loew, found a thriving metropolis ripe for the taking and perfect for making motion pictures.[2]

Early movies introduced audiences to an array of on-screen images and archetypal characters that could tell a story quickly: the hero, the villain, the damsel in distress, and the fallen woman. The hero characters were brave, bold, and true, and the actors who played them became the audience's modern-day heroes. Based on research conducted at the Library of Congress for the documentary *The Bronze Screen: 100 Years of the Latino Image in Hollywood Cinema* (2002), most of the 'heroic' roles were given to actors who were of

Anglo descent, white actors. Researchers also found that most of the negative roles were given to actors of color: Latinos, Blacks, and Asians.[3] Author George Hadley-García, in his book *Hispanic Hollywood: The Latins in Motion Pictures*,[4] also cites "historical competition" as one explanation, stating the American media were quick to mirror the bigotry inflamed by the Mexican Revolution, which some felt to be a barbaric civil war.

As Frank Javier García Berumen writes in his book *The Chicano/Hispanic Image in American Film*, ". . .there were only two types of Hispanics (in film): Docile and/or violent. . . . Neither could think for themselves." Berumen continues that the Yankee heroes of early films, and some decades later, were portrayed as superior to Hispanic characters in love and war, always winning the girl. He also states it was an "established practice" to present Blacks and Asians in negative portrayals.[5]

For audiences, many times what is seen on the screen is what one might expect in life. The sheer power of films can have an effect on our emotions and beliefs, and it cannot be denied that motion pictures can and do move, inspire, and sometimes, educate us. If the image of a person or culture one sees in motion pictures is continually the same or similar image, it only can lead to the belief that that depiction is based in truth and, therefore, a true representation.

In his book, *Latino Images in Film*, film scholar Charles Ramírez Berg speaks of "a fairly new critical approach" to the study of stereotypes in film, that of "representational studies."[6] Hollywood filmmakers rarely claim any film character portrayal to be a true-to-life or an exact representation of any person, even one presented in a film biography. A portrayal, of say Abraham Lincoln, is seen through the eyes of the writer and/or director; artistic license will mostly likely be utilized. And while filmmakers do not state that any film characterization is meant as a literal reflection of a person, culture, or community, looking at movies through *representational studies* we could come to a different conclusion. If a person, culture, or community is continually portrayed in the same manner, with the same accent, the same moral compass (or lack of), the same reactions to similar situations, without any digression from that portrayal, that very portrayal can and often does become the basis on which that person, culture, or community is known and judged.

In regard to the Latino male characters in films, he continues,

> If that were the only or rare instance of a Latino being a bad guy in a U.S. movie, there might be some validity to this argument (that movie characters do not represent reality). But the (negative Latino male) character is a descendant of a long line of Latino movie antagonists, stretching back to the silent-era "greaser" bandits.

In *The Bronze Screen: 100 Years of the Latino Image in Hollywood Cinema*, actor Edward James Olmos states: "I think this (the motion picture) is the strongest medium ever created in the history of the human species, bar none. It attacks the subconscious mind in a way that we have no idea of what the impact is." Some feel that moviegoers either believe what they see to be true, or use the information gained by seeing a movie as a foundation upon which to build their own beliefs. Actor Rita Moreno adds, in regard to the Latino image, "Hollywood is very influential in placing in the minds of people images of what we Latinos are." Actor John Leguizamo echoed those ideas in his interview for *The Bronze Screen*: "Movies become what you're represented as." Actor Esai Morales adds: "They [movies] become the subconscious images [of people] that the rest of the world will have." Unfortunately, many times, those images lead to the conclusion that Hispanic, African American, and Asian people are not of good character.[7]

It all began with the industry's first films. Early motion pictures were **MOS**, "without sound," but often accompanied by music, telling simple stories with easily identifiable characters. The hero was usually a handsome Anglo dressed in light-colored clothing and donning the proverbial "white hat." The villain was usually not attractive and sometimes had a mustache. If it was a western, the bad guy was often Native American or Mexican.

While many of these early silent films have been lost with time, a few remain and reflect the negative roles thrust upon actors of color and negative images presented to audiences. Director D.W. Griffith's 1915 film, *The Birth of a Nation*, portrayed black men as "unintelligent and sexually aggressive towards white women." Some of these roles, adding injury to insult, were played by white actors in **blackface**. The NAACP attempted to have the film banned, yet this film was seen as a commercial success and became the first film to be screened by a sitting President at the White House, Woodrow Wilson in 1915.[8]

During this time, Asian women were also given little consideration in film, with very few portrayals. Female Asian characters were usually depicted as stereotypical "dragon ladies," attractive but domineering and conniving. As early Hollywood film actress Anna May Wong said in a 1993 *Los Angeles Times* interview, "Why is it that the screen Chinese is nearly always the villain of the piece, and so cruel a villain—murderous, treacherous, a snake in the grass? We are not like that. . . . We have our own virtues. We have our rigid code of behavior, of honor. Why do they never show these on the screen?"[9]

It could be argued that the Latino image was given some of the worst treatment, perhaps due to Mexico's proximity geographically, historically, and economically to California and Los Angeles. During the early decades of the twentieth century, Mexico was struggling to rebuild itself from a civil war, the Mexican Revolution, and was looked upon as a nation in distress and flux with little effort to adhere to the law of the land. Mexico was also considered to be a place to escape from the law, and "let loose."

To California residents, 1930s Tijuana, just over the border, was little more than a convenient playground for drinking and carousing—an escape from the restraints of the **Prohibition Era**. Many early filmmakers and actors joined in the fun over the border at the horseraces, gambling establishments, and nightlife.

Maybe unjustly extrapolating, visitors who consorted with the Mexicans who worked in the nightclubs and bars as dancers, bartenders, and gamblers, felt these few represented the general Mexican population. Filmmakers often work with what they have experienced, and these visits may have influenced their opinions and formulated their perceptions of the Mexican people and their culture. Thus Latinos, mostly Mexicans, became the underbelly characters in films produced during that time.

The Greaser Movies

Some of the movies' first bad guys were Mexicans called "**greasers**." The term "greaser" has its roots in myth and in reality. During the late 1800s, many of the workers who tanned hides for a living were Mexican, or of Mexican heritage, and used a greasy mixture for use in converting animal hides for manufacturing shoes and saddles. Another version of the same story has Mexican men working on wagon wheels and adding grease to the wheels to keep them running smoothly. In early movies, "greaser" took on a negative connotation and was used to label the Mexican movie villain. The "greaser" characters were dangerous and prone to violence and mayhem. Some of the film titles reflect the attitude U.S. Anglos had in relation to their neighbors to the south. *Licking the Greaser* (1914), *Broncho Billy and The Greaser* (1914), *Tony the Greaser* (1911), they all presented the Mexican as short-tempered, violent, and downright mean—a bad *hombre*. In *Broncho Billy's Redemption* (1910), it is a Mexican who steals the dying man's money. In *The Gun Fighter* (1917), the Mexican villain kicks a young child clinging to its mother and carries the mother away. In *Arizona Wooing* (1915), the Mexican cowboy character— a *bandido* wearing a *sombrero*—ties up the film's Anglo hero, taunting him and slapping him in the face. In the 1910 film *The Cowboy's Baby*, the greaser was especially evil and even sadistic, throwing the hero's child into a rushing river.

This was not a great start for the Latino image in film, and it is important to note that, while U.S. audiences cheered at these films, Hispanics did not. In 1922, Mexico threatened to boycott all U.S. films with negative depictions that portrayed its people as dumb and violent "greasers."[10] Some Latin American countries supported the ban, resulting in concern for U.S. and South American trade relations. President Woodrow Wilson implored the movie studios to "be a little kinder to the Mexicans."[11]

These early negative images of Latinos continue to this day. The gang member or cartel drug runner is the new *bandido*. With so many negative depictions of Latinos in films, let's pose this question: What do you think of when you think of Latino roles in Hollywood movies? Is it Tony Montana of "Say hello to my little friend" fame, from *Scarface* (1983) and played by non-Hispanic Al Pacino? Or maybe it's Esai Morales in *Bad Boys* (1983) or any of the Puerto Rican Sharks in *West Side Story* (1961).

Movies are not just entertainment. They can often be the basis on which many people build their opinions of what others are like in reality. If the portrayals of a particular group are limited to negative portrayals, one can only assume that these portrayals will become the foundations of what people believe a community, a racial group, an ethnic group is. In some cases, this negative image is the only role model available for those very people to aspire. As Ramírez Berg offers in *Latino Images in Film*, "With repetition . . . narration becomes representation."[12]

From "Bandidos" to Latin Lovers

After the period of the "Greaser Films," Latino portrayals took a 180-degree turn. In the early 1920s, Latinos lost their *sombreros* and mustaches, replacing them with a much-desired look—that of slicked-back hair and bedroom eyes. The Latin Lover was born. Both Latino men and women were sexualized, romanticized as spicy sex symbols. The change began, interestingly enough, with a non-Hispanic, Rudolph Valentino, portraying a sensual Spanish bull-fighter in *Blood and Sand* (1922). Following that success, Hollywood filmmakers embraced the "Latin type," opening the doors to actors Gilbert Roland, Ramón Navarro, Lupe Vélez, and Dolores del Río.

With his good looks, Mexican stage actor Ramón Novarro was the first Latin American star and one of the first male sex symbols. He had the good fortune to be cast as the lead in *Ben Hur* (1926), the most expensive silent movie ever made, and a huge success. But Hollywood filmmakers still had this hang-up about their actors being "Mexican." Author George Hadley García puts it this way,

> Dolores del Río was from Mexico, and proud of it. She came from a semi-aristocratic family, but Hollywood Europeanized her (her producers wanted her bio to refer to her as "Spanish").[13] She resented this, but the only background that was esteemed in Hollywood at that time, and for a long time after, was the European background.

On a lighter note, the Latin Lover character was so successful that Austrian Jewish actor, Jacob Krantz, in an effort to be more "sellable," changed his name to the Latin-sounding Ricardo Cortez. Only in Hollywood.

Talkies Change the Movies

Before the first **talkies** came to the screen (*The Jazz Singer*, 1927), only looks counted. With the advent of the 'talkies' audiences would now also be *hearing* the actors' voices. Along with this improvement in storytelling came a boatload of trouble for actors with an accent. Some felt that speaking with an accent made one sound too foreign. Hadley-García says it best in *The Bronze Screen*:

It was a disaster for anyone who had a foreign accent, unless perhaps you were British. Many people's careers were ruined, Hungarians as well as Mexicans. Men with accents, like Gilbert Roland and Antonio Moreno, became supporting actors overnight because the American male establishment was threatened by the foreign men.[14]

But female actors with an accent were given a pass. Hadley-García adds, "Lupe Vélez and Dolores del Río, continued right on with their careers as though nothing had happened."[15] Spoken by a woman, an accent was considered sexy and acceptable. Vélez, best remembered for her *Mexican Spitfire* comedy films, used her accent to create self-deprecating characters, and laughed all the way to the bank. Although she did complain that she portrayed "Chinese, Eskimos, Japanese, Indian squaws, Hindus, Swedes, Malays and Javanese, but seldom Latin,"[16] it was her role as a Mexican in eight *Mexican Spitfire* films (1940–1943) that garnered enough commercial success to have her name above the film's title.

The world was shrinking, and Hollywood films were supplying a shared experience for audiences worldwide. Silent films were easily exported; all that was needed was to translate the "dialogue cards" within a film from English to whatever language necessary. The talkies changed that. In order to keep the international market supplied with the movies other countries craved, Hollywood studios filmed movies in English during the daytime, and using the same sets, camera set-ups, and sometimes even costumes, shot the same films with foreign language actors. One of the most successful films shot during the "Graveyard Shift" production schedule was the Spanish-language version of *Dracula* (1931), starring Mexican-born actress the late Lupita Tovar. In an interview for *The Bronze Screen*, Tovar spoke about the production:

> It was very difficult. We reported to makeup at 6 o'clock and we started shooting at 8. The English cast had gone out and then we go in and worked all night. We were one take, one take. We were very, very good. We wanted to prove that we were better, if not the same, than the American actors. We were paid less. I didn't care because it was enough for me and happy to have a job.[17]

The Great Depression (1929–1939) began with the economic crash of the U.S. stock market and resulted in many jobs being lost in the United States. Some felt that Mexicans were taking jobs from U.S. citizens, and the government responded with the sometimes-forced deportation of Mexicans and Mexican Americans to Mexico, known as **repatriation**. At the same time, U.S. movie audiences needed and wanted the movie experience to be one of escapism. In a cinematic **dichotomy**, the image of Latinos in film during this time was one of aristocratic South Americans in escapist fantasies. The Mexican actress Dolores del Río starred in a number of these films, including *Flying Down to Río* (1933)

Figure 4.1 Dolores del Río mural on Hollywood boulevard.
Meunierd/Shutterstock

as a Brazilian beauty who must choose between her Latino boyfriend and an American bandleader. The exquisite del Río headlined the film that co-starred newcomers Fred Astaire and Ginger Rogers. No spoiler alert here, but can you guess who she marries in the end?

The roles for Latino actors continued to be more of the same: villains, peons, cantina girls, and buffoons. One of the first Hollywood film Latino heroes was a fictional Mexican-American in the 1933 film *Bordertown*. Although the hero is Latino, he is a flawed character, and the film offers a peek into the racial prejudice experienced by Latinos at that time. It stars Paul Muni as a young man from the *barrio*, Johnny Ramírez, who graduates from law school. During his very first appearance in court, he loses his temper, punches out the opposing attorney, and is immediately disbarred. Ramírez has no choice but to go to a Mexican bordertown and run a casino. He falls in love with a beautiful and wealthy blond client, who rejects his advances, telling him, "You belong to a different tribe, Savage."[18] Yes, she calls him "savage." As film historian Charles Ramírez Berg states, "*Bordertown* becomes a cautionary tale to Mexican-Americans: Don't go outside the barrio, don't try for mainstream success. Stay where you are. That's where you belong."[19]

During this time in our country, Latinos were treated as second-class citizens, as were African Americans. In Texas and California, Mexican-American children were taught in separate schools; across the country Latino families were denied the purchase of homes in white neighborhoods; and on the east coast Puerto

Ricans were kept in their *barrios*. In the southwest it was common and acceptable for restaurants and establishments to have signs in their front windows that commanded, "No Dogs. Negros. Mexicans."

Paradoxically, the biggest boost to the Latin image in Hollywood films resulted from world events an ocean away.

Good Neighbors

In early 1930s Germany, Adolf Hitler was rising to power, setting up the scenario for World War II. The United States felt that, in order to protect itself from land and sea attacks by the German army or Japanese navy, its shores and borders needed to be secure. Therefore, the country needed to develop a better relationship with its neighbors to the south. Thus, the **Good Neighbor Policy** was created. And, to strengthen "hemispheric unity," then President Franklin Roosevelt reached out to the Motion Picture Division of the Office of the Coordinator of Inter-American Affairs to squash the stereotypes of Latin Americans that existed throughout society as a result of their portrayals in films. Film studios were urged to show Latin Americans in a more favorable light, and not perpetuate negative stereotypes as Latinos being lazy, unsophisticated, and downright, well, savage.

From this policy, a number of Hispanic and Latino actors were welcomed and given the star treatment. One successful recipient was Brazilian entertainer Carmen Miranda. She starred in a number of films as a happy and likeable character. Walt Disney got into the picture with a number of animated films, including the colorful *Three Caballeros* (1944), with a magical, musical tour throughout Latin America. Cuban Desi Arnaz was given a role in a drama film as a heroic U.S. soldier; Anthony Quinn played a key role in the epic *Guadalcanal Diary* (1943); and, in one of the most remarkable films of the decade, Latino military servicemen who were honored with the Congressional Medal of Honor were at the center of a modest, but heartfelt film, *A Medal For Benny* (1945).

During this time, sultry bombshell actress Margarita Cansino emerged, known as "The Love Goddess," and U.S.-born of Irish and Spanish descent, but studios, and maybe audiences, were not quite ready for their movie-star dream girls to be Hispanic. Cansino was reinvented with lighter hair and a new name, and transformed into the classic 1940s glamour girl with intelligence and humor as the newly minted Rita Hayworth.

Hayworth was not the only one asked to change her name, and many actors of that time did change their names to be more suitable for the marquee. But, for Latinos, the name change fell under the umbrella of hiding who you were— Latin. In *The Bronze Screen* documentary film, Ricardo Montalban stated that his studio wanted to change his name to Ricky Martin. Cesar Romero's producers suggested the Anglicization of "Cesar" to "Caesar." Contemporary actors were often given the same advice, as the late Elizabeth Peña shared, "My agent

Cuban Producer, Actor, and Musician

Desi Arnaz

Desiderio Alberto Arnaz y de Acha III, professionally known as Desi Arnaz, was a Cuban-born producer, actor, and musician who was most known for his role on the *I Love Lucy* (1951–1957) television show. He started his career appearing in Broadway musicals and several movies, including *Bataan* (1943). Soon after, he appeared with his wife, Lucille Ball, in *I Love Lucy*. His role allowed him to be the most successful entrepreneur on television at that time. He created Desilu Productions with his wife, which allowed him to create and produce many shows and movies. He passed away in 1986.

Sources: People.com, Biography.com, NY Times

Figure 4.2 U.S. postage stamp from 1999, featuring Lucille Ball and Desi Arnaz from the popular television sitcom *I Love Lucy.*

Tony Baggett/Shutterstock

seriously told me that, if I wanted to work, to change my name to Elizabeth Sterling. And I said . . . I have a banana stain all over my body."[20] Miss Peña did not agree and neither did the great character actress Lupe Ontiveros, who was told her name sounded "too ethnic." The feisty Miss Ontiveros replied, "Have you looked at me? I am ethnic!" Actor and comedian John Leguizamo (*To Wong Foo . . .*) adds, "Lecubano, Legs and Ammo, Legs and Gumbo, nobody could never say it. I said, 'I'm stickin' with it. It's made me who I am.'"[21]

Beginning the 1940s, films continued to have a politicized message, reflecting the United States' temperature [shift] from liberal to conservative. In the 1940s, the U.S. initiated "The Bracero Program," which brought much-needed workers from Mexico to fill agricultural jobs left behind by those who enlisted for military duty. The Bracero Program gave a legal opportunity to Mexicans to enter the U.S. and work, but it was not without abuses, which were reflected in the film *Border Incident* (1949), starring Ricardo Montalban. Montalban reflects on the film, "It showed the American public an aspect of the honorable working man, who is not somebody you sneeze at because he's a peon, because he comes to work in the lettuce fields."[22]

Changing Reels

By the early 1950s, the **Hollywood Blacklist**, spearheaded by then U.S. Senator Joseph McCarthy (R-WI) and the FBI, claimed the careers of many in the film industry. Many successful, left-leaning writers were banned from being hired by Hollywood studios. Writer Herbert Biberman was imprisoned for not giving up names and information about colleagues who were communists and, upon his release, directed one of the most remarkable films to depict the Mexican-American working-class community, *Salt of the Earth* (1954). The film is remarkable on a number of levels. It is based on a true story of Mexican and Mexican-American miners striking for better working and living conditions. And, it tells the story from a Latina point of view. Film historian Rosa Linda Fregoso states, "The film deals with issues of race and class. That's revolutionary. Most importantly, the subjective voiceover of the film is a voice of a woman— the voice of a Chicana."[23] The film starred Mexican actress Rosaura Revueltas. After the film's completion she was arrested and deported for working on the film. Ramírez-Berg adds, "I count it as the beginning of Chicano cinema. Many of the actual Mexican-American workers played themselves. They also collaborated on the screenplay and they demanded the screenwriter to make some changes in the script."[24]

There were a number of milestones for Latinos in film during this time, including Puerto Rican actor José Ferrer starring in the film *Cyrano De Bergerac* (1950), being honored with the Academy Award as Best Actor, and becoming the first Latino to win an Oscar. During this same time, a young Puerto Rican actress was starting out in films, and co-starred in *The Ring* (1952). Rita Moreno played the girlfriend to an up-and-coming boxer from East Los Angeles. Moreno is proud of that film and its portrayals: "Everyone in the film and in the family are good people. He's not a gangster, he's not a bad boy. She's a good girl. She has very traditional Mexican values. She doesn't want him to box."[25] Filmmaker Luis Valdez says of the film, "Where it absolutely failed is that the character failed, he didn't make it, he was a failure, and he had to learn to go back and live with his own people at his own level. That was the point of the movie."[26]

Ten years later, for her role in *West Side Story* (1961), Moreno would become the first Latina to be awarded an Oscar. Moreno and Ferrer's prestigious accolades proved that Latin actors have the talent to star in a film and carry it to critical success, and yet Hollywood continues, even to this day, to offer primo Latin character roles to non-Latino actors. For most Latino actors, starring roles in film were few and far between. At the same time, though, there was Anthony Quinn, Mexican-American, who was chosen to play many ethnicities, including Arab, Italian, Native American, and Greek.

Non-Latinos Playing Latinos

Over the years, it has been rare for many Latino actors to be selected for roles that are Latino and heroic, which are often given to non-Latino actors to play. Beginning with non-Latino Paul Muni playing Mexican president Benito Juárez in the 1939 film *Juárez*; Natalie Wood as "María" in *West Side Story* (1961), portraying a Puerto Rican; Marlon Brando starring as Mexican revolutionary Emiliano Zapata in *Viva Zapata!* (1952); and continuing to more recent films, including Alicia Lardé Nash, the supportive wife to Russell Crowe's John Nash in *A Beautiful Mind* (2001). Alicia Lardé Nash is El Salvadorian but was played by non-Latina Jennifer Connelly. Ben Affleck portrayed heroic CIA agent Antonio Mendez, whose heritage is Mexican in the film that he also directed, *Argo* (2012). One important film that did have a Latino as star and hero is the aforementioned *Border Incident* (1949). Ricardo Montalban co-starred as a Mexican federal agent working to expose the exploitation of Mexican farmworkers. This is the Latino actor-as-star-hero needle in the very huge Hollywood haystack.

While some may have felt in past decades that there just were not enough talented Latino actors to play Latino roles, one must question why in today's world Latinos are not given the opportunity to play these heroic roles? Often film executives answer they need 'star power' for a film to have the best chance to be a financial success, but it has been proven time and again that big named movie stars can still have failing commercial successes. *Ishtar* (1987) with then superstar actors Warren Beatty and Dustin Hoffman comes to mind, with a $55 million budget that grossed $15 million; or *Heaven's Gate* (1980), with then A-list actors Kris Kristofferson and Christopher Walken, which had costs of $44 million and a $3.5 million gross; or, even more recently, *Suburbicon* (2017), starring Oscar nominee Matt Damon, and directed by George Clooney, had a $25 million budget and a $3.8 million box office gross. The bottom line—"star power" is not a true nor viable gauge for box office success.

A New Point of View (POV)

By the 1960s, more Latinos were found working behind the camera, including music composer Lalo Schifrin, who worked on a number of iconic films, including *Cool Hand Luke* (1967) and *Bullit* (1968), and wrote the theme to *Mission*

Impossible for television, which was used in the 1996 movie. Cuban-American Pablo Ferro offered his talents to countless opening titles, including *Bullitt* and the film classic, *Dr. Strangelove* (1964). Soon more Latinos would join the production ranks, including cinematographers Emmanuel Lubezki and John Alonzo.

But it was not until the 1970s and 1980s that we see the fruition of the Civil Rights Movement (1960s) reflected on the silver screen. U.S. Latino filmmakers began making their own movies, telling stories in a voice that had not been heard before and presenting new images for the cinema. According to film scholar Chon Noriega,

> the first and probably major achievement of Latino filmmakers making feature films (beginning in the 1970s) is that without almost any support from the industry, they have managed to make as many feature films about Latinos as the industry made in the previous 70 years.[27]

Latino filmmakers told stories that focused on their own communities. These films presented a different **POV** of the immigrant experience, of Latino life in the U.S., and of Latino families. *Zoot Suit* (1981) and *La Bamba* (1986), directed by Luis Valdez, *American Me* (1992), directed by Edward James Olmos, *Crossover Dreams* (1985), directed by Leon Ichasco, *El Norte* (1983), directed by Gregory Nava, *Up In Smoke* (1978), written by Cheech Marin and Tommy Chong, *Stand and Deliver* (1987), directed by Ramón Melendez, *Born in East LA* (1987), directed by Cheech Marin, and *The Milagro Beanfield War* (1988), produced by Moctezuma Esparza. All these films were seeded during the seventies. It must be noted that, while many of these films offered opportunities to Latina actresses, most notably Elizabeth Peña, Sonia Braga, and Lupe Ontiveros, none of these films were written or directed by Latinas. The sexism ceiling had yet to be addressed.

There was also a change in casting for mainstream studio films with the inclusion of a few Latino actors: Andy García in his Oscar-nominated *The Godfather, Part 3*, Rosie Perez in *White Men Can't Jump*, and her Oscar-nominated role in *Fearless*, Benicio Del Toro in the same film, and his Academy Award-winning role in *Traffic*, Raul Julia in *The Addams Family*. These are a just a few, among many others. All these talented actors proved that with the right break comes the opportunity to shine.

African-American actress Viola Davis said it best at her acceptance speech for her 2015 Emmy Award: "The only thing that separates women of color from anyone else is opportunity. You cannot win an Emmy for roles that are simply not there."[28]

No discussion of the Latino image in films during the twentieth century can be had without highlighting two sensational stars that were created during its last decade. In 1991, a young man in Texas with a guitar, a gun, a turtle, and money raised from participating in a medical testing study told the story of a traveling mariachi musician who is mistaken for a murderous criminal—and a director was born. Robert Rodriguez thrilled audiences with his film *El Mariachi* (1992), and

Music, Film, and TV Crossover Icon

Jennifer Lopez

Jennifer Lynn Lopez, known as Jennifer Lopez or J-Lo, is a singer, actress, and dancer. She is of Puerto Rican descent and landed her first major role as Selena Quintanilla in the movie *Selena* (1997). Lopez has also starred in many films, including *The Wedding Planner* (2001) and *Anaconda* (1997). She also released her first album in 1999. Lopez became a hit in both the film and the music industries. *Forbes* has ranked Lopez as the thirty-eighth most powerful woman in the world and as one of the most powerful celebrities in the world. *Time* has ranked her as one of the top twenty-five most influential Hispanic Americans.

Sources: Biography.com, TVGuide.com, *W Magazine*

Figure 4.3 Jennifer Lopez
DFree/Shutterstock

continued to contribute to the Latino image on the silver screen as well as mainstream studio pictures with *Desperado*, (1995), *From Dusk to Dawn* (1996), *Spy Kids* (2001), and continues today to be a leading Hollywood filmmaker.

The life of the Tejano singing sensation, Selena Quintanilla, was celebrated in the motion picture *Selena* (1997), by writer/director Gregory Nava, and produced by Moctezuma Esparza. Actor Jennifer López had a few movies under her belt, including a breakout role in Nava's *My Family, Mi Familia* (1991), but it was Selena that catapulted López into international stardom as an actor, entertainer, and producer.

The New Movie World

As we head toward the second decade of the twenty-first century, what expectations are there for Latino writers, producers, directors, and writers? What can the movie-going audience expect? According to the 2017 Hollywood Diversity Report, the people of color population, which is 23% of the U.S. population, "In 2015 . . . purchased 45% of all movie tickets sold in the United States." That is significant. And, the report states, adding to that mountain of movie tickets, Latinos were, "well represented . . . accounting for 23% of ticket purchases alone." That is a lot of tickets.[29]

Everyone wants to see themselves on the big screen. We all want to be the hero in the movie. We all want to get the boy or the girl in the end, and walk into the sunset, happy. The need and desire of ethnic groups and women to see themselves in heroic starring roles is monumental to the growth of Hollywood, and to the deepening of understanding between all communities. But, Hollywood, while happy to sell movie tickets to everyone, continues to ignore a large segment of the population, namely women and people of color.

According to the July 2017 "Media, Diversity, and Social Change Initiative," published by The Annenberg Foundation and the USC Annenberg School of Communications and Journalism,[30] Hollywood is missing the mark on including these two groups in their film productions. Taking into account the top 100 fictional films of 2016, with a total of 4,583 speaking characters, 68.6% of the speaking roles were male and 31.4% were female. And, it's been that way for a long time. Since 2007, the increase of female speaking parts has only been 1.5%.

For people of color, the numbers are even more dismal. Of those characters in these top 100 films whose race and or ethnicity could be determined, 70.8% were white, 13.6% black, 5.7% Asian, 3.1% Hispanic/Latino, and 3.4% Middle Eastern, with less than 1% American Indian/Alaskan Native and 1% Native Hawaiian. In total, 29.2% of all characters were from underrepresented racial/ethnic groups, which is well below U.S. Census figures of 38.7%. That number is also well below the non-Caucasian movie-going audience in this country which is 49%.[31]

Given the opportunity to shine, Latino, black, and Asian actors can and do step into the spotlight and do well. The 2017 runaway family-film hit was an animated movie, *Coco*, with a story set during the sacred Mexican holiday, *Día de los Muertos*. With characters written by a team that included a Latino writer, Adrían Molina, direction from Molina and Lee Unkrich, a cast of Latino actors in all major voice roles, and Latino musicians, the film became a financial success.

For continued change in this direction and in order for more films to include women and people of color, Hollywood film studios need to open the door to

---

Award-Winning Actor

Benicio del Toro

Benicio del Toro, born Benicio Monserrate Rafael del Toro Sánchez, is a Puerto Rican native who is well-known for his successful acting career. He started acting in the 1980s and has starred in several films, including *The Usual Suspects* (1995) and *Traffic* (2000). He has won a British Academy Film Award, Golden Globe Award, Screen Actors Guild Award, and an Academy Award for his role in *Traffic*. Del Toro was also voted as one of the '50 Most Beautiful People' by *People* magazine. He has also directed films and is still starring in upcoming films and TV series.

Sources: *Rolling Stone*, Biography.com, *Hello!* Magazine

Figure 4.4 Benicio Del Toro
Featureflash Photo Agency/Shutterstock

women and people of color as creative partners. For film to present images and roles that truly reflect an authentic experience, and thus be successful, those roles must be created, written, directed, and produced by members of those groups. That is where the real change begins. It is only when women, Latinos, Blacks, Asians, and the LGBT communities are invited through the gated walls of the studio and their stories are embraced as important and relevant stories that studio-produced films will offer a true reflection of this country.

Comedian, Actor, and Author

George López

George López is a Mexican-American comedian and actor best known for his self-titled *George López* (2002–2007) television sitcom. He also hosted his own late-night television show called, *López Tonight* (2009–2011). López received the Latino Spirit Award for Excellence in Television in 2003 and in 2005, and *Time* magazine has named him as one of "The Top 25 Most Influential Hispanics in America." López is also a published author, has appeared in films and TV shows, and continues to perform in comedy shows across the nation.

Sources: GeorgeLopez.com, Biography.com, *Time*

Figure 4.5 George López
Tinseltown/Shutterstock

Until that time, we will turn to independently produced films, films created by cable outlets, films created for distribution on the internet to offer a true view of each of us in these United States. Since the dawn of man, human beings have placed their handprints in the caves they called home. They wanted all who came after them to know they were here. They existed. They mattered. And they had a story to tell. This same desire and goal is what fuels the evolution of the Latino Image in Hollywood films.

From Showbiz to Activism

Eva Longoria

Eva Jacqueline Longoria Bastón, known as Eva Longoria, is a Mexican-American actress known for her breakout role starring in *Desperate Housewives* (2004–2012). In fact, Longoria received a Golden Globe in 2006 and multiple Screen Actors Guild Awards for her role on *Desperate Housewives*. She has also starred in films and other shows, such as *Harsh Times* (2005) and *Over Her Dead Body* (2008). In recent years, Longoria has been a vocal activist for voter mobilization. She has spoken publicly about the importance of voting and is an advocate for immigrant and farm workers' rights.

Sources: Biography.com, TVGuide.com, TheTimes.co.uk

Figure 4.6 Eva Longoria
DFree/Shutterstock

Broadway Star Shines in Hollywood

Lin-Manuel Miranda

Lin-Manuel Miranda was born in New York City and is of Puerto Rican descent. He is a lyricist and performer most known for his role in the hit Broadway show *Hamilton*, which premiered in 2015. He received Tony Awards for the Best Book and Best Score for his work with *Hamilton* in 2016. Miranda has also contributed and starred in other Broadway shows, including *In the Heights* (2008) and *Bring it On: The Musical* (2011). He recently helped write the music for the Disney movie *Moana* (2016) and is set to appear in many upcoming films and shows.

Sources: Broadway.com, LinManuel.com, *Rolling Stone*

Figure 4.7 Lin-Manuel Miranda
Lev Radin/Shutterstock

Vocabulary Words

Bandido   MOS
Blackface   POV
Dichotomy   Prohibition Era
Good Neighbor Policy   Repatriation
Greasers   Talkies
Hollywood Blacklist

Points to Remember

- In early movies, hero roles were often played by actors who were of Anglo descent, and white. Researchers have found that most of the negative roles at that time were given to actors of color: Latinos, Blacks, and Asians.
- Latinos lost their *sombreros* and mustaches, replacing them with a much-desired look—that of slicked-back hair and bedroom eyes. The "Latin Lover" was born in the 1920s. Both Latino men and women were sexualized, romanticized as spicy sex symbols in films during this time period.
- Latinos reached a number of milestones in 1950s films, including Puerto Rican actor José Ferrer starring in the film *Cyrano De Bergerac* (1950), being honored with the Academy Award as Best Actor, and becoming the first Latino to win an Oscar.
- In the 1980s, films like *La Bamba* were produced from a different point of view—that of the Latino immigrant experience.
- The 2017 runaway family-film hit *Coco* featured a story set during the sacred Mexican holiday, *Día de los Muertos*. With characters written by a team that included a Latino writer, Adrían Molina, direction from Molina and Lee Unkrich, a cast of Latino actors in all major voice roles, and the use of Latino musicians, the film became a financial success.

Names to Remember

Dolores del Río
Edward James Olmos
Esai Morales
Gregory Nava
Leon Ischaso
Luis Valdez
Lupe Vélez
Lupita Tovar
Moctezuma Esparza
Ricardo Montalban
Rita Moreno

Practice Questions

1   If repeated images of Latinos in films have influenced audience perceptions of Latinos in real life over time, what have you observed in recent years as the effects of those images today? How can the current film industry improve and work toward reversing those effects?

2   Which would you rather have and why? (A) Your image presented in a motion picture in a negative light. (B) No mention of you or your image in a motion picture. (C) None of the above. Explain your answer.

3   In this chapter, you learned about non-Hispanic actors who played Latino characters in films over the years. This practice still happens today. Do you think it is problematic or harmless? Support your answer with facts from the chapter and outside sources.

Activities

1   Search the internet for any of the film titles noted, and spend a weekend binging on Latino film history. Some of my "must-sees" are *Bordertown*, *The Three Caballeros*, *A Medal for Benny*, *My Family*, *Mi Familia*, *Selena*, *Crossover Dreams*, *Zoot Suit*, and anything from the "*Spitfire*" series starring Lupe Vélez.
2   Create a Latino History Film Festival. Choose a particular decade and gather as many films from those 10 years. Exhibit the film, shown on a big screen with an audience for a one-day Latino Film Festival. Conduct a question-and-answer session after each film to ponder the image of Latinos in Hollywood films.

Timeline

1900s: Motion pictures are introduced to audiences around the world. Many of these early films are MOS, without sound.

1920s: Most Latino movie portrayals are of villains or servants: *The Mexican's Revenge* (1909), *The Mexican's Jealousy* (1910), *Bronco Billy and the Greaser* (1914), *His Mexican Sweetheart* (1912), and *Chiquita the Dancer* (1912).

1926: Mexican actor Ramon Novarro stars in the most expensive silent film to be made, *Ben Hur*.

1927: The first motion picture with synchronized sound exhibited, *The Jazz Singer*.

1933: The Good Neighbor Policy—President Franklin Delano Roosevelt's plan to improve relations with the nations of Central and South America, and prevent them from supporting Germany.

1947: The Hollywood Blacklist—ten Hollywood writers and directors are accused of being Communists and banned from being hired by film studios.

1950: José Ferrer becomes the first Latino to win an Academy Award for "Best Actor," *Cyrano de Bergerac*.

1954: *Salt of the Earth* by Blacklisted director Herbert Biberman, writer Michael Wilson, and producer Paul Jarrico tells the story of a Mexican-American miners' strike with an all-Latino cast; for many it's the birth of the Mexican-American film.

1962: Rita Moreno is the first Latina to win an Academy Award: "Best Supporting Actress" Academy Award for *West Side Story*.

1983:   Gregory Nava directs and co-writes *El Norte* with Anna Thomas, original screenplay nominated for Academy Award.

1987:   Luis Valdez write and directs *La Bamba*, a commercial success for Universal Pictures.

1997:   Jennifer Lopez stars in *Selena*, portraying singer Selena Quintanilla. The role launches Lopez into stardom.

2017:   Adrían Molina and Lee Unkrich direct the animated film *Coco*, which featured a cast of Latino actors in all major voice roles, as well as Latino musicians.

Additional Resources

Berumen, Frank Javier, *Brown Celluloid* (Vantage Press, 2003).

Berumen, Frank Javier, *The Chicano/Hispanic Image in American Film* (Berumen Vantage Press, 1995).

Hadley-García, George, *Hispanic Hollywood: The Latins in Motion Pictures* (Citadel Press Book, 1990).

Ramírez-Berg, Charles, *Latino Images in Film: Stereotypes Subversion, Resistance* (University of Texas Press, 2002).

Reyes, Luis, and Rubie, Peter, *Hispanics in Hollywood: A Celebration of 100 Years in Film and Television* (Lone Eagle, 2000).

Rodriguez, Carla E., *Heroes, Lovers, and Others* (Smithsonian Books, 2004).

About the Author

Nancy De Los Santos-Reza

Photo courtesy of Nancy De Los Santos-Reza

Born and raised in Chicago, Nancy De Los Santos-Reza, M.A., began her career as Assistant Producer and Producer for film critics Roger Ebert and Gene Siskel's film review programs *Sneak Previews* (PBS) and *At the Movies* (Syndicated). Nancy has written for Lifetime and the Disney Channel, as well as the Showtime drama series *Resurrection Blvd.*, the PBS series *American Family*, and Hulu's *East Los High*. She's also been on the writing staff for the National Council of La Raza's Alma Awards, hosted by Eva Longoria.

She is co-writer and co-producer with Susan Racho of *The Bronze Screen: One Hundred Years of the Latino Image in Hollywood Cinema*, directed by Alberto Dominguez. The feature documentary aired on Cinemax/HBO and was presented on the PBS series, *Voces*. While researching for the film, De Los Santos discovered 1940s Latina actresses being referred to as "glamorous tamales," and claimed the title for her production company. She is also the co-producer and co-writer of a documentary on the life of legendary Chicano troubadour and composer, Lalo Guerrero. *Lalo Guerrero: The Original Chicano*, aired on PBS, as part of the LPB series, *Voces*.

She is the Associate Producer on the feature films *Selena* starring Jennifer López and Edward James Olmos, and *My Family*, *Mi Familia* starring Olmos, López, and Jimmy Smits. De Los Santos received her B.S. degree in Radio, Television, and Film from the University of Texas at Austin and holds a Masters in Communications from the University of Michigan at Ann Arbor.

Notes

1 Luis Reyes and Peter Rubie, *Hispanics in Hollywood: A Celebration of 100 Years in Film and Television* (Hollywood, CA: Lone Eagle, 2000).
2 Rudy Behlmer, *Memo from David O. Selznick* (New York: Viking Press, 1972).
3 George Hadley-García, *Hispanic Hollywood: The Latins in Motion Pictures* (New York: Citadel Press, 1990), 6; Charles Ramírez-Berg, *Latino Images in Film: Stereotypes Subversion, Resistance* (Austin, TX: University of Texas Press, 2002); Berumen, *The Chicano/Hispanic Image in American Film*.
4 Hadley-García, *Hispanic Hollywood: The Latins in Motion Pictures*, 32.
5 Frank J. Berumen, *The Chicano/Hispanic Image in American Film* (New York: Vantage Press, 1995).
6 Ramírez-Berg, *Latino Images in Film: Stereotypes Subversion, Resistance*.
7 *The Bronze Screen: 100 Years of the Latino Image in Hollywood*, dir. Nancy De Los Santos, Susan Racho, and Alberto Domínguez (United States: Questar, 2002), DVD.
8 *Thirteen: Media With Impact*, "D.W. Griffith's The Birth of a Nation," www. thirteen.org/wnet/jimcrow/stories_events_birth.html.
9 Edward Sakamoto, "Anna May Wong and the Dragon-Lady Syndrome," *Los Angeles Times*, July 12, 1987, http://articles.latimes.com/1987-07-12/entertainment/ca-32 79_1_dragon-lady.
10 *The New York Times*, "How Hollywood has Portrayed Hispanics," March 1, 1981, www.nytimes.com/1981/03/01/movies/how-hollywood-has-portrayed-hispanics. html?pagewanted=all.
11 Hadley-García, *Hispanic Hollywood: The Latins in Motion Pictures*.
12 Ramírez-Berg, *Latino Images in Film: Stereotypes Subversion, Resistance*.
13 *The Bronze Screen*.
14 Ibid.
15 Ibid.
16 Ibid.
17 Ibid.
18 *Bordertown*, dir. Archie Mayo, perf. Paul Muni and Bette Davis (United States: Warner Bros. Pictures, 1935).
19 *The Bronze Screen*.
20 Ibid.
21 Ibid.
22 Ibid.
23 Ibid.
24 Ibid.
25 Ibid.
26 Ibid.

27 Ibid.
28 Soraya N. MacDonald, "You Cannot Win an Emmy for Roles that are Simply Not There': Viola Davis on her Historic Emmys Win," *The Washington Post*, September 21, 2015, www.washingtonpost.com/news/arts-and-entertainment/wp/2015/09/21/you-cannot-win-an-emmy-for-roles-that-are-simply-not-there-viola-davis-on-her-historic-emmys-win.
29 Bunche Center for African American Studies at UCLA, "2017 Hollywood Diversity Report: Settling the Record Straight," 2017, http://expre.ss.ucla.edu/wp-content/uploads/2017/04/2017-Hollywood-Diversity-Report-2-21-17.pdf.
30 Stacy L. Smith, Kevin Yao, and Katherine Pieper, "Inequality in 900 Popular Films: Examining Portrayals of Gender, Race/Ethnicity, LGBT, and Disability from 2007–2016," July, 2017, http://annenberg.usc.edu/sites/default/files/Dr_Stacy_L_Smith-Inequality_in_900_Popular_Films.pdf.
31 Ibid.

5   *El Ritmo Latino*

Hispanic/LatinX Music Influences in the U.S.

Javier F. Leon, Ph.D.

Director of Latin American Music Center,
Indiana University

The history of Hispanic or LatinX music in the United States has been diverse, involving different musical genres, styles, and influences that stretch from various regions of the country to Mexico, the Caribbean, and Central and South America. The people behind these influences have been equally varied and have included men and women whose families come from multiple socio-economic, cultural, and ethnic backgrounds. Over the last several decades, the terms Hispanic and LatinX have provided a useful way to bring together and recognize the needs of a number of these different communities, many of which had previously been turned into "invisible" minorities by virtue of being categorized as "white."[1] Yet, many of the people who today are generally deemed to fall within this category, while recognizing its potential usefulness, also continue to debate what exactly it means to be Hispanic or LatinX in the United States. Music has been a particularly active arena in which these debates continue to take place, providing members of these communities ways of fostering collective identity, and negotiating how they are perceived and defined by others, as well as making important contributions of their own to mainstream American music and popular culture.

For nearly two centuries, if not longer, a number of musical traditions have flourished in different parts of the United States and informed much of the music associated with Hispanic or LatinX communities. These traditions have varied regionally. Some grew out of the musical activities of immigrant communities originally from Latin America or the Caribbean. Others are associated with communities whose histories in a particular geographical region pre-date their incorporation into the United States. This, however, does not mean that these different forms of music developed in isolation. In most cases, these musical forms have a history of cross-pollinating, not only with one another, but also with musical traditions from Anglo-Americans, African-Americans, and other neighboring groups. Understanding this complex musical landscape involves focusing our attention on three interrelated areas: (1) the broad number of communities whose musical production can fall into the broader category of Hispanic or LatinX, the way in which these communities differ from each other, and how have they changed over time; (2) the parallel fascination that American mainstream culture has had with what it has perceived as "Latin" music and how members of Hispanic or LatinX communities have engaged with it; (3) the role that crossover artists and genres have had in negotiating stylistic, social, and cultural boundaries between these two other areas.

Mexican-American Traditions and the Southwest

Musical traditions associated with Mexican-Americans, particularly in the Southwest of the United States, constitute a particularly rich repository of musical influences. Although many of these traditions share some historical, musical, and stylistic continuity with traditions on the other side of the U.S.–Mexico border, they have also developed their own local particularities over many generations. Genres like the **corrido**, a narrative ballad that historically served as a type of oral newspaper that chronicled important events, usually through the tragic exploits of folk heroes, were used to document local histories.[2] Early examples of *corrido* and *corrido*-like songs include accounts of how Californian Spanish authorities put down an insurrection in Santa Barbara in 1824, and of the deaths of outlaws and dissidents in New Mexico (1832) and Texas (1841). In the twentieth century, the genre became a vehicle for chronicling the abuses of Mexican-Americans by Anglo-Americans, such as the Texas Rangers. It also became a way of memorializing important events that impacted the community, such as the assassination of John F. Kennedy,[3] and as a vehicle for social protest as part of Chicano activism, especially during the 1960s and 1970s.[4] Since the 1990s, a variant known as the *narcocorrido* has emerged on both sides of the border and, although in some aspects it has continued to chronicle some of the hardships experienced by poor people, it has also become controversial for its romanticization of the exploits of drug cartel kingpins who are cast in the role of contemporary folk heroes.[5]

In addition to the *corrido*, a number of other genres have historically formed an integral part of the musical traditions associated with the Southwest, including another more romantic or sentimental ballad tradition known as the **ranchera**, dance forms based on waltz and polka rhythms, and others based on traditional Mexican regional music like the *huapango*. These forms have been played in a variety of different styles and formats, some having origins in Mexico, like *mariachi* and *son jarocho* ensembles. Others were the result of musical innovations taking place in the Southwest, particularly in Texas, as is the case with the **conjunto** and *orquesta* ensembles that began to develop in the 1930s.

Conjunto music became strongly associated with working-class roots. It is an ensemble centered on the **button accordion**, an instrument introduced by neighboring German and Eastern European settlers in the area, and the **bajo**

sexto, a twelve-string guitar found throughout Northern Mexico. In contrast, the **orquesta** was a more varied dance band ensemble that included brass and reed instruments, electric guitar and bass, and different types of percussion. Orquestas reflected the tastes and sensibilities of more urban, middle-class Mexican Americans, expanding their repertoires to also include genres and influences from other parts of Latin America and the Caribbean, as well as from Anglo-American and African-American dance band genres like the foxtrot and boogie-woogie, and later on, jazz, rhythm and blues, rock and roll, and country music.[6] After World War II, both of these musics also began to move out of the Southwest as many Mexican-Americans migrated to the Midwest and other parts of the country, looking for new work opportunities.[7]

By the 1980s and 1990s, conjunto and orquesta music, along with a more contemporary-sounding style featuring electronic keyboards, electric guitar, bass, drum set, and, increasingly the accordion, became very influential, not only in Texas but throughout the Southwest and Mexico. Conversely, however, these musical exchanges also contributed to the growing popularity of musical styles from Northern Mexico on the U.S. side of the border, including the brass band-centered genre known as *banda* originally from the region of Sinaloa.[8] Another important example of these ebbs and flows is the prominence that **cumbia** gained in this region during these decades. Originally a dance genre from

Figure 5.1 Ozomatli at the 2010 MusiCares Person of the Year tribute to Neil Young.
s_bukley/Shutterstock

Colombia and Panama, in the 1950s *cumbia* began to migrate to other countries in Latin America, going as far south as Argentina and as north as Mexico.

By the 1970s, *cumbia* was a staple of the norteño ensembles of Northeastern Mexico, an ensemble similar to the conjunto groups on the Texas side of the border, but which identified more closely with immigrant sensibilities. In the late 1980s and early 1990s, Selena Quintanilla's more pop- and R&B-influenced version of this *cumbia* style not only became synonymous with a more modern Tejano or Tex-Mex style, but also managed to crossover not only into the U.S. mainstream but back across the border to many other parts of Latin America. At the same time, other styles of cumbia that had been developing and circulating internationally had found their way to other communities in the Southwest.[9] More recently in California, a stronger influence of more tropical-sounding *cumbia* styles led groups like Ozomatli to synthesize these multiple versions while further infusing them with elements of hip hop, jazz, funk, rock, and reggae that speak not only to Mexican-American and Chicano sensibilities, but to a number of other Hispanic and LatinX communities.

Caribbean Connections

Another important set of musical and cultural influences is associated with communities originally from the Spanish-speaking Caribbean region. Cuba, in particular, has had a long history of musical contact with the United States, and part of that early history can be traced to nineteenth-century New Orleans. The **habanera**, a Cuban salon dance that gained international popularity during that time, made a strong impact in the musical life of that city, through music arriving not only from Cuba, but also Mexico and other parts of Latin America, where the *habanera* rhythm had also taken root.[10] There was also sustained and ongoing contact between musicians in New Orleans and Havana, so that, by the turn of the twentieth century, a number of rhythmic influences associated with Cuban and Afro-Cuban musical genres can be found in the music of the early jazz music scene.[11] Another Cuban genre that developed during the latter part of the nineteenth century was the **bolero**, a type of guitar-accompanied ballad that by the first decades of the twentieth century had spread throughout Latin America and the Caribbean, forming the basis for a pan-Latin American style that could also be heard in the United States.[12]

In the 1930s, taking advantage of mainstream audiences' growing fascination with Latin American music, particularly in New York, a number of Cuban musicians and band leaders began to flourish, playing different forms of Cuban dance music. In these settings, Cuban musicians came into contact with Puerto Rican musicians and a few musicians from other parts of Latin America. The resulting music combined various blends of dance music genres from those islands with elements of jazz, and American dance band music, echoing the type of cosmopolitan sensibility that Southwestern orquestas had also begun to pursue, but with a more decidedly Caribbean influence. One particularly important outgrowth of this activity is the emergence of **mambo**, a genre that coalesced between the 1940s and 1950s as a result of dialogues between enclaves of Cuban musicians and other collaborators as they moved between Havana and New York.[13] By the mid 1950s, *mambo*'s popularity exploded, particularly in New York where a number of bands led by both Cuban and Puerto Rican musicians became extremely influential.

The 1950s and 1960s brought about a number of social and political changes that would impact these communities greatly over the next several decades. Although, Puerto Ricans had had U.S. citizenship since 1917, advances in air travel during the 1950s made it easier for people to travel from the island to the United States. As a result, more traditional forms of Puerto Rican music, such as *bomba* and *plena*, which had been performed in New York City since the 1920s, but was little known outside Puerto Rican neighborhoods, became increasingly visible.[14] The Cuban Revolution in 1959 curtailed the ability of many musicians to travel back and forth and to some degree stifled some of the musical creativity and innovation that had grown out of those exchanges. In the years following the revolution, hundreds of thousands of Cubans left the island, creating new and important enclaves particularly in the Miami area, which eventually became a new site for the cultivation of Cuban music. Meanwhile, in New York, the growing Puerto Rican population remained actively involved in the musical scene, fusing *mambo* and other Cuban forms that were still popular in the area with soul and rhythm and blues to create boogaloo.[15] Going into the 1970s, **salsa**, a type of music developed mainly by Puerto Ricans in New York City, became a remarkable local and later commercial success that soon spread to various parts of the Caribbean and Latin America, becoming to many a symbol of pan-Latino identity.[16] In the 1980s and 1990s, **merengue** and **bachata**, two genres from the Dominican Republic, began to rival the popularity of *salsa* in New York, partly the result of the sharp growth of the Dominican immigrant population that started in the 1960s.[17]

The Celia That I Knew

by Omer Pardillo Cid
Celia Cruz's Former Manager and Current Estate Manager
The author's personal testimonial has been translated from Spanish.

"I learned many values from her. One of the most valuable was her humility."

In life there are no coincidences, from the day you are born everything is written. That is, precisely, what united me to Celia, destiny.

Our way of thinking was the same, and we used to talk a lot, especially on long trips. One day she tells me: "Omer, you and I were predestined

Figure 5.2 Celia Cruz
Photo courtesy of Omer Pardillo Cid

to meet and work together," and I can say with complete faith that I became her confidant. I had the honor and the enormous pleasure of knowing, beyond the artist, the person, a woman who, in addition to her energy, Cuban, and colorful extravagance in the costumes for the stage, had a lot of faith, was a Catholic, a good wife, good sister, good aunt, good friend and, above all, for me, a good boss, who eventually became like a mother.

Celia and Pedro spent more time with me than with their own family, and I spent more time with them than with my family. Thank God I could show them how much I admired them and loved them in their most difficult moments. During Celia's illness, and until the moment her body left the earth, I did not separate from her and did everything possible to make her illness less difficult.

Celia, Pedro, and I shared the same zodiac sign, Libra, which made us similar in many things. On innumerable occasions, without speaking, we already knew what we wanted to say in a situation.

I learned many values from Celia. One of the most valuable was her humility; despite her being the greatest, she was always the simplest and that led her to win the hearts and admiration of many. She did not approach power; power approached Celia Cruz. With her, I had the opportunity to meet presidents from different countries, kings and businessmen, and also humble people. Celia treated everyone equally, always with a smile on her face and a word of kindness for anyone who approached her.

I never saw her deny an autograph to anyone. She would even give autographs when she was in church, especially in Ermita de la Caridad, "Hermitage of Charity," a sanctuary that she used to visit every time we traveled to Miami, and if someone approached her, she kindly answered: "Look, wait outside and I'll give it to you, because in here we have to respect the Virgin and it is the only moment that I have to be Celia the person, not the artist."

In my memory, I carry many of her confessions as well as the difficult moments to reach triumph. She always knew how to fight the few enemies she had. One day she gave me a life lesson and said: "Omer, that journalist who is coming has always written very badly about me, but he will never know that I have read all his articles. I will greet him so kindly that he will say: 'Celia doesn't even know that I wrote badly about her.'" Just like that, she showed me once again her human caliber. She repeatedly told me to ignore people who wanted to harm us; it is the best thing that one can do, because you minimize the importance of it and that hurts more than facing them, something that she knew how to do very well.

Figure 5.3 Celia Cruz
Photo courtesy of Omer Pardillo

Figure 5.4 Celia Cruz
Photo courtesy of Omer Pardillo Cid

In New York, she loved to go unnoticed through the streets of Soho. I enjoyed walking a lot and, on those occasions, she and I went alone because if Pedro was there, she was immediately noticed. On Saturdays during the winter season when we were in New York, she put on a long mink coat, Prada tennis shoes, a turban, and giant eyeglasses adorned with sequins and she would tell me, "Omer, we're going to enjoy the streets of New York." Then, we went to her favorite restaurant, Balthazar in Soho, and shopping afterwards. Even if she tried to hide, people always recognized her and, in reality, I will confess that she loved it. Celia lived to shine on the stages of the world, to give interviews, to sign autographs—that was the world in which she took refuge from the personal problems that, like any human being, she had.

She was the one who did not know how to say "no."

It was hard for her to say no to something she was asked to do. She always had as a rule that she did not perform on a stage where there was an artist who lived in Cuba and she tried to avoid encounters. On one occasion, at a concert in Venezuela, a businessman who worked a lot with Celia told her: "I want to ask you to take a picture with someone whom I am going to bring now and wants to meet you." It was an artist based in Cuba and I prefer to omit his name.

Celia, very cordially, posed for the photo and had a short conversation with the person in the dressing room, and after he left she said: "Omer, that's why you have to always ask who these private meetings are with because I'm sure that they are going to show that photo to everyone and then my compatriots in exile are going to say, with good reason: 'Look at Celia sharing with a certain person.'" Over time, that orchestra came to Miami and the first thing they brought to the news was the photo with Celia in Venezuela and she, in an interview from Buenos Aires, told a Miami television station: "The photo is not a montage. It's me. It's one of those things that happen in life that I did not provoke."

In her repertoire it is very difficult to find a song that refers to something political, but I can confirm that, without any fear, she denounced the Cuban reality throughout the world. To any journalist who asked her, "What do you think of Fidel Castro?," she replied, "The day you ask Fidel Castro about me and get a comment, then I will respond."

For more than 50 years she was a singer who gave Cuba great glory, but on her island they did not know her triumphs. The world did recognize them. Today her legacy lives with many distinctions, a United States postage stamp, and a tribute on her birthday with the Google Doodle dedicated to her. She has left us all with her charisma and eternal smile; with me, the privilege and pride of having shared with her so many triumphs, and personal moments, joyful and difficult, that I carry on with me.

Thank you, Celia and Pedro for making me part of your family.

South and Central American Influences

Throughout the twentieth century, there have been a number of musical influences from South and Central America that have found their way into the United States, although in many cases these initially came as imported and exotic novelties aimed at mainstream American audiences rather than being cultivated by Hispanic or LatinX populations. Historically, the United States has gone through several moments in which mainstream audiences have "discovered" and then become enamored with music perceived as "Latin."[18] The first of these love affairs was with **tango**, a dance genre originally from Argentina that arrived in the United States via Paris during the 1920s. Tango's arrival quickly led to the emergence of American emulators, some with little experience or familiarity with Latin American musical genres, laying the groundwork for what would become a decades-long tradition of "mainstreaming" Latin American songs, musical instruments, and ensembles as novelties under the generic label of "Latin" music. These included the introduction of the marimba, an instrument that was widely used in folk traditions in Central America and Southern Mexico, and the bolero.[19]

These interpretations of "Latin" music continued into the 1950s and 1960s, perhaps best represented at that time by the genre known as exotica. One of the most memorable of these performers was Peruvian singer Yma Sumac (Zoila Chávarri del Castillo), who became well-known for her operatic renditions of songs from various parts of South America, performed while dressed as an "Inca Princess" and accompanied by a boisterous mambo orchestra.[20] Other musical trends, however, veered more strongly toward more substantive musical engagement with Latin American music. This was the case with bossa nova, a jazz-influenced genre that migrated from Brazil, also during the 1950s and 1960s, and which, along with some of the jazz-influenced Cuban forms that were being heard in New York, became the two main foundations of what came to be known as **Latin jazz**.[21]

During the second half of the twentieth century, immigrants from Central and South America, many of them escaping political and economic hardships in their home countries, began to establish sustainable communities throughout the United States. Like their Mexican, Puerto Rican, and Dominican counterparts, many of these communities were concerned with the continued cultivation of more traditional folk and popular music, which led to the creation of cultural associations and folklore schools where younger generations of musicians could learn a variety of different folk music and dance from their home countries. People originally from the Andean region (Bolivia, Chile, Colombia, Ecuador, Peru, and northern parts of Argentina) introduced a number of dances and forms of music associated with the indigenous and mestizo traditions for which the region is known. In the 1990s and 2000s, many of these organizations had also grown to include musical practices associated with other minority populations from those countries, in particular those associated with Afro-descendant communities.

There was also a resurgence of the cultivation of popular music genres like the tango, cumbia, and samba, along with the introduction of other genres like the Colombian vallenato, the Venezuelan joropo, and the Brazilian capoeira. Central American communities similarly introduced a number of folk dance ensembles, as well as popular forms of music influenced by both Mexican and Caribbean genres such as norteño and salsa, and even English-speaking Caribbean forms such as soca, ska, and reggae. Two particularly important minority Central American genres that gained prominence in the United States in the 1990s, particularly in New York, were punta and punta rock.[22] These were traditional and contemporary incarnations of musical practices cultivated by the Garifuna, a mixed Afro-Indigenous group from Honduras, Guatemala, Nicaragua, and Belize.

Challenging and Expanding Boundaries

The musical influence of Hispanic and LatinX communities in the United States also goes beyond their involvement with musical genres originally

Figure 5.5 Gloria and Emilio Estefan have received several Grammys for their
work. Their story of success is the focus of the hit Broadway musical
On Your Feet.

Tinseltown/Shutterstock

associated with or derived from Latin American and Caribbean genres. Although
not always recognized, Hispanic and LatinX musicians have made important
contributions to a number of different styles of American popular music, in
some cases creating subgenres of their own. A number of Hispanic and LatinX
musicians of multiple backgrounds were actively involved in jazz and some of
its precursors going back to the late nineteenth century, and over the decades
made important contributions to the development of various styles of jazz, as
was the case with Machito (Francisco Gutiérrez Grillo), Mongo Santamaría,
Antonio Carlos Jobim, Eddie Palmieri, and more recently Poncho Sánchez.[23]
A similar long and varied history can be found in rock and pop music, ranging
from the early rock and roll contributions of Ritchie Valens to the music of
Carlos Santana and Joan Baez in the 1970s, Gloria Estefan, Selena Quintanilla,

Figure 5.6
Marc Anthony is one of the most
prominent salsa singers of this era.

Kathy Hutchins/Shutterstock

Figure 5.7
Ricky Martin is a Puerto Rican singer,
author, and actor. Martin has received
multiple Grammy nominations after his
first English album, which was self-titled
Ricky Martin.

DFree/Shutterstock

and the crossover success of early 2000s pop stars like Ricky Martin, Christina
Aguilera, and Marc Anthony, who paved the way for a more recent generation
of young performers.[24]

Freddy Fender was also influential in the country music realm.[25] Hispanic
and LatinX youth, particularly Puerto Ricans, growing up in the Upper
Manhattan, Brooklyn, the Bronx, and other major urban areas in the United
States were also actively involved in the emergence of genres like freestyle, not
to mention rap and hip hop.[26] Freestyle, an early style of electronic dance music
that emerged in the 1980s, introduced mainstream audiences to a new generation
of Hispanic and LatinX artists, many of them female, most important among
them Lisa Lisa and Cult Jam. In the realm of hip hop, artists have contributed
to the creation of multiple subgenres and regional styles, which have included
important contributions by seminal West Coast performers like Mellow Man
Ace, Kid Frost, and Cypress Hill; East Coast artists Frankie Cutlass and more
recently Immortal Technique, Texas pioneer Johnny Z; and a strong Miami-
based contingent currently represented by rapper Pitbull, born Armando
Christian Pérez. Perhaps one of the most influential of these has been reggaetón,
which developed in Puerto Rico in the late 1990s, and which, thanks to artists
like Daddy Yankee, Don Omar, and Ivy Queen, has been the subject of yet
another crossover phenomenon not only in the United States but all over the
Caribbean and Latin America.[27]

Figure 5.9
Armando Christian Pérez, who is professionally known as Pitbull, and often Mr. Worldwide, is of Cuban descent. He is a well-known rapper in the United States and around the world.

Kathy Hutchins/Shutterstock

Figure 5.8
Christina Aguilera is of Ecuadorian descent. She is most known for her accomplishments as a singer and an actress.

Featureflash Photo Agency/Shutterstock

Figure 5.10
Pop sensation Selena Gomez is of Mexican descent and has sold millions of albums and singles worldwide.

Tinseltown/Shutterstock

The "King of Latin Pop"

Enrique Iglesias

Enrique Miguel Iglesias Preysler, known as Enrique Iglesias, was born in Madrid, Spain. He is often referred to as the "King of Latin Pop" and has sold over 159 million records worldwide. Enrique Iglesias broke a record for 27 number-one singles on *Billboard's Hot Latin Tracks*.

Sources: Billboard.com, Biography.com, *The Guardian*

Figure 5.11 Enrique Iglesias
Joe Seer/Shutterstock

These and many other artists have made use of their roles as performers, composers, band leaders, managers, producers, radio and television personalities, record label creators, and media entrepreneurs to help establish a better infrastructure for the creation and dissemination of many different kinds of music. As they have for decades, New York, California, and Texas continue to be important centers of this type of music industry activity. In more recent decades, Miami has also risen in prominence, becoming an important nexus through which many Latin American and Caribbean artists move their music to other countries in the region, as well as an entry point to the mainstream American market.[28] Going into the twenty-first century, this growing influence has afforded artists and music entrepreneurs a larger voice in showcasing the complex variety and diversity that characterizes the musical heritages of all of these distinct but interrelated Hispanic or LatinX communities.

Vocabulary Words

Bachata

Bajo Sexto

Bolero

Button Accordion

Conjunto

Corrido

Cumbia

Habanera

Latin Jazz

Mambo

Merengue

Orquesta

Ranchera

Salsa

Tango

Points to Remember

- Hispanic or LatinX music is an overarching category that includes communities originally from a variety of different parts of Latin America, the Caribbean, and areas that eventually became a part of the United States.
- Musical traditions in these different communities did not develop in isolation, but rather in dialogue and contact with one another and with musical traditions associated with neighboring Anglo-American and African-American groups.
- American mainstream perceptions of what they have come to term "Latin" music have not always squared with how musicians Hispanic or LatinX musicians themselves and their communities have chosen to musically represent themselves.
- Hispanic or LatinX musicians have made important contributions to a number of American popular music genres including jazz, rock, country, electronic dance music, rap, and hip hop.
- Over time, artists and music entrepreneurs have been able to gain greater visibility and influence within American mainstream media, using music to expand and redefine what it means to be Hispanic or LatinX in the United States.

Names to Remember

Antonio Carlos Jobim

Eddie Palmieri

Machito

Mongo Santamaría
Ozomatli
Pitbull
Selena Quintanilla
Yma Sumac

Practice Questions

1   What are some of the musical and cultural differences that characterize Hispanic or LatinX music in different parts of the United States?
2   How have the forms of music in these different communities interacted with one another and mainstream American audiences?
3   Discuss the contributions that Hispanic and LatinX artists have made to the development of other forms of American popular music.
4   Can you give examples of musical genres or types of music that, while initially associated with one particular community or group, have come to have broader appeal or relevance to multiple communities?
5   How has the changing panorama of Hispanic or LatinX music over the last century influenced the ability of musicians to define themselves and their communities?

Activity

While some forms of Hispanic or LatinX music tend to be associated with musical practices that are originally from a particular Latin American or Caribbean country (i.e., samba is played by Brazilians, merengue by Dominicans, etc.), nearly all of the musicians discussed in this chapter have been supported with contributions from musicians from a variety of different heritages. This activity will have two parts: (1) Use online sites like americansabor.org to search through artist biographies for information about their background. Work in small groups, with each researching either the different backgrounds of musicians who participated in a particular type of music, or the contributions that artists with backgrounds in a particular Latin American or Caribbean country have made to different genres. Consult with your instructor to make sure that you are not choosing a category that is too broad or narrow. (2) Use your preferred online audio and video streaming service to find three or four representative musical examples to share and discuss with the class either at a later class meeting or your class's website, blog, or online discussion site.

Timeline

1920s: The Argentinian genre *tango* is introduced in the U.S.
1930s: Conjunto and orquesta ensembles begin to form. Cuban musicians and band leaders began to blossom.

1940s–1950s: The *mambo* genre begins to flourish as a result of the collaboration of Cuban and other musicians.

1950s: The *cumbia* genre originates in Colombia and Panama and then migrates south. Air travel advances facilitate the migration of Puerto Ricans to the U.S.

1959: Cuban Revolution impedes musicians from freely traveling to and from the U.S.

1960s: Dominican immigration to the U.S. begins to increase significantly. Genre *Latin jazz* is formed as a combination of the Brazilian genre bossa nova and jazz-influenced Cuban forms.

1970s: The emergence of the *salsa* genre becomes an identity symbol of Latinos.

1980s–1990s: Contemporary *conjunto* and *orquesta* music becomes more influential in Texas, the Southwest, and Mexico. Dominican genres, *merengue* and *bachata*, begin to compete for the spotlight against *salsa* in New York.

1990s: *Punta* and *punta rock* gain popularity in the U.S., particularly in New York.

Additional Resources

American Sabor, www.americansabor.org—a companion website to the Smithsonian Travelling Exhibit *American Sabor: Latinos in U.S. Popular Music*. It contains artist biographies, historical sketches, classroom teaching guides, and interactive audio tools.

Latin Music USA, dir. by Pamela A. Aguilar and Daniel McCabe (Arlington, VA: PBS Distribution, 2009), DVD.

Pacini Hernández, Deborah, *Oye Como Va! Hybridity and Identity in Latino Popular Music* (Philadelphia, PA: Temple University Press, 2009).

Javier F. León

Photo courtesy of Javier F. León

About the Author

Javier F. León, Ph.D., is an ethnomusicologist specializing in popular music, heritage, nationalism, and African diasporic identity in Latin America. He currently is the Director of the Latin American Music Center at the Indiana University Jacobs School of Music. His work has been published in multiple journals and edited volumes including *Latin American Music Review*, *Black Music Research Journal*, *Ethnomusicology Forum*, and *Music and Cultural Rights*. He is also the editor of the special Music and Neoliberalism issue in the journal *Culture, Theory and Critique* and co-editor of *A Latin American Music Reader: Views from the South*.

Notes

1 Cristina G. Mora, *Making Hispanics: How Activists, Bureaucrats, and Media Constructed a New American* (Chicago, IL: University of Chicago Press, 2014).

2 Cathy Ragland, *Musica Norteña: Mexican Americans Creating a Nation Between Nations* (Philadelphia, PA: Temple University Press, 2009), 7–8.

3 Dan W. Dickey, *The Kennedy Corridos: A Study of the Ballads of a Mexican American Hero* (Austin, TX: Center for Mexican American Studies, University of Texas, 1978).

4 José E. Limón, *Mexican Ballads, Chicano Poems: History and Influence in Mexican-American Social Poetry* (Berkeley, CA: University of California Press, 1992), 90–91.

5 Ragland, *Música Norteña*, 10–11.

6 Manuel Peña, "Música Fronteriza/Border Music," *Aztlan: A Journal of Chicano Studies* 21, nos 1–2 (1996): 48–49, www.lib.utexas.edu/benson/border/arhoolie2/pena.html.

7 María Herrera-Sobek, *Chicano Folklore: A Handbook* (Westport, CT: Greenwood Publishing Group, 2006), 48–49.

8 Helena Simonett, *Banda: Mexican Musical Life Across Borders* (Middletown, CT: Wesleyan University Press, 2001).

9 Deborah P. Hernández, *Oye Como Va!: Hybridity and Identity in Latino Popular Music* (Philadelphia, PA: Temple University Press, 2010), 120–127.

10 John S. Roberts, *The Latin Tinge: The Impact of Latin American Music on the United States* (New York: Oxford University Press, 1999), 35.

11 Alejandro L. Madrid and Robin D. Moore, *Danzón: Circum-Caribbean Dialogues in Music and Dance* (Oxford, NY: Oxford University Press, 2013), 118.

12 Mark Brill, *Music of Latin America and the Caribbean* (Boston, MA: Prentice Hall, 2011), 131–132.

13 Rubén López Cano, "Notes for a Prehistory of Mambo," in León, Javier F. and Helena Simonett, *A Latin American Music Reader: Views from the South* (Urbana, IL: University of Illinois Press, 2016), 221–249.

14 Juan Flores, *From Bomba to Hip-Hop: Puerto Rican Culture and Latino Identity* (New York: Columbia University Press, 2000), 67–69.

15 Ibid., 83–95.

16 Marisol Berríos-Miranda, "Is Salsa a Musical Genre?" in Waxer, Lisa, *Situating Salsa: Global Markets and Local Meaning in Latin Popular Music* (New York: Routledge, 2002), 23–50; Christopher Washburne, *Sounding Salsa: Performing Latin Music in New York City* (Philadelphia, PA: Temple University Press, 2008).

17 Deborah Pacini Hernández, *Bachata: A Social History of a Dominican Popular Music* (Philadelphia: Temple University Press, 1995), 108–114.

18 Maria Elena Cepeda, "Columbus Effect(s): Chronology and Crossover in the Latin(o) Music Boom," *Discourse* 23, no. 1 (2001): 63–81.

19 Roberts, *The Latin Tinge*, 50–57.

20 Francesco Adinolfi, *Mondo Exotica: Sounds, Visions, Obsessions of the Cocktail Generation* (Durham, NC: Duke University Press, 2008), 105–108.

21 Brill, *Music of Latin America and the Caribbean*, 245–247.

22 Oliver N. Greene, "Ethnicity, Modernity and REtention in the Garifuna Punta," *Black Music Research Journal* 22, no. 2 (2002): 189–216.

23 John Storm Roberts, *Latin Jazz: The First of the Fusions, 1880s to Today* (New York: Schirmer Books, 1999).

24 Daniel Party, "The Miamization of Latin-American Pop Music," in Madrid, Alejandro L. and Ignacio Corona, *Postnational Musical Identities: Cultural Production and Consumption in a Globalized Scenario* (Lanham, MD: Lexington Books, 2008),

66–67; Roberto Avant-Mier, *Rock the Nation: Latin/o Identities and the Latin Rock Diaspora* (London: Continuum, 2010), 46–48; 127–128; 131.

25 Roberts, *The Latin Tinge*, 180–181.

26 Flores, *From Bomba to Hip-Hop*, 126–127; 137–139; Hernández, *Oye Como Va!*, 63–65.

27 Raquel Z. Rivera, Wayne Marshall, and Deborah Pacini Hernández, *Reggaetón* (Durham, NC: Duke University Press, 2009).

28 Party, "The Miamization of Latin-American Pop Music," 67.

6 Hispanic/LatinX Art in the U.S.

Past and Present

Ilenia Colón Mendoza, Ph.D.

Associate Professor of Art History,
University of Central Florida

The cultures inherited by Latinos predate the formation of the United States. From the Olmecs to the Aztecs in Central America, the Taino in the Caribbean, and the Chavín and Inca in South America, these ancient civilizations serve as a foundation for the formation of a modern-day Latino community. These populations had sophisticated calendar systems, monumental architecture, and structured civilizations. Their important historical contributions are often overlooked when we study Western Art. Many Latino artists use the **iconography** of formative cultures in their work. Two major historical events heightened the influence of Latinos in the United States: the Mexican–American War (1846–1848), with its annexation of Mexico's northern territories, and the Spanish–American War (1898) in which Spain ceded Puerto Rico to the United States.

Early Artists Paving the Way

Early twentieth-century artists, such as Frida Kahlo, Diego Rivera, José Clemente Orozco, David Alfaro Siqueiros, and Ana Mendieta, incorporated their cultural heritage into their creations as well as important historical and political events. These artists were the first to come and work in the U.S. and their influence on American art is well documented. After working in San Francisco in 1930 and in Detroit from 1932 to 1933, Mexican artist Diego Rivera was invited by the Rockefellers to create a mural for the Rockefeller center in 1933. The **mural** (large-scale painting painted directly on the wall), entitled *Man at the Crossroads*, was proposed and accepted. Midway through completion Rivera added a depiction of Vladimir Lenin that was poorly received by the Rockefellers because of its communist leanings. A letter was written by the Rockefellers requesting Lenin be eliminated from the mural, citing that the portrait was not part of the original proposal. Rivera refused to eliminate the figure and therefore was removed from the project; after he was paid a lump sum for his work, the **mural** was destroyed.[1] This controversial work was one of the first instances of a Latin American artist being featured in the mainstream press. The news behind the controversy was widespread, and Rivera later recreated the work in Mexico.

Frida Kahlo was married to Diego Rivera and traveled with him to the United States. She was also Mexican, and although less known at the time her work is now very popular and influential. Frida is well known for her biography; she suffered from polio as a child and on September 17, 1925, was in an accident in which the wooden bus she was riding collided with a streetcar. An iron handrail impaled her through her pelvis, fracturing the bone; she also fractured several ribs, her legs, and her collarbone.[2] She became an artist while she was recovering in bed from her injuries. While traveling with Diego Rivera she was often referred to as Mrs. Rivera. Her painting *Self-Portrait along the borderline between Mexico and the United States* (1932), shows her on a pedestal marked Carmen Rivera, as she was known in the U.S. She paints the Detroit industry in contrast to the nature of Mexico and clearly sides with her Mexican heritage as she proudly holds a Mexican flag and wears a necklace inspired by Aztec art. This work represents how many Latino immigrants feel trapped between cultures.

Mexican muralist Orozco lived in the United States from 1927 to 1934. He is known as one of the "three great muralists" along with Rivera. He created murals at Pomona College, Claremont, in California, the New School for

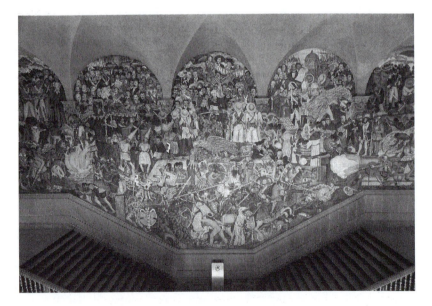

Figure 6.1 The History of Mexico, Diego Rivera fresco mural, National Palace, Mexico City.

Florian Augustin/Shutterstock

Figure 6.2 Mural by José Clemente Orozco in a classroom of the University of
Guadalajara, Mexico.

Bill Perry/Shutterstock

Social Research in New York, and Dartmouth College, Hanover, in New
Hampshire. This last mural, housed in the library of the university, is one of
his most influential works. The *Epic of American Civilization* was painted between
1932 and 1934 and covers almost 300 m² (3,200 square feet) in twenty-four
panels. Topics shown include Migrations, Human Sacrifices, The Appearance
of Quetzalcóatl, Corn Culture, Anglo-America, Hispano-America, Science,
and Modern Migration of the Spirit.[3] In one scene Orozco criticizes the
academic life and, although this work was met with controversy by some
alumni, the board of directors of the university decided to keep the work in
the spirit of creative freedom.

The third member of the "three great muralists" is David Siqueiros,
who first traveled to New York in 1932 and returned in 1936 after traveling
to Los Angeles. In New York, Siqueiros was the artist in residence at the
"Contemporary Arts" exhibition at the St. Regis gallery. It was there he ran a
political art workshop in preparation for the 1936 General Strike for Peace and
May Day parade. Jackson Pollock, one of the most famous and impactful
American artists, attended the workshop and helped build floats for the parade.[4]
Siqueiros has been credited with teaching drip and pour techniques to Pollock
that mark his career in Abstract Expressionist action painting.

Cuban-born Ana Mendieta immigrated to Iowa as a child as part of Operation
Peter Pan, which helped Cuban children escape Fidel's regime. She attended
graduate school at the University of Iowa.[5] Her works deal with displacement

and exile, and have been referred to as eco-feminism because of their connection of nature and feminist ideologies. Mendieta also did film projects and influential **performance** pieces such as the *Untitled* (*Rape Scene*) in 1973, which recreated a rape scene in her apartment to comment on the brutal rape and murder of a fellow student. Mendieta died in New York under suspicious circumstances after falling from her thirty-fourth-floor apartment; her husband at the time, Carl Andre, was accused and later acquitted of her murder. She is still discussed widely in the media and the feminist protest group, No Wave Performance Task Force, often perform in her honor. These aforementioned canonical artists, among many others, serve as a stepping stone for the contemporary artists that will follow in the twenty-first century.

When discussing Latinos in the U.S. and their involvement in the art world, we find that certain cities such as New York, Miami, Chicago, and Los Angeles have become important centers. Chicano, Cuban–American, and Puerto Rican artists have a strong hold on contemporary art production. Puerto Ricans, for example, started immigrating to New York in the 1950s. Because Puerto Ricans have U.S. passports they can remain in the U.S. without requiring a visa. Some of the artists we will look at in this chapter are **first-generation**, meaning their parents were born in their country of origin while they were born of Hispanic families but in the mainland U.S.

Today, there are a large number of Hispanic and Latino artists working in the U.S. Major themes of their work include identity politics, issues of isolation and cultural displacement, politics, race, and gender. In this chapter, you will learn about Latino artists who interact with media and reflect on the issues media bring. The preferred **genre** (a category of artistic works characterized by similarities in form, style, or subject matter) of many of these artists includes performance; a presentation to an audience within a fine art context. This can be either scripted or unscripted. It can be done with or without audience participation; by using video, **installations**, as an artistic genre of three-dimensional works that can be site-specific and designed to transform a space, and multimedia experiences.

Coco Fusco and Guillermo Gómez-Peña

Coco Fusco is a Cuban-American interdisciplinary artist and writer. At present, she is the Andrew Banks Endowed Professor at the College of Art at the University of Florida.[6] Her work deals with issues of gender and race; she studies the impact of media and cultural constructs on Latino identity. Guillermo Gómez-Peña is a **Chicano** (Mexican-American born in Mexico City) performance artist, writer, and vocal activist. He created work in multiple media, including performance art, video, and installation.[7] These two artists collaborated on the work *Two Undiscovered Amerindians Visit the West* performed in 1992–1994. The work dates to the late twentieth century and is pivotal to establishing performance as a platform for Latino artists.

The piece premiered at Columbus Plaza in Madrid as part of the Edge '92 Biennial in May of 1992, and it toured for about two years. This year marked the 500 years of the "discovery" of the Americas. The artists sought to comment on the treatment of native populations that were decimated during colonization and their treatment as curiosities. **Conquistadors** took natives to the Kings of Spain as if they were items to be displayed. Fusco and Peña occupied a large cage and impersonated natives belonging to a made-up island off the coast of Mexico that was untouched by European culture called Guatianau.[8]

Fusco wore a costume that consisted of a hula grass skirt and a leopard print bikini top. She was adorned with shell necklaces and body paint and covered her eyes with sunglasses. Peña had an elaborate headdress and a wrestling mask, as one would see in Mexican *lucha libre*, wrestling characterized by exaggerated gestures, costumes, and masked characters. The work was interactive with the public. Fusco ate bananas presented from outside the cage, and she would also dance while Peña would tell stories of his people in a made-up language. This storytelling was the only time the artists spoke. They also worked with filmmaker Paula Heredia to create *The Couple in the Cage: Guatianaui Odyssey* (1992–1993) to document the performances and audience reactions. Some visitors were so confused they actually thought these were real natives.[9] This work emphasizes the connection between display and the idea of curiosity. As the "other," the Amerindian—like the Latino—becomes an object to be stereotyped and misunderstood. The artists also call attention to the ignorance regarding Latino culture in general.

Pepón Osorio

Pepón Osorio was born in Santurce, Puerto Rico, in 1955. Osorio's pieces, influenced by his experience as a social worker in the Bronx, usually evolve from an interaction with the neighborhoods and people among which he is working. He said: "My principal commitment as an artist is to return art to the community."[10] In order to prepare for the *Scene of a Crime*, shown in the 1993 **Whitney Biennial**, an exhibition of contemporary art in New York that takes place every two years, the artist rode around with detectives to make sure his work was authentic as possible.

He later invited the detectives back to solve the crime in his work because he had asked them many suspicious questions about what happens when you use an ice pick to hit somebody in the head.[11] This piece is an installation and we see a wife murdered by her husband. The wife is a mannequin and her body is placed face down and it is roped off. Personal photos, **bric a brac**, miscellaneous objects, ornaments of little value, and trophies, are the only way to approach the real Latino body. The welcome mat reads: "Only if you can understand that it has taken years of pain to gather into our homes our most valuable possessions; but the greater pain is to see how in movies others make fun of the way we live." The artist seeks to highlight issues of domestic violence.

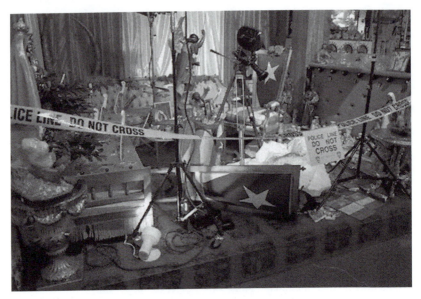

Figure 6.3 Scene of a Crime installation by Pepón Osorio, 1993, shown at the Whitney
Museum in New York.

Photo courtesy of Pepón Osorio

He created a link between the wounded body and the body in cultural
productions such as movies. The real body is also linked to the represented
body. Videotape boxes are included with statements made by the Latino
community about Hollywood films.

Osorio states how Latinos are shown in film:

> We are either seen as violent, horny or on welfare. They never show our
> humanity or our struggles and empowerment. You see the negative
> stereotypes portrayed in the movies so many times that at some point you
> start believing them yourself. The more I see the stereotypes, the more I
> feel excluded from the world, almost as if I'm living a reality that is
> common to others.[12]

The cycle of cultural wounding and healing is presented by a video monitor
placed in the mirror above the body that shows a blood-filled urn, which breaks
after falling, shatters, and puts itself together again. This represents the assault
on Latino culture by mainstream media. *The New York Times* reviewed this
piece, at which point Osorio realized the community did not regularly see the
newspaper. For future installations, he decided to show work in the community
first and then at a gallery.

Wanda Raimundi-Ortiz

Wanda Raimundi-Ortiz was born in Bronx, New York, in 1973 and is an assistant professor of art at the University of Central Florida. Internationally recognized for her performance art, her alter ego *Chuleta* has gained popularity in the art world.

Her character, whose name translates to "pork chop," which is a typical food in the Puerto Rican diet, gives advice on everything from decorating to fine art. Using the YouTube platform as her medium, she manipulates media as an instrument. Fulfilling the idea of a Nuyorican stereotype right down to the **doobie**, a wrapping of the hair with bobby pins commonly used in Puerto Rico and the Dominican Republic where the hair is placed in rollers to make it straight, the artist is confronting preconceived cultural constructs. *Chuleta* speaks Spanglish, and she dresses from the Rainbow Shops but curiously debates the value of **appropriation** and Andy Warhol's work. In video number six, "Identity Art," *Chuleta* discusses Wanda Raimundi-Ortiz, and mentions "you gotta do you!" and that she is "a hood-ass feminist." This interesting dynamic of alter ego discussing the artist is clever and innovative.

Raimundi-Ortiz's construction of *Chuleta* is a direct embrace of the stereotypes she stayed away from growing up. She was brought up to exemplify the "best most dignified Latina" and to steer clear of doobies and rollers in

Figure 6.4 Puerto Rican artist Wanda Raimundi-Ortiz is well known for her visual and performance art.

Photo courtesy of Wanda Raimundi-Ortiz

A Latina Artist's Experience

Wanda Raimundi-Ortiz

Can you describe a moment in your career, or a piece of your work, that made you feel especially proud to be a Latina? Can you describe a specific time when you tapped into your Hispanic heritage to inspire your work?

This is a tricky question since my work is firmly anchored in my *Latinidad*. However, my work also intends to pick some of the inner workings of *Latinidad* apart, especially as a stateside-born Puerto Rican, aka

Figure 6.5 Film stills of Wanda Raimundi-Ortiz as *Chuleta*, from *Ask Chuleta #6 Identity Art* video, 2010.

Photo courtesy of Wanda Raimundi-Ortiz

American (as if the islanders are not also technically Americans . . . that note is for those that still don't know that Puerto Rico is a U.S. commonwealth, not a state, nor an independent country). So much of my work is a direct response to feeling displaced while living in the very country where I was born and raised. Reared to be a proudly Boricua woman from immigrant parents, my first-generation Puerto Rican-American experience is not unlike so many other first-gen people. We have similar, often funny stories about our old school upbringings clashing loudly with new world expectations and codes, and navigating the choppy waters between adhering to and upholding old-school traditions and moving upward on the shiny gilded ladder of "equal" opportunity that lured our parents here.

However, as an art maker, it became increasingly difficult to make work that I thought would resound with the art viewing public. I assumed that audiences were predominantly white and that making work about *Latinidad* would alienate me from visibility and acceptance in the art world. Tailoring of my visual and creative language left me stunted, feeling disingenuous and uninspired. It wasn't until I encountered the masterful work of Pepón Osorio that I felt my Latina voice validated. I learned that I could be powerfully critical of my people (Latinos and Americans, as well as the art world), and still be proud. I could speak of disenchantment, marginalization, critique intersections where these worlds met for me. I began making work about living in the fracture of multiple lives, all the while challenging the parts of our culture that are problematic.

Some of my proudest and gut-wrenching moments were documented in murals I created at the Museo de Arte de Puerto Rico and at the Hunter College Center for Puerto Rican studies in New York. I chronicled the voyage of Wepa Woman's return to her *patria*, Puerto Rico, in reverence and awe of the island's splendor, only to be devastated and rendered powerless by the very people and nation whose code she is sworn to defend and uphold. Loosely autobiographical, the works tackle displacement and bewilderment between two cultures, neither of which fully accepts you because you are neither American enough nor Puerto Rican enough. Too stubbornly Latino to fully assimilate and too American to understand island life, but expected to represent both wholly, proudly. I could not have been prouder to be Puerto Rican and invited to exhibit at the Museo—and I couldn't have been more devastated than to *not* have been acknowledged as Puerto Rican since I was born on the mainland. To quote the poet Maria Teresa Fernández, aka *Mariposa*, "*No nací en Puerto Rico, Puerto Rico nació en Mi*" (I wasn't born in Puerto Rico, Puerto Rico was born in me).

public.[13] Growing up, she chose neither; she was not representative of the inner city nor the dignified Latina her family wanted her to be; she rebelled and embraced other cultures, such as **New Wave** and Punk. Wanda comments that representations of Latinos in the media are "flat, formulaic" and notes that, when you do not fit these molds, you become ambiguous and your own community does not acknowledge you. She has taken on personalities that deal with the hyper-sexualization of Latinas, such as Wepa Woman. But in this case, she wanted *Chuleta* to be someone you would know. *Chuleta*'s own growth is seen in the progression of the videos she creates, how they are edited and shot, and also in the topics she chooses. The work is controversial and has received backlash from some who may not realize that the artist's intention is deliberate. By appropriating cultural stereotypes she wants to call attention to the expectations of what Latinas should look like. In her words, "Latinas are packaged to be acceptable to a white consumer, white women want to be you and white men want to be with you."[14]

Nao Bustamante

Nao Bustamante is an internationally known Chicana (Mexican-American) artist who lives in Los Angeles, California. Her **oeuvre**, or body of work, includes performance art, video installation, filmmaking, and writing. She is Associate Professor and Vice Dean of Art at the USC Roski School of Art and Design.[15] Her work *America, the Beautiful* is a 50-minute performance from 1995 that shows the artist binding her curvy Latina body with tape. This performance fulfils the definition of **body art**, as it uses the body as medium or material. The artist is commenting on how women punish themselves for beauty.

She argues Latina women, in particular, find it harder to conform to these constructed ideas of beauty seen in magazines and television because of body type, hair color, and texture. To begin the performance, the artist removes her clothing completely. She then sits and places a paper toilet seat cover around her neck. She then begins her beauty ritual by curling her eyelashes, applying red lipstick, and brushing gold dust on her face. Bustamante puts on a blonde wig and uses an entire hairspray bottle to set her hair. Using packing tape, she creates an hourglass figure that is the part of the idealized American beauty. Bustamante then climbs a small ladder and proceeds to put on high heels and fingerless white gloves. Throughout the piece, she uses a record player that she manipulates to play the appropriate music for her actions. After getting down from the small ladder, she climbs to the top of a larger one, which she straddles while she smokes a cigarette. The ladder, much like the concept of a corporate ladder, is a metaphor for reaching professional heights. At the top of the ladder, she makes rabbit shadow puppets. Later, she climbs down after hanging onto the ladder in various uncomfortable positions. She gets a bouquet of roses and is temporarily happy, then, in anger, she chews one of the roses off. At the end of her performance, she plays the American national anthem by blowing on bottles.

The performance shows how the artist sacrifices her body, a body which is strained physically by a tape that makes her immobile but also a body that she exposes to the public for scrutiny. While she is applying the spray to her hair, you can see that Bustamante is having difficulty breathing and gags on the fumes of the spray. These demonstrations of physicality echo the daily beauty rituals of women. Her attempt to conform to beauty standards outside her cultural Mexican background is painful but also unattainable.

The artists you have learned about grew up seeing stereotypical images of Latinos in the media and have often been victims of prejudice. They have often been presumed incompetent and faced racism. Historically, the art world has not embraced artists of color and women as openly as white males. As the world changes, so will the art that future generations produce. The artists you have learned about deal with important issues of identity. How are Latinos perceived? How are they portrayed in movies, TV shows? What is known about Latino culture? What is true and what is fiction? Often, Latinos are seen as the "other," the non-western, the minority. **Second-generation** Latinos are particularly displaced as they are in between the culture of their parents and the North American culture in which they have grown up. As populations grow and shift, more and more Latinos occupy and make their presence known using media, video, and performance as tools for communication and advocacy. Surely, the portrayal of Latinos in media will continue to change in the upcoming years, and artists will continue to shed light on those portrayals.

Vocabulary Words

Appropriation
Body Art
Bric a Brac
Chicano(a)
Conquistador
Doobie
First-Generation
Genre
Iconography

Installation
Lucha Libre
Mural
New Wave
Oeuvre
Performance
Second-Generation
Whitney Biennial

Points to Remember

- The *Two Undiscovered Amerindians Visit the West* (1992–1994), a theatrical piece by Coco Fusco and Guillermo Gómez-Peña, was groundbreaking for Latino artists.
- Pepón Osorio's art sheds light on how Latinos are stereotyped as being violent, sexualized, or on welfare.

- Wanda Raimundi-Ortiz's alter ego, *Chuleta*, is a symbol of non-conformist, empowered, feminist Latinas who want to remove the stigma from their cultural stereotypes.
- Nao Bustamante's performance in *America, the Beautiful* (1995) depicts how Latina women desperately attempt and struggle to achieve societal standards of beauty in America.

Names to Remember

Ana Mendieta
Coco Fusco
David Alfaro Siqueiros
Diego Rivera
Frida Kahlo
Guillermo Gómez-Peña
José Clemente Orozco
Neo Bustamante
Paula Herida
Pepón Osorio
Wanda Raimundi-Ortiz

Practice Questions

1   The work by Coco Fusco and Guillermo Gómez-Peña coincided with the celebration of what event? Explain what their work attempted to communicate in regards to native populations.
2   What work did Pepón do before he became an artist? What kind of issue did his performances aim to underline? Name the work that reflected this.
3   Why does Pepón Osorio want to bring art to the community?
4   What is Wanda Raimundi-Ortiz's alter ego called? Explain what her impersonation intends to convey about Latinas and the kind of responses that it has prompted from audiences.
5   What medium does Nao Bustamante use and what is the purpose of her work? Give a specific example of how her work emphasizes the social standards that women attempt to achieve.

Activity

Create collages of positive media images of Latinos you see in magazines, newspapers, and computer screenshots. Cut and paste the images on foam board keeping artistic design in mind, or make virtual collages on the computer. The board will be discussed in class with the following prompts.

1 Why did you select these images?
2 Why do you see these images of Latinos as positive?
3 Was it hard to find these positive images? Did you encounter stereotypes in your search?
4 What can you do to help promote healthy and positive images of Latinos in the media?

Timeline

1846: Beginning of Mexican–American War
1848: End of Mexican–American War.
1898: Beginning of Spanish–American War.
1925: On September 17, Frida Kahlo gets into a car accident on that leaves her with extensive injuries. She becomes an artist during her recovery time.
1927: Artist José Clemente Orozco lives in the U.S. until 1934.
1932: Frida Kahlo paints *Self-Portrait* along the borderline between Mexico and the United States; artist José Clemente Orozco begins painting *The Epic of American Civilization*, completed in1934; David Siqueiros travels to New York and returns in 1936 after traveling to Los Angeles.
1933: Mexican artist Diego Rivera is invited to create the mural for the Rockefeller center by the Rockefellers.
1936: General Strike for Peace and May Day parade.
1950s: Migration of Puerto Ricans to New York begins.
1955: Artist Pepón Osorio is born in Santurce, Puerto Rico.
1973: Wanda Raimundi-Ortiz is born in Bronx, New York; Ana Mendieta creates *Untitled (Rape Scene)* in her apartment after the rape and murder of a fellow student.
1992: Coco Fusco and Guillermo Peña collaborated on the performance *Two Undiscovered Amerindians Visit the West.*
1993: *Scene of a Crime* is shown at Whitney Biennial.
1995: Nao Bustamante's work *America, the Beautiful* performance.

Additional Resources

Coco Fusco and Guillermo Gomez Peña, *Two Undiscovered Amerindians visit the West*: www.youtube.com/watch?v=gLX2Lk2tdcw.
Pepón Osorio on Art 21: www.art21.org/videos/segment-pepon-osorio-in-place.
Wanda a Chuleta on Identity Art #6: www.youtube.com/watch?v=FpeGFOF1Wic.
Nao Bustamante: www.naobustamante.com/ and http://hidvl.nyu.edu/video/0010184 39.html.

About the Author

Ilenia Colón Mendoza

Photo courtesy of University
of Central Florida

Ilenia Colón Mendoza, Ph.D., received a bachelor's degree in Art History and Archaeology from the University of Evansville in Indiana, a master's degree in Latin American Art, and a Spanish Baroque Ph.D. from the Pennsylvania State University. She is associate professor of Art History at the School of Visual Arts and Design of the University of Central Florida. Her book entitled *The Cristos yacentes of Gregorio Fernandez: Polychrome Sculptures of the Supine Christ in Seventeenth-Century Spain* (Routledge: Ashgate, 2015) examines the significance of the Cristo yacente sculptural type within the context of the theatrical elaborations of the Catholic Holy Week in Baroque Spain.

Notes

1 Patrick Frank, *Readings in Latin American Modern Art* (New Haven: Yale University Press, 2004), 36.
2 Hayden Herrera, *Frida: A Biography of Frida Kahlo* (New York: Harper Perrenial, 2002), 47–50.
3 *Dartmouth*, "Dartmouth Digital Orozco," www.dartmouth.edu/digitalorozco.
4 Laurance Hurlburt, "The Siqueiros Experimental Workshop: New York, 1936," *Art Journal* 35, no. 3 (1976): 237–246.
5 Kaira Cabañas, "Ana Mendieta: Pain of Cuba, Body I Am," *Woman's Art Journal* 20 (1990): 12–17.
6 Coco Fusco, "Biography," www.cocofusco.com.
7 "Guillermo Gómez-Peña," *Video Data Bank*, www.vdb.org/artists/guillermo-g%C3 %B3mez-pe%C3%B1-0.
8 Whitney Chadwick, *Women, Art and Society* (New York: Thames & Hudson, 2012), 393.
9 Coco Fusco and Paula Herida, "The Couple in the Cage: Guatianaui Odyssey," *Video Data Bank* (1993), www.vdb.org/titles/couple-cage-guatianaui-odyssey.
10 Pepón Osorio, "Artist Lecture," presentation at Bloomsburg University of Pennsylvania, Bloomsburg, Pennsylvania, April 1, 2010.
11 Pepón Osorio, "Artist Lecture."
12 Ibid.
13 Wanda Raimundi-Ortiz, interviewed by Ilenia Colón Mendoza, September 30, 2016.
14 Raimundi-Ortiz, interview.
15 Nao Bustamante, "Biography," www.naobustamante.com/about.html.

Unit 3

The LatinX Impact on Electronic and Digital Media

7 From Grassroots to Big Business

The Emergence and Development of Hispanic/LatinX Radio in the U.S.

William Kinnally, Ph.D.

Associate Professor of Radio-Television,
University of Central Florida

People looking carefully at the history and development of Hispanic radio will see that an entrepreneurial spirit and desire to build a sense of community are at its core. Hispanic radio emerged in the early days of radio as one of many foreign-language media endeavors like newspapers and radio broadcasts in German, Polish, and even Lithuanian. These media outlets served as unique public voices in ethnic communities.[1] The Hispanic radio pioneers offered vibrant music, alternative news, and colorful personalities to audiences who largely lived in the American Southwest and West. This radio programming grew slowly at first. However, by the mid-twentieth century, it was outpacing all of the other foreign-language programming. The latter part of the twentieth century brought exponential growth, and numerous niche program **formats** were adopted by more and more stations in the effort to serve their ever-growing Hispanic and Latino communities in cities and towns all across the country.

Brokered Time to Full-Time

The beginnings of Hispanic radio reflect what was happening in the radio industry during its early decades. Through the 1950s, radio was quite different from the way it is today. Rather than offering one kind of music all day every day, station schedules consisted of **blocks** of programs.[2] The schedule was somewhat like what we see on a TV channel today. From the late 1920s to the 1940s, radio station owners offered mostly English-language programs and made their money by either having sponsors for their programs or "renting" the "air time" to independent program producers, also known as **brokers**. The radio owners felt compelled to fill as much air time as possible.[3] Naturally, some periods of the day were less desirable to producers than others. Even then, they realized most people were not going to listen to the radio late at night or early in the morning.

As a result, these English-language stations rented the air time during the less desirable hours to brokers who created programs that served various immigrant communities, including Spanish-speaking communities. In New York City, Julio Roque became a radio broker. He actually had a career as a dentist, but he was also a musician and composer. So, in the mid-1920s, he created *Revista Roque*, which was the first Spanish-language radio program in New York. The show included a variety of Latin American music including Roque's compositions and performances by his own orchestra. He even used the radio show to sell his own brand of toothpaste and mouthwash. On the West Coast, brokers such as Rodolfo Hoyos were accomplishing the same goals. Hoyos was also a musician who performed on his daily show but his program also included poetry, drama, and discussions of community issues.[4] In his case, the station charged him nearly $200 per month for an hour-long daily time slot.[5] He then would travel around the community visiting local businesses such as **bodegas** to take music requests, find out what issues were important to the community, and sell them advertising. Unlike most of the produced radio commercials we hear on the radio today, the advertisements consisted of simple mentions of the businesses and their products during the program.[6]

Obviously, the owners of stations featuring foreign-language broadcasts were pleased to be making money by selling the late night and early morning air time, and they had little interest in supervising or interfering with what was being broadcast during those hours. However, during World War II (1939–1945), the U.S. Office of Censorship imposed restrictions on all radio stations, especially those that carried foreign-language programs.[7] Although government censors mostly paid attention to Japanese, German, Italian, and Polish broadcasters, Spanish-language programs were also subjected to limitations. One broker in San Antonio, Raoul Cortez, recognized the government's concerns and saw an opportunity. Cortez applied to the **Federal Communications Commission (FCC)** to build a new radio station that would only feature Spanish-language programming. Recognizing that the national climate did not exactly favor the idea of increasing the amount of foreign-language radio, Cortez argued that the station could be helpful to the government because it could generate greater support for the war among Mexican-Americans.[8] In 1946, after the war, the FCC approved the application and KCOR-AM became the first full-time, Spanish-language radio station in the U.S.[9] Their slogan was "*La Voz Mexicana*" or "The Mexican Voice." As important, KCOR was the first Hispanic-owned station in the country and is still operating as a full-service, Spanish-language station today. Cortez would later launch the first full-time, Spanish-language television station, KCOR-TV.[10]

In the early 1940s, stations with Spanish-language programs represented about a quarter of all the stations broadcasting foreign-language programming. By the early 1960s, the percentage increased to two-thirds.[11] The industry evolved during the 1950s and 1960s. More full-time Spanish-language stations were launched in various cities such as Denver and New York. The era of the industrious broker who served as host/performer/producer/salesman had largely passed. This period also saw a move toward more standardization in programming as Spanish-language radio networks were created. Raoul Cortez's "Sombrero" radio network, which started in 1956 and eventually included as many as fifteen stations, is a great example. These kinds of networks helped coordinate and distribute programs to multiple stations. They also sold advertising that could be placed on multiple stations and conducted promotions across wider areas.[12]

The next two decades saw Spanish-language radio begin its true ascent. In the mid-1960s, after lobbying by Hispanic radio broadcasters, Arbitron, Inc., the primary U.S. company collecting radio listening data for advertisers and stations at that time, began measuring the audiences for Spanish-language stations.[13] This signaled that advertiser interest in reaching the Hispanic consumers was increasing. During the 1970s and 1980s, there was more investment in stations and programming as well as greater interest in the Spanish-language market.[14] By 1980, there were more than 500 stations that offered some Spanish-language programming and there were 104 stations that were reported as having a Spanish-language format—meaning that all their programming was targeting Hispanic/Latino audiences. Although there were stations scattered throughout the U.S., a high concentration—more than half—were located in California and Texas.[15]

The 1990s saw further growth in the industry. For example, there were more than 500 Spanish-language stations in the U.S.[16] The radio industry went through a number of changes in the late 1990s as a result of the Telecommunications Act of 1996, which had a dramatic influence on how many broadcast stations one company could own.[17] The Spanish-language market did not escape the effects of this regulatory change. Within the decade after the 1996 legislation, there was an increase in the concentration of ownership—that is, more stations were owned by fewer companies. Generally, the total number of radio stations, regardless of format, increased by a little more than 5% but the number of owners decreased by more than 30%.[18] The new regulations had an impact on the ethnic diversity of the broadcast ownership. By 2006, only 3% of all radio stations were owned by Hispanics/Latinos, while approximately 7.5% of stations had a Hispanic radio format.[19]

Cable and Satellite Radio

Up to this point, the conversation has focused on terrestrial radio, i.e., radio programming that is sent over-the-air using ground-based antennas. However, in the late 1980s, new radio competitors came on the scene with a goal of reaching national audiences. The early station lineup on Digital Cable Radio, now called Music Choice, was limited and focused on traditional popular music

Managing Radio Sales

by Lourdes Lora Washington
Director of Sales and Promotions for Hola 104.9FM in
Port St. Lucie, Florida

I can proudly say that I'm one of the pioneers of Spanish-language media in the Washington, D.C. Metropolitan Area. I fell in love with radio in 1984, when I was interviewed live in the studio of the first Spanish radio station in Washington (*Radio Mundo*). That's when I decided I wanted to be a DJ, or a news anchor. I was majoring in business management, which I hated, as it really bored me. My life changed after I became the secretary for the First Lady of Washington, D.C., Mrs. Effie Barry. I admired her so much that she became my mentor. I wanted to be like her, so I changed majors to marketing and public relations. In 1993, after having my second child, I decided to get into radio. My friend from college, Alejandro Carrasco, had been hired as the general manager at a Spanish radio station, and he mentioned to me he was looking for bilingual sales people. I told him I was interested in the position, and he hired me.

I started selling an AM station with 1,000 watts. It was a sunrise to sunset station, which means the signal was limited, and it had to be turned down to 500 mhz at sunset. WILC-AM 90 Radio Borinquen was a Tropical format station, which was the hot format back then.

Figure 7.1 Lourdes Lora Washington
Photo courtesy of Lourdes Lora Washington

The Hispanic community in the Washington metropolitan area was growing rapidly due to the war in Central America. The newly arrived immigrants needed guidance, so the station became the voice of the community. The music was in LPs and 8 tracks! I learned how to erase 8 tracks, how to record reel to reel, how to tape them, how to write my own scripts, copy points, produce commercials, type news from the IP (which was our only news source), and how to read an insertion order (orders that came from agencies). There was no internet, so we negotiated contracts in person or by phone, and the orders and contracts were faxed to us or signed personally. The commercial logs were done manually. I became an expert selling to the agencies with no ratings. WILC-AM was the most popular Spanish station in the market.

We organized the best Latin music festivals in the city. In 1996, I left to help my friend open a new station, Radio America. I was his national sales manager. I had to travel to different markets to sell the station. Even though it was an AM station, we had ratings, so I was able to get business from the national and regional agencies. It was very challenging to sell the market, since Washington, D.C. was not a top ten Hispanic market. I had to educate the English-speaking clients about how to sell to Hispanics. I created a lot of my own scripts that would actually make sense to our listeners. So I had to culturize a lot of the ads. In 1999, I was hired by ZGS Broadcasting, an affiliate of Telemundo. Telemundo was new in the market and had to compete with the goliath of Spanish TV networks: Univision. The station was not on cable so we had to do strenuous local marketing and promotion—what is known as "guerilla marketing"! It was one of the hardest media to sell. It was a big challenge for me, but I did not give up. Once the station was on cable and the numbers increased it got better; it was a matter of convincing the business owners and the agencies they would get results (ROI, or return on investment). I was able to get the best accounts in the station and I was at the top of my game.

In 2001, ZGS Broadcasting leased a radio station, and I was asked by the owner to be part of the team. I helped develop the format, the team, the image, and entire structure of the station. I accepted the general sales manager position. It was another challenge for me! The station was in red numbers. In less than a year, we brought the station back to life! We surpassed the sales goal, and the station was back on the radar. Viva 900AM was alive! Then, the 9/11 tragedy impacted our industry in unexpected ways. It was a very difficult time for the economy. The marketing budgets were cut, and we started to feel it. In 2003, I was hired as local sales manager for WBZS-FM 92.7/94.3 and WKDL-730AM. They were the strongest stations in the Hispanic market and the ones with the best ratings. WBZS-FM La Mega was the only FM station in Spanish in the area. WKDL-730AM, Radio Capital was the only Regional Mexican format in the market. The majority of the Hispanic population in the Washington Metro area was from Mexico and Central America back then, hence the popularity of the stations. The stations were doing well in ratings, but the community outreach was a disaster. I had to mend a lot of bridges that had been burned by previous managers. I had a very good reputation in the Hispanic market, so I started to create relationships with community organizations, and a lot of the clients returned to advertise in the stations; 2004 was the best year in radio I ever had! We had successful promotions and very successful festivals.

In 2006, the stations were sold to Red Zebra Communications. They flipped the stations to sports radio. I gave it a try, but the community was very much affected by that. I begged them to leave the AM station in Spanish, but it didn't happen. I then decided to move to Miami, Florida, where I worked at another regional Mexican station, which did not do well in Miami. I'm presently working for Hola Broadcasting LLC as director of sales and promotions. Previously I was at iHeartRadio in West Palm Beach, where I represented ten stations, one being the number one Spanish Station in the area: WRLX-FM, MIA 92.1FM. My philosophy for selling radio to the Latino Market? It is all about the relationships you build; they are not my clients, they are my friends. Once they have my trust, and they know I will use my experience and expertise to help their business grow and get their return on investment, they will advertise with me and listen to me.

formats. However, as they increased the number of channels being offered, they seized the opportunity to offer programming for audiences with a Hispanic or Latino heritage. By 2010, their channel lineup included Musica Urbana (featuring reggaeton and Latin rap), Tropicales (including bachata, salsa, and merengue), Pop Latino (Latin hits), Mexicana (playing ranchera and mariachi), Tejano (Tejano music), and Romances (Spanish love songs).[20]

The satellite radio era opened in 2001 when XM Satellite Radio played reggae superstar Bob Marley's "One Love."[21] The message of inclusiveness associated with that classic Marley song was exemplified in 100 music and talk channels, five of which were dedicated to Latin music. The channels included *Rock en Español*, Tejano, and Caribbean.[22] Sirius Satellite Radio started in 2002 and included as many as eight Latin music channels.[23] The two companies merged in 2008, and one of the conditions set by the FCC was that the new company had to make a concerted effort to include programming that was relevant to underserved communities.[24]

Following the merger, the company launched SiriusXM Latino as part of their new channel expansion and included channels such as *Radio Formula Mexico* and *Playboy Radio Español*. SiriusXM partnered with National Latino Broadcasting to provide content for four new Latin channels such as *En Vivo*,

From Print to TV to Radio

Cristina Saralegui

Cristina Saralegui was born in Havana, Cuba, in 1948. She later immigrated to the United States in 1960 and studied communications and creative writing at the University of Miami. She worked for *Vanidades*, the *Miami Herald*, and *Cosmopolitan*. Cristina Saralegui eventually became the editor-in-chief for the *Cosmopolitan en Español*. She is also known for her television show on Univision, *El Show de Cristina*; a daily radio show titled *Cristina Opina*; and a magazine called *Cristina la Revista*. She received a star on the Hollywood Walk of Fame and was inducted into the Broadcasting & Cable Hall of Fame for her hard work.

Sources: Biography.com, *Contemporary Hispanic Biography*

Figure 7.2 Cristina Saralegui
Featureflash Photo Agency/Shutterstock

featuring Spanish and English hits, as well as Cristina Radio, a talk show hosted by Cristina Saralegui.[25] In all, the Latino lineup included ten commercial-free music channels such as *La Mezcla* (Mix), *Aguila* (Eagle), and *La Kueva*. However, in 2016, SiriusXM created a stir in the Latin music industry when it moved eight of their Latin music channels, including *Aguila* (regional Mexican music) and *La Kueva* (Latin rock), from their satellite service to their online service.[26] This left two music channels on the satellite, including *En Vivo* (English and Spanish hits), *Caliente* (Tropical), and several Spanish-language talk/news channels such as ESPN Deportes, CNN en Español, and American Latino Radio.

Hispanic Radio Online and On the Go

As more people begin to use online services for radio programming, Hispanic audiences are also finding channels, apps, and other internet-based sources to satisfy their listening needs. Although Pandora is not immediately thought of as a Hispanic or Latino audio service, they have attracted more than 19 million monthly unique visitors (MUV) who are Hispanic. Pandora's success is due to their investment in their wide-ranging library of Latin music to be used on twenty-seven channels as well as a range of Mexican music for fifteen other channels. On top of that, they also offer Puerto Rican music channels.[27] Spotify gives fans of Hispanic music a wide range of listening options. It offers genre-specific playlists focusing on reggaeton, bachata, salsa, and more. It also provides access to informational podcasts such as *El Show de Piolín* or *Latino Rebels Radio*.[28]

The major Hispanic broadcasting companies are maintaining a mobile and online presence, too. In 2013, Univision launched Uforia, a music app that allows people to listen to one of the traditional radio stations owned by Univision as well as other specialty stations. Recognizing their targeted younger audience is interested in a wide range of music, their music selection goes beyond Hispanic/Latin music to include R&B and pop.[29] They recently expanded their interface to allow people to select channels based on emotion. You can click on one of several buttons like "energized" or "relaxed" to automatically stream Latin and popular music to suit your mood. Increasing the competition in the online music market, the Spanish Broadcasting System (SBS) developed LaMusica, their Latin streaming music app. Like Uforia, LaMusica was developed specifically for the Hispanic/Latino community and enables people to listen to stations owned by SBS as well as curated channels where the listener can balance up to five different music genres and listen to a stream of music that reflects that balance.[30]

The Sound on the Air

In the 1940s, Spanish-language programs were predominantly music based but they also included news, talk, drama, and other programming such as quiz shows and promotional discussions, etc. (see Figure 7.3).

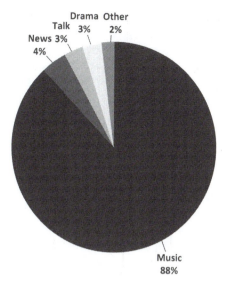

Figure 7.3 Programming content on Spanish-language radio in 1941.
Arnheim and Bayne, 1941

Between the 1980s and 1990s, the Hispanic/Latino population grew by about 50%.[31] That kind of dramatic increase in the population spurred an increase in the number of stations offering a Spanish-oriented format (see Figure 7.4) and contributed to its success. In the top markets such as Los Angeles and New York, the Spanish-language music stations were becoming more competitive by attracting larger audiences, so much so that they rivaled more traditional formatted stations carrying smooth jazz or adult contemporary music.[32] Recognizing the financial potential of these stations inspired programmers to place more restrictions on the programming than had been allowed in the past. The kinds of restrictions included reducing the range of music styles and limiting the number of songs the DJs were allowed to choose on their own. This helped the stations present a more consistent sound throughout the day. They also began to offer a mix of Spanish and English songs.[33]

As the number of Hispanics in the U.S. grows, the markets that have been known for their sizable Hispanic populations are becoming more diverse and including people from a wider range of Hispanic/Latino origins (see the current top markets in Table 7.1). With greater ratings success, the range of formats in markets all around the country increased. In 2010, there were as many as 10 different Hispanic and Spanish-language formats. Mexican Regional and Spanish Contemporary have been the most popular around the U.S.[34] Mexican Regional stations play music by Mexican and Latin American artists who specialize in a variety of music styles such as norteña, **ranchera**, and even cumbia. Other formats include Spanish News/Talk, Tejano, and Spanish Sports. There were also notable differences in the Spanish programming formats favored by audiences in different regions. The most obvious difference is that Hispanic audiences in the Northeast and Central and South Atlantic states (e.g., New York, Florida, etc.) favor Spanish tropical and Spanish contemporary formats, whereas audiences in the Central, Mountain, and Pacific states (California, Texas, Arizona) favor the regional Mexican format.[35]

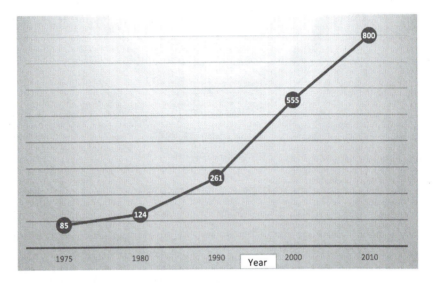

Figure 7.4 Number of Spanish-language format radio stations in the U.S. 1975-2010.

Note: Station count includes stations identifying as having a Tejano format.

Broadcasting Yearbook 1975, 1980 and *Broadcasting & Cable Yearbook* 1990, 2000, and 2010

Table 7.1 Top 10 Hispanic Markets in the U.S (12+)

Rank	Market	Hispanic 12+ Population
1	Los Angeles	4,803,400
2	New York	3,802,300
3	Miami/Ft. Lauderdale/Hollywood	1,891,600
4	Houston/Galveston	1,801,500
5	Chicago	1,591,500
6	Dallas/Ft. Worth	1,487,600
7	San Francisco	1,446,000
8	Riverside/San Bernardino	1,003,400
9	San Antonio	991,900
10	Phoenix	927,300

Nielson 2014, April *State of the Media: Audio Today: A Focus on African American and Hispanic Audiences*

Spanish-Language Formats

- *Mexican Regional*—This is the most common Spanish-language format in the U.S. As the title suggests, the nature of this music-oriented format can vary based on which part of the country a station serves. Stations in the Southwest are most likely to feature music styles that originated in Mexico such as banda, ranchera, and norteño. However, stations in the Southeast may offer a mix that includes other styles as well, such as cumbia from Colombia and bachata from the Dominican Republic.

- *Spanish Contemporary*—This is the second most common Spanish-language format in the U.S. Programs often include a mix of Spanish and English pop music. From the Spanish perspective, there is a blend of Spanish-language ballads along with bachata and reggaetón. These are likely to be presented alongside English-language dance hits.

- *Spanish Adult Hits*—This format offers a blend of classic, English-language hits from the 1960s to the 1990s as well as legends of Latin popular music such as the Mexican band Los Tigres del Norte and the "Queen of Ranchera," Rocio Durcal. As with the Regional Mexican, the music mix can vary a great deal based on the station's location.

- *Spanish Tropical*—Sometimes called Caribbean Tropical, this format is most frequently found along the East Coast. The blend includes reggaeton, bachata, and salsa, as well as English-language crossover hits.

- *Spanish News/Talk*—This format is a staple for Spanish-language audiences seeking a culturally oriented perspective on the issues of the day. These stations typically offer news in the morning and afternoon drive times and present topical talk programs during middays and evenings. The wide range of discussion topics includes health, immigration, and sports.

- *Spanish Religious*—This inspirational talk and music format has been more popular among women than men. The music often focuses on Spanish-language contemporary Christian artists.

- *Spanish Variety*—This format has a strong community orientation and features a combination of spoken word/talk and music programs. Older Hispanics (65+), whose primary language is English, make up a significant portion of the audience for this format.

- *Tejano*—The name of this format is Spanish for "Texan." This is a predominantly English-language format found primarily in central and southern areas of the Lone Star State. The Tex-Mex music reflects a blend of European and Mexican sensibilities for a unique sound that remains popular in Texas.

- **Spanish/Mexican Oldies**—This format fills a niche by providing classic songs that have been mainstays on Mexican Regional stations mixed in with music by international superstars. The eras represented range from the 1970s to the 2000s.
- **Spanish Sports**—This format typically follows the model of English-language sports stations. The primary difference is heard in the kinds of sports being discussed, i.e., soccer as opposed to American football. The deals made with local professional sports franchises such as the NBA and NFL to offer live, Spanish-language play-by-play of games has brought greater attention to these stations.

Networking and Syndicated Programming

As the development of the Raoul Cortez's "Sombrero" network in the 1950s suggests, it did not take long for brokers to see the value in finding several outlets for the programming they worked so hard to produce. By the 1970s, it became more common for stations to collaborate and broadcast shared programming. The size of the networks remained small, about ten to fifteen stations. The National Spanish Language Network was among the largest with as many as twenty-six stations.[36] Of course, the networks operating today generally have a greater reach and offer numerous special programs and formats.

Univision is the media company that is the most committed to Hispanic radio, which is evident in their ownership of seventy stations in the U.S. and five in Puerto Rico. The stations they own in top markets such as Los Angeles, Houston, Dallas, and Miami have been among the most popular. In 2016, Univision owned three stations among the top ten in the Los Angeles market and the top-rated station in Houston.[37] Besides owning a large number of stations, in 2012, they launched a radio network among their AM stations in nine of the top markets.[38] Those stations offer shows selected from the numerous Univision **syndicated** programming that are available for other Spanish-language stations around the country to purchase. Case in point, they have several morning shows, each with a unique tone and character that is well-suited for one of the common formats used around the country. For example, *El Bueno, La Mala, y El Feo* (The Good, the Bad, and the Ugly) combines Regional Mexican music with humor and is popular among audiences in the advertisers' favorite age range, 18–49. Another, *The Enrique Santos Morning Show*, is a talk program with notable political and entertainment guests such as presidential candidates and celebrities from films and television such as the reality program *Bordertown: Laredo*. The network also offers the weekly *El Hit*

Parade de America hosted by Javier Romero, who counts down the top fifteen popular/contemporary songs.

The Hispanic Communications Network (HCN) began in 1982 as the Hispanic Radio Network and now includes 270 radio stations and provides other media services like marketing and promotion as well. From the radio perspective, the network focuses on daily and weekly information segments directed at Hispanic audiences in the U.S. and Puerto Rico.[39] These programs encompass a variety of topics such as the environment (*Planeta Azul*), health (*Fuente de Salud*), and lifestyles/culture (*Para Vivir Mejor*).

The Spanish Broadcasting System (SBS) owns nine stations in major markets like Los Angeles, New York, and Miami as well as four stations in Puerto Rico. The company launched their "Aire Network" to provide Hispanic/Latino stations around the country with the chance to subscribe to several programming feeds such as 24/7 music formats titled La Raza, Tropical, and Latino Pop. The network programming is modeled after what they program on their company's successful large-market stations. They also offer a 2-hour, high-energy mix on the weekend called La Mezcla hosted by DJ Alex Sensation, a native Colombian whose show originates on New York City's La Mega 97.9 FM.[40]

Audiences

Today, Hispanic/Latino radio is prospering. Forty million Hispanics tune in to radio. That means 93.5% of all Hispanics listen to radio at least once a week and the average amount of time the Hispanic listener spends with radio is a little more than 12 hours a week. Men comprise 53% of the Hispanic radio listening audience. Unlike many other audiences, Hispanic audiences spend the most time listening to radio during the middle of the day (10 a.m. to 3 p.m.). The most popular Hispanic radio format is Mexican Regional.[41]

Hispanic audiences are generally characterized in the same way as other audiences, according to demographics such as age, location, and socio-economic status. However, they are also categorized based on their preference for using English or Spanish as their primary language (i.e., English-dominant or Spanish-dominant). Nielsen, the major audience research company in the U.S., learned that language preference is associated with different patterns of general radio use, and particularly with regard to station formats. Among all U.S. listeners between the ages of 18 and 49, the Spanish-dominant population spends the most time listening to radio. They even spend over an hour more with radio each week than their English-dominant counterparts. The most popular formats for Hispanics who are "English-dominant" include Contemporary Hit Radio (CHR), Rhythmic Contemporary Hit Radio, Adult Contemporary (AC), and Country. As you may have noticed, these are English-language formats. However, "Spanish-dominant" listeners are more likely to listen to stations with Mexican Regional, Spanish Contemporary, and Spanish Adult Hits formats. They still enjoy English-language CHR and AC stations but they just tune in much less frequently.[42]

'Radio Found Me Just in Time'

Gilda Mirós
Spanish-Language Radio Host, Producer, Actress, and Author

Thanks to the Creator, I have lived 79 years, have had a marvelous, long career, and still am very active. I pray that I may leave this physical world while doing something I love, performing. I feel happy, at peace, and satisfied with my life.

I am also proud and grateful to have a large part of my professional life captured on films, photographs, newspaper clippings, audios, videos, and books, because I know that pleasant memories should be shared, especially if they have been positive and productive, if we have served the community, and if we have shared our talents with others, enhancing their lives. I believe, then, that we can celebrate our entry into this world; I do believe that we as eternal souls come to this world to learn, serve, and progress.

Figure 7.5 Gilda Mirós (left) in 1975, at her first talk radio show *Tu Mundo Feminino*, interviewing Ana Standard, who was a Puerto Rican nutritionist representing Cornell University NYC. Mirós has recently received a "Hall de La Fama" recognition by a Puerto Rican Cultural Institute in New York for her work in the Spanish Language Theater.

Photo courtesy of Gilda Mirós

With all these images, we will be traveling together toward the memories of the past and creating new memories with facts that marked history in the performing arts. I love sharing with everyone the miracle of life and art in all its manifestations.

As a broadcaster, my radio and television interviews were simple and honest, always interested in exploring the human side, the soul of my guests; what they really were like. It didn't matter where they came from; I wanted to share with my audience their personal stories and talents.

I was born in Puerto Rico, later a Bronx teenager going to Art School in Manhattan, graduating and traveling with my loving, gentle, kind mother to Mexico City. I studied drama and eventually became a TV model and singing and dancing film actress. Constantly traveling back and forth between New York City, Mexico, and Puerto Rico, I was doing TV, films, commercials, soap operas, and theatre, with much success in all phases.

In 1975, divorced and with two children, radio found me just in time. I got a job as a staff DJ at WADO, 1280 AM, in NYC, doing exactly what the male announcers did. My mom helped with the children, and I was on my way to learning the ropes. I later signed with WJIT, and finally SBS imported me into Miami, doing the first coast to coast broadcast in Spanish: NYC, MIA, LA.

Figure 7.6 Gilda Mirós with radio pioneer Raúl Alarcón Sr., founder of the Spanish Broadcasting System.

Photo courtesy of Gilda Mirós

I am sure that my experience in the theatre, including studying diction, gave me an advantage in radio. Besides playing music, and doing news, commercials, and weather, I produced a one-hour show daily that was then extended to four hours daily, using all the entertaining elements that I had learned while producing and co-hosting a weekly, live four-hour talk show in Spanish for SIN in 1970.

I also opened my doors to all Latinos and all ages in my radio show in the capitals of the world: NYC, Miami, and Spain. My programs were divided into blocks: community, medicine, entertainment, and music, plus opened phone lines and also remotes from different countries. It was a winning format anywhere.

Over the years, I've had the privilege of interviewing hundreds of performers from all over Latin America, on radio and TV, and from a great variety of musical and theatrical genres. On my mother's advice, I started recording these fascinating interviews with my guests, understanding that they were precious oral histories, that they are priceless. My intention is to preserve the stories of these notable performers and their music. They are all entertainers irreplaceable in the memory and culture of Latin America; all truly icons. I invite you to read my books, watch my films and videos, and to listen to my audio interviews, always hoping that you can enjoy this material, as much as I have enjoyed living it. Blessings.

Hispanic Radio and Community Connections

Hispanic radio, and Spanish-language media in general, has been vital because it has fostered both **social integration** and **differentiation**. That is to say, people for whom Spanish was their dominant language and who had strong emotional connections to their Spanish heritage relied on Spanish-language radio to keep them informed about the world at large while staying connected to their cultural roots. In spite of the fact that the majority of the programming time on radio throughout Hispanic radio's early years was dedicated to music, Spanish-language stations were more than just ways for audiences to stay entertained. They were important because the brokers—and later the station programmers—maintained deep ties to their communities. In many ways, the early block programs were developed and sustained by cultivating groups of artists/performers and businesses that were drawn from and appealed to the Spanish-speaking communities. But the programs often offered more. In the 1940s, the music was primarily Mexican and the source of news heard on Hispanic/Latino radio was nearly as likely to be from Mexico (18%) as the U.S. (22%).[43] As such, the stations reflected cultural roots and frequently the radio personalities were engaged in their communities. For example, Pedro González hosted *Los Madrugadores* in Los Angeles and used his program as a forum

Bilingual Radio Personality and Media Entrepreneur

Paco López

Figure 7.7 Paco López
Photo courtesy of Paco López

Cuban-born Paco López moved to the United States at the age of two and eventually settled with his parents in Tampa, Florida. He eventually became a morning and/or afternoon radio personality and programmed radio stations in Miami, Houston, Phoenix, Washington, D.C., New York, and Jacksonville and eventually settled in Orlando, Florida.

López was recognized by *Hispanic Magazine* in 1992 as one of ten up-and-coming Latino broadcasters in the mainstream media, and eventually hosted multiple nationally syndicated radio shows. Among his accolades are his Billboard Airplay Monitor Magazine's National Radio Show Host of the Year nominations. He also hosted his own highly rated television program while in Houston, Texas, Phoenix, and Arizona, and has appeared on MTV, USA Network.

As a bilingual broadcaster, López has also appeared on Telemundo's Disney Christmas program. He also created, programmed *Oyeme!*, a tropical music satellite channel on the World Space Satellite Radio Network, and hosted *Musica Caliente*, an English/Spanish bilingual program. He has appeared in two feature film theatrical releases, *Streetwise* (1998), and *Black Spring Break II, The Sequel* (2001).

He currently owns Paco Lopez Media and has done commercial voiceover work for Johnson & Johnson, Walt Disney World, Universal Orlando Resorts, Campbell's Soup Company, V-8, All State Insurance, and even Spanish television dubs for Bernie Sanders during the New York Presidential primaries in 2016.

He is currently developing multiple radio programs for companies and stations in the United States, Costa Rica, and Brazil.

Source: Paco López

to discuss causes, effects, and responses to the U.S. government's treatment of Mexicans and Mexican immigrants in the 1930s.[44]

The Hispanic population in New York differed from that of Los Angeles due to migration from Puerto Rico as opposed to Mexico, particularly in the 1950s. As a result, programmers developed different formats to resonate with the dominant population in their cities. Today, the news offered by Spanish-language media is more likely to include national and international political information as well as issues relating to the border and immigration than media that target other demographics.[45]

These days, stations that offer Spanish-language news and talk programs discuss issues that speak directly to their audience's experiences, such as health issues, real estate, interactions with police, and even offering legal guidance regarding immigration.[46] There have also been efforts to use Spanish-language radio to promote health education. For example, in the 1980s, the *Tu No Me Conoces* (You Don't Know Me) campaign was a successful effort to promote awareness of HIV risk and testing.[47] Radio has also been used as a means for promoting diabetes awareness among older Spanish-dominant audiences in California. More recently, **"edutainment"** approaches have been tested. Edutainment campaigns try to promote important health information, such as the value of the HPV vaccine in fighting cervical cancer, by integrating educational messages into entertainment-oriented programming like radio dramas or "Radionovelas."[48] These kinds of efforts are evidence of how valuable Hispanic radio has been to the well-being of the communities they serve.

Hispanic/Latino radio has been at the forefront of political movements such as opposing legislation that proposed double-layered fencing along the Mexico–U.S. border and mandating employer verification and penalties for employing illegal workers, among other stipulations. Eduardo Sotelo, also known as *El Piolin* ("Tweety bird"), was a prominent host in Los Angeles and outspoken opponent of the bill. He and other Hispanic radio personalities helped defeat such legislation by conducting persuasive interviews and encouraging their audiences to participate in civil actions such as marches organized by pro-immigrant organizations.[49]

The Future

Hispanic radio had humble beginnings. It first appeared in the form of specialty programs performed live during air times that radio station owners thought had little value. The success those programs achieved can be linked to the energy and enthusiasm of the brokers. The creative men who sold the advertising also assembled musicians and actors, hosted, and even performed in the programs themselves because they understood the value and the need for their communities to have a voice on the air. The challenges facing Hispanic radio owners, producers, and talent are different today but the energy and enthusiasm remains. The Hispanic/Latino population is growing and, by extension, the potential radio audience is growing too. That growth brings more attention, greater competition, and higher expectations.

The increased attention has fostered a better understanding of how diverse the Hispanic/Latino audience is. Whereas the early brokers had a reasonably good understanding of the communities they were reaching out to, today's

The Alarcón Legacy

Raúl Alarcón Sr. and Raúl Alarcón Jr.

Raúl Alarcón Sr. was a Cuban-American media executive. He is known for founding the Spanish Broadcasting System (SBS) after leaving behind multiple radio stations in Cuba. Alarcón served as the chairman of SBS until 1999. He died in Miami in 2008. His son, Raúl Alarcón Jr., is also a Cuban-American media executive. In fact, Raúl Alarcón Jr. became the president of SBS in 1985 and the CEO of SBS in 1994. He currently still holds these positions, and SBS now operates over twenty radio stations.

Sources: Bloomberg.com, *Investopedia*, and *CNN Money*

Figure 7.8 Raúl Alarcón Sr. and son Raúl Alarcón Jr. receiving the National Parkinson's Foundation—President's Medal in 1989.

Raúl Alarcón Jr.

"Hispanic" audience is broad and multidimensional. In spite of the many challenges facing Hispanic media in the twenty-first century, traditional, satellite, and online radio services continue to resonate with Hispanic/Latino audiences due to their strong desire to entertain and inform.

Vocabulary Words

Blocks
Bodegas
Brokers
Differentiation
Edutainment
Federal Communication
  Commission (FCC)
Format
Social Integration
Syndication
Telecommunications Act of 1996

Points to Remember

- Hispanic radio began with the desire to take advantage of less desirable radio times to give the community entertainment and news that connected audiences to their cultural roots.
- The rise in popularity and financial success of Hispanic radio is closely tied to the growth of the Hispanic/Latino population in the U.S.
- There are two patterns of radio use, based on the audience's preference for English or Spanish as their primary language.
- Hispanic talk radio hosts select and discuss topics in a way that reflects a perspective that can differ from the mainstream radio approach.

Names to Remember

Cristina Saralegui
Eduardo Sotelo
Julio Roque
Pedro González
Raoul Cortez
Rodolfo Hoyos

Practice Questions

1   Explain the broker system and how radio stations filled airtime during hours of downtime on air.
2   How did Raoul Cortez convince the FCC to allow him to start a Spanish-language radio station? What was his rationale as to how it would benefit the U.S. government?
3   In which decade did Arbitron, Inc. begin measuring audiences of Spanish-language stations?

4   Spanish-language radio stations used a syndication system to share content. Explain this system and provide examples of this practice from the chapter.

5   Define social integration and differentiation. How can these two concepts influence the type of content that ends up on the radio?

Activity

Programming Analysis: Identify one Spanish Adult Contemporary (Spanish AC) station and one traditional Adult Contemporary (AC) station in your market or region. Listen to or record one hour of each station from the same period of day (morning 6 a.m.–10 a.m., midday 10 a.m.–2 p.m., afternoon 4 p.m.–7 p.m.). Compare the two stations by examining the songs they play, the language they use, the news that is presented, the commercials they play, etc. Discuss how the programming is different. In what ways do the stations reflect the community? Do you notice cultural differences in the music or announcing? How do the commercials differ? (Many popular radio stations stream their programming on the Web. So, if you cannot find stations in your area, you can likely find ones online.)

Timeline

1939–1945:   World War II. Restrictions on all radio stations were established by the U.S. Office of Censorship, particularly on those with foreign-language programming.

1940s: Spanish-language stations represented only about a quarter of all the foreign-language stations and the majority of programming was music.

1946:   The first full-time, Spanish-language radio station in the U.S., KCOR-AM, was established.

1956:   Sombrero Radio Network by Raoul Cortez was created.

Early 1960s: Two-thirds of stations accounted for two-thirds of all stations.

Mid 1960s: Radio listening data began to be collected by Arbitron, Inc., signaling advertisers' interest in Spanish-language listeners.

1970s: It became more common for stations to collaborate and broadcast shared programming.

1970s and 1980s: Spanish-language stations began to receive much more attention.

1980s: Many radio competitors emerged in attempts to reach national audiences. Hispanic/Latino population grew by about 50%.

1980:   Over 500 stations offered Spanish-language programming and 104 stations had a Spanish-language format.

1982:   The Hispanic Communications Network (HCN) was founded and currently includes 270 radio stations and other media services.

1990s: The industry experienced significant growth.

1996: The **Telecommunications Act** caused concentration of ownership to increase and ethnic diversity ownership to decrease.

2001: XM Satellite Radio brought forth a new era of radio listening.

2002: Sirius Satellite Radio is established and includes eight Latin Channels.

2006: About 3% of all radio stations were owned by Hispanics/Latinos, and about 7.5% of stations had a Hispanic radio format in the U.S.

2008: XM Satellite Radio and Sirius Satellite Radio merge under the condition set by the FCC to offer programming that served underserved communities.

2010: Digital Cable Radio, now known as Music Choice, began to include Musica Urbana in their programming to appeal to Hispanic/Latino audiences.

2012: Univision launched a radio network among their AM stations in nine of the top markets.

2013: Univision created the music app Uforia to offer audiences a variety of Spanish-language stations.

Additional Resources

Fowler, Gene, and Bill Crawford. *Border Radio: Quacks, Yodelers, Pitchmen, Psychics, and Other Amazing Broadcasters of the American Airwaves*. (Austin, TX: University of Texas, 2002).

Gutiérrez, Félix F., and Jorge Reina Schement. *Spanish-language Radio in the Southwestern United States* (Austin, TX: University of Texas, 1979).

Rodríguez, America. "Creating an Audience and Remapping a Nation: A Brief History of US Spanish Language Broadcasting 1930–1980," *Quarterly Review of Film and Video* 16, no. 3–4 (1997): 357–374. doi:10.1080/10509209709361470.

About the Author

William Kinnally

Photo courtesy of University of Central Florida

William Kinnally, Ph.D., has 25 years of experience working as a producer, programmer, director, and manager in public, non-commercial, and cable radio. His area of interest spanned jazz, blues, international, and new age music. He produced concert recordings for local and national broadcast and contributed jazz features, profiles, columns, and reviews to various national and regional publications such as *Jazziz* magazine and *The Gainesville Sun*. His teaching interests include audio production, media management, and media programming. His research interests include examining media effects, especially how news presentations affect our understanding of issues as well as examining factors that influence our selection and enjoyment of entertainment media.

Notes

1 Félix F. Gutiérrez and Jorge Reina Schement, *Spanish-Language Radio in the Southwestern United States* (Austin, TX: University of Texas, 1979).
2 Michael A. McGregor, Paul D. Driscoll, Walter McDowell, and Sydney W. Head, *Head's Broadcasting in America: A Survey of Electronic Media* (Boston, MA: Allyn & Bacon, 2010).
3 America Rodríguez, *Making Latino News: Race, Language, Class* (Thousand Oaks, CA: Sage, 1999).
4 America Rodríguez, "Creating an Audience and Remapping a Nation: A Brief History of US Spanish Language Broadcasting 1930–1980," *Quarterly Review of Film and Video* 16, no. 3–4 (1997): 357–374. doi:10.1080/10509209709361470.
5 Félix F. Gutiérrez and Jorge Reina Schement, *Spanish-Language Radio in the Southwestern United States*.
6 Rudolf Arnheim and Martha Collins Bayne, "Foreign Language Broadcasts over Local American Stations," in Lazarsfeld, Paul F., and Frank N. Stanton, *Radio Research 1941* (New York: Duell, Sloan and Pearce, 1941), 3–64.
7 Bryant Putney, "Censorship of Press and Radio," in *Editorial Research Reports 1939*, vol. II, 221–238 (Washington, DC: CQ Press, 1939), http://library.cqpress.com/cqresearcher/cqresrre1939092000.
8 Mari Castaneda, "Spanish-language Radio," in Tatum, Charles M., *Encyclopedia of Latino Culture: From Calaveras to Quinceañeras* (Santa Barbara, CA: Greenwood, 2014), 824–835.
9 Rene A. Guzman, "Spanish-language TV Born in S.A.," *San Antonio Express-News*, June 21, 2015, www.expressnews.com/150years/culture/article/San-Antonio-is-home-to-the-nation-s-first-6340586.php.
10 Ibid.
11 Jane McNab Christian and Chester C. Christian, Jr., "Spanish Language and Culture in the United States," in Fishman, Joshua A. *Language Loyalty in the United States: The Maintenance and Perpetuation of Non-English Mother Tongues by American Ethnic and Religious Groups* (The Hague, the Netherlands: Mouton, 1966).
12 Kenton T. Wilkinson, *Spanish-language Television in the United States: Fifty Years of Development* (New York, NY: Routledge, 2016).
13 Rodríguez, *Making Latino News*.
14 Kenton T. Wilkinson, "Spanish Language Media in the United States," in Albarran, Alan B., *The Handbook of Spanish Language Media* (New York: Routledge, 2009).
15 Broadcasting Yearbook, *Broadcasting Publications* (Washington, D.C.: Blackburn & Co., 1980).
16 *Arbitron*, "Hispanic Radio Today 2013: How Hispanic America Listens to Radio," 2013, www.arbitron.com/downloads/Hispanic_Radio_Today_2013_execsum.pdf.
17 Todd Chambers, "Losing Owners: Deregulation and Small Radio Markets," *Journal of Radio Studies* 8, no. 2 (2001): 292–315. doi:10.1207/s15506843jrs0802_6.
18 Todd Chambers, "The State of Spanish-Language Radio," *Journal of Radio Studies* 13, no. 1 (2006): 34–50. doi:10.1207/s15506843jrs1301_3.
19 Arie Beresteanu and Paul B. Ellickson, "Minority and Female Ownership in Media Enterprises," *Washington, DC: Federal Communications Commission*, 2007, https://pdfs.semanticscholar.org/6361/6f6412bbc37ae9118a1815709e5fe01897f8.pdf.
20 Music Choice, "Channel Line Up Change," April 15, 2009, http://corporate.music choice.com. Accessed September 6, 2016.
21 *Billboard*, "Marley Song Launches XM Satellite Radio Feed," September 26, 2001, www.billboard.com/articles/news/78299/marley-song-launches-xm-satellite-radio-feed.

22 Steve Carney, "Radio Enters a New Orbit," *Los Angeles Times*, September 28, 2001, http://articles.latimes.com/2001/sep/28/entertainment/ca-50755.

23 Eric A. Taub, "Drive-Time Radio on 100 Channels; Digital Transmissions Could Transform Radio in the Car and at Home," *The New York Times*, October 19, 2000, www.nytimes.com/2000/10/19/technology/drive-time-radio-100-channels-digital-transmissions-could-transform-radio-car.html.

24 Olga Kharif, "The FCC Approves the XM-Sirius Merger," *Bloomberg*, July 26, 2008, www.bloomberg.com/news/articles/2008-07-25/the-fcc-approves-the-xm-sirius-mergerbusinessweek-business-news-stock-market-and-financial-advice.

25 National Latino Broadcasting LLC, "Announces First-Of-Its-Kind Political Programming from Washington DC Targeting US Hispanics," *Cision PR Newswire*, January 18, 2012, www.prnewswire.com/news-releases/national-latino-broadcasting-announces-first-of-its-kind-political-programming-from-washington-dc-targeting-us-hispanics-137558328.html.

26 Hannah Karp, "SiriusXM Cuts Several Latin-Music Channels From Its Satellite-Radio Service," *Wall Street Journal*, May 31, 2016, www.wsj.com/articles/siriusxm-cuts-several-latin-music-channels-from-its-satellite-radio-service-1464738791.

27 Leila Cobo, "Why Pandora is Booming with Hispanic Listeners," *Billboard*, August 15, 2014, www.billboard.com/biz/articles/news/digital-and-mobile/6221657/why-pandora-is-booming-with-hispanic-users.

28 "Spotify Launches Multimedia Hub to Celebrate Hispanic Heritage Month—Vents Magazine," *Vents Magazine*, September 15, 2016, http://corrientelatina.com/music/spotify-launches-multimedia-hub-celebrate-hispanic-heritage-month/.

29 Leila Cobo, "Univision's Uforia App Now Picks Music Based on Your Mood," *Billboard*, March 14, 2016, www.billboard.com/articles/columns/latin/7256354/univision-uforia-app-new-features.

30 Leila Cobo, "SBS Relaunches Pandora-Like LaMusica App for Latin Listeners," *Billboard*, December 2, 2015, www.billboard.com/articles/columns/latin/6784806/sbs-lamusica-radio-streaming-app-latin-mobile-marketplace.

31 U.S. Bureau of the Census, *Statistical Abstract of the United States: 1993*, 113th edition (Washington, DC: U.S. Bureau of the Census, 1993), www.census.gov/library/publications/1993/compendia/statab/113ed.html.

32 Donna Petrozzello, "Hispanic Radio Formats Going Strong," *Broadcasting & Cable*, November 18, 1996.

33 Ibid.

34 *Arbitron*, "Hispanic Radio Today."

35 Ibid.

36 Ward L. Quaal and James A. Brown, *Broadcast Management: Radio, Television* (New York: Hastings House, 1976).

37 *Radio Online*, "Nielsen Audio Ratings," http://ratings.radio-online.com/cgi-bin/rol.exe/arb_menu_rank.

38 Carl Marcucci, "Univision Details Lineup for 'Univision America,'" *Radio and Television Business Report RSS*, July 3, 2012, http://rbr.com/univision-details-lineup-for-univision-america.

39 *Hispanic Communications Network*, "Who We Are," www.hcnmedia.com/who-we-are.

40 *Aire Radio Networks*, "About Us," www.aireradionetworks.com/about-us.

41 *Arbitron*, "Hispanic Radio Today."

42 Ibid.

43 Rudolf Arnheim and Martha Collins Bayne, "Foreign Language Broadcasts over Local American Stations."

44 Rodríguez, *Making Latino News*.

45 Yann P. Kerevel, "The Influence of Spanish-Language Media on Latino Public Opinion and Group Consciousness," *Social Science Quarterly* 92, no. 2 (2011): 509–534. doi:10.1111/j.1540-6237.2011.00780.x.

46 Nelson Harvey, "Latino Radio Stations Connect Immigrant Communities," *High Country News*, June 19, 2013, www.hcn.org/issues/45.10/latino-radio-stations-connect-immigrant-communities.

47 John P. Elder, Guadalupe X. Ayala, Deborah Parra-Medina, and Gregory A. Talavera, "Health Communication in the Latino Community: Issues and Approaches," *Annu. Rev. Public Health Annual Review of Public Health* 30, no. 1 (2009): 227–251. doi:10.1146/annurev.publhealth.031308.100300.

48 Deanna Kepka, Gloria D. Coronado, Hector P. Rodríguez, and Beti Thompson, "Evaluation of a Radionovela to Promote HPV Vaccine Awareness and Knowledge Among Hispanic Parents," *Journal of Community Health* 36, no. 6 (2011): 957–965. doi:10.1007/s10900-011-9395-1.

49 Mari Castaneda Paredes, "The Significance of U.S. Spanish-language Radio," in Montilla, Particia M. (ed.), *Latinos and American Popular Culture* (Santa Barbara: Praeger, 2013), 68–85.

8   From Radio Stations to Television Networks

The Evolution of Spanish-Language Broadcasting in the U.S.

Kenton T. Wilkinson, Ph.D.

Professor and Director of the Thomas Jay Harris
Institute for Hispanic and International Communication,
Texas Tech University

This chapter is adapted from the book *Spanish-Language Television in the United States: Fifty Years of Development*, written by Kenton T. Wilkinson.

In the 1920s and 1930s, entrepreneurs, who were usually musicians as well, began producing music programs in Spanish that aired at off-peak hours on English-language radio stations. Two interesting examples were Pedro J. González in Los Angeles and Julio Roqué in New York, both of whom led bands that played live over the airwaves. Because major advertisers in English were skeptical about the size and profit-potential of the Spanish-speaking audience, the early radio pioneers employed a broker system whereby they collected fees for over-the-air advertising from businesses in the Latino community, then paid the station for airtime. The broadcasts in Spanish also provided cohesion for the Latino community by announcing relevant news, events, and job openings, and transmitting personal messages for listeners. In 1946, Raoul Cortez, a Mexican immigrant, established KCOR-AM in San Antonio, the country's first full-time Spanish-language radio station owned by a Latino. This marked an important transition away from the broker system, moving Spanish-language radio to function more like its mainstream counterpart in English. Like other stations that quickly followed, KCOR-AM not only reached listeners in the city, but also many households in surrounding rural areas.

Raoul Cortez is also credited with establishing the first full-time television station in Spanish. KCOR-TV began broadcasting in 1955 and, after failing to generate a profit, was acquired in 1961 by an investor group that changed the call letters to KWEX-TV. This was the first property in a station group named Spanish International Communications Corp. (SICC), which would build KMEX-TV in Los Angeles in 1962 and acquire WXTV serving New York in 1968 and WLTV in Miami in 1971. SICC continued expanding to other regions with high concentrations of Spanish speakers through the 1970s and 1980s, not only through broadcasting but rapidly growing cable television systems as well.

SICC's principal owners were U.S. business associates of Emilio Azcárraga Vidaurreta, a Mexican citizen, pioneering broadcaster, and co-founder of the Televisa conglomerate whose ownership and control of the SICC stations were limited to 20% by U.S. broadcasting law, section 310(b) of the Communications Act of 1934. The same restriction does not apply to broadcast networks, permitting Azcárraga to legally hold a larger percentage of Spanish International Network (SIN), a sister company that distributed programming and sold advertising for SICC. The executive at the center of both operations was Rene Anselmo, a U.S. citizen of Italian descent who had worked for Azcárraga and his partners in Mexico. Anselmo took on the challenging tasks of convincing viewers, cable system operators, and advertisers of Spanish-language television's viability, as well as enlarging SIN programming's reach through **Ultra High Frequency (UHF)** stations, satellites/repeater stations, low-power television, and cable TV systems. These became the foundations of a formal, organized industry; in fact, SIN became the first national network to regularly distribute its programming via satellite.

Spanish-language radio also became more structured during the 1960s and 1970s as station groups expanded and national networks such as the Spanish Broadcasting System, Caballero Spanish Media, and Katz Hispanic Radio coalesced. It is important to recognize that these changes toward mainstreaming the Spanish broadcasting industries occurred during a period of substantial upheaval in American society, marked by the civil rights movement, mounting opposition to the Vietnam War, questioning of the status quo by many youth, and assassinations of leading American political figures. Farmworkers' rights movements and the Chicano Movement, which was also known as the Brown Power Movement, brought new public attention to the needs and interests of Latino populations, even if those movements and their leaders were largely kept at a distance by commercial Spanish-language broadcasters.

The "Decade of the Hispanic"

The 1980s, dubbed the Decade of the Hispanic, brought a different type of attention to the U.S. Latino population, one embraced by commercial broadcasters. The 1980 U.S. Census showed a 62% increase in the population over the previous 10 years, prompting projections of growing political, economic power, and cultural influence by Latinos. During the decade, the first Latino was elected mayor of a major city—Henry Cisneros of San Antonio—two

Latinos were appointed to cabinet positions in George H.W. Bush's administration, and Latino performers and athletes gained new prominence in American popular culture. Examples include the musicians Carlos Santana, Linda Rondstadt, and Los Lobos; actors such as Ricardo Montalban and Jimmy Smits; and athletes such as Fernando Valenzuela and Roberto Durán. Spanish-language television also received increased attention from the mainstream press, but not all of it was positive.

Two investors in the Spanish International station group, SICC, had filed suit against the company in 1976 claiming that the network, SIN, took unfair financial advantage of the stations, creating a pipeline for sending revenues back to Mexico in violation of the foreign ownership and control restrictions mentioned above. A federal judge agreed, ruling in 1986 that the stations must be sold to new owners. After a contentious bidding process, during which some advocates demanded that the new proprietors be U.S. Latinos, the Anglo-controlled companies Hallmark Cards Corp. and First Capital of Chicago emerged as the new owners, paying $301.5 million for ten stations (five of them low-power). Within a year's time the companies paid another $300 million for the network, SIN, which was renamed Univision. The network's essential value was its right-of-first-refusal to Televisa programming for 10 years, an asset that remains lucrative today as many Televisa programs air in primetime and are highly rated.

And They Said We Wouldn't Last . . .

Maria Elena Salinas
Longtime Univision Network Anchor

"There is no future in Spanish-language media." That was one of the most common phrases I would hear when I began my career at KMEX Channel 34 in Los Angeles in April of 1981. Of course, those who would say it did not work in Spanish-language media. The logic behind that statement was that the Latino community in the United States would eventually assimilate, learn English, and not watch TV in Spanish anymore. Well, fast-forward three-and-half decades later, it turns out they were only half right. Hispanics have assimilated, but what was not taken into consideration is that to Latinos assimilation doesn't mean leaving behind their language and culture but rather embracing a new one.

I should know, because I am part of that community I have been reporting to for over three decades. Born in Los Angeles, as the daughter of Mexican immigrant parents, I grew up in a bilingual and bicultural environment. Fortunately, my parents spoke to me only in Spanish at home, which allowed me to learn the language well enough to have a career in communications utilizing their mother tongue.

Things were very different back then. Spanish-language media was in its infancy—just a few cable stations around the country linked together to form the Spanish International Network, SIN. In the summer of 1981, the network newscast was born in a trailer at Howard University in Washington D.C. where we had half an hour of satellite time to broadcast nationwide. Any major news that broke outside of that half hour would have to be reported by the local stations.

Our founders were visionaries but not clairvoyants. They knew there was a great need in the Latino community for information not just entertainment. They knew the community would grow, and more and more cities across the country would begin to broadcast in their language. But who would have imagined that 14 million Latinos in the early 1980s would quadruple and become the largest minority in the U.S. three decades later?

The growth of the Latino community is unequivocally tied to the growth in Spanish-language media, and not just in numbers, but in the level of sophistication. No longer are Hispanic viewers mostly recently

Figure 8.1 Maria Elena Salinas
Photo courtesy of Univision Network

arrived immigrants who, back then, were trying to learn how to survive in their newly adopted country. Now they are also immigrants turned into naturalized citizens or U.S.-born Hispanics ready to demand their place in our society. Latino viewers are now professionals, entrepreneurs, college-educated individuals, and voters. Having a choice of getting their information in English or Spanish, most still gravitate toward Spanish, not just because of the language but because of the content. It's information they can relate to that cannot be found in so-called "mainstream media."

Early on in my career, I realized that my duty, and that of those of us who work in Spanish-language media, would be to empower the Latino community. We needed to inform them of their rights and their responsibilities. Whether through reporting on issues that affect Hispanics, immigration, healthcare, education, or participating in campaigns to motivate them to become citizens, register to vote, and participate in the electoral process, the empowerment of the Latino community has always been my mission and will continue to be until the contributions of Latinos to our society are fully recognized.

So, I guess those who predicted there was no future for Spanish-language media truly underestimated the power of the Latino community and the influence it would exert in our society. As for me, I didn't only make a career out of working in Spanish-language media. Serving that community gave me a sense of responsibility, a sense of purpose that goes beyond performing my journalistic duties.

Trailblazer in TV News

Cecilia Alvear

Born in the island of San Cristobal, Galapagos Island, Ecuador, Cecilia Alvear was a pioneer journalist that advocated for diversity inclusion in newsrooms in the U.S. She believed that journalism could be more honest if there was more diversity. Alvear moved to the California in 1960s, a time when Hispanic women journalists in the U.S. were scarce. She began her career working for several local television stations in Los Angeles and eventually became the first Latina producer of NBC news in Burbank. She also served as president of the National Association of Hispanic Journalists (NAHJ) for two years. As a journalist, her work ranged from covering the war in Nicaragua and El Salvador and natural disasters in Mexico, El Salvador, and Ecuador, to interviewing Cuban revolutionary Fidel Castro, narcos, coyotes, artists, and more. Among other roles, she served as a board member and vice president of the California Chicano News Media Association, an organization dedicated to improving opportunities of Latino journalists. Alvear mentored, influenced, and inspired new generations of LatinX journalists. Even though she did not have a college degree, she was the first Latina to receive the honorary Nieman Fellowship from Harvard University in 1988. In addition, *Hispanic Business* chose her as one of the "100 Most Influential Hispanics in the United States," in 2000. Alvear passed away at the age of 77.

Sources: LA Times, NY Times, *Nieman Reports*

Figure 8.2 Cecilia Alvear

Photo courtesy of The National Association of Hispanic Journalists

Also in 1986, Reliance Capital Corp. acquired John Blair & Co., which owned broadcast stations in Puerto Rico and Florida. This became the base for Telemundo Network, which quickly began buying or building stations in key Spanish-speaking cities as SICC had done two decades earlier. Mainstream U.S. corporations had come to recognize the profit-potential of Latinos and were calculating that growing numbers of large-budget advertisers would do the same. Thus, competition entered the industry and became evident in a rivalry to produce Spanish programs within the U.S., principally in Miami. A key strategic element was to recover a portion of the (comparatively high) domestic production costs by exporting programs to other Spanish-speaking countries.

Castañeda (2003) reports that in 1980 there were sixty-seven Spanish-oriented radio stations in the U.S., a number that grew to over 600 by 2002. Clearly the 1980s and 1990s were important decades for the industry's growth, including in areas not previously reached by radio. Not only did listener and stations numbers increase during this period, but so did the quality and quantity of audience research. Companies such as Gallup and Arbitron used sophisticated sampling procedures for large regional and national studies of the Spanish-speaking audience at the same time as more refined studies were being conducted by academic researchers (e.g., O'Guinn & Meyer, 1983/1984). Deep-pocketed media corporations and advertisers were taking a keener interest in Latino-oriented broadcasting. Following the general market trend, Spanish-language radio experienced ownership consolidation during the 1990s, fueled by the Telecommunications Act of 1996, which accelerated media **deregulation**.

Changes in Technology, Ownership, and Politics

Returning to television, the 1990s were characterized by Univision's dominance, deepening international connections, and the beginning of profound technological change. In 1992, Univision changed ownership again, with the Hollywood mogul Jerrold Perenchio heading an investor group that returned Emilio Azcárraga Milmo, son of the founder, to the U.S. industry, this time joined by Gustavo Cisneros of Venevision as a third partner. The purchase price was $509 million. Telemundo took on high debt from its station expansion binge, and had difficulty obtaining or producing competitive programs; the network and its twenty-three owned-and-operated stations were acquired by Sony and Liberty Media for $539 million in 1997.

During the 1990s, pay television systems continued to grow in the U.S. and overseas, creating greater demand for content to fill the increasing hours of broadcast time. Simultaneously, the costs of distributing such content decreased as signal compression enabled by digital technology boosted satellites' data-carrying capacity, and **Panamsat** emerged as the first privately held satellite service with global reach (the post-SIN/SICC project of Rene Anselmo). **Direct-to-home (DTH)** satellite broadcasting also spread throughout Latin

The Man Behind Sábado Gigante

Don Francisco

Don Francisco, born in 1940 as Mario Kreutzberger Blumenfeld, is a Chilean-born entertainer known for his contributions to television. In 1962, he began hosting *Sábado Gigante*, the longest-running variety show on television in the world, according to the *Guinness Book of Records*. In 1986, the show then made its way to Miami, Florida, becoming one of Univision's biggest hits, and aired its last episode on September 2015. In 2001, Kreutzberger was inducted into the Hollywood Walk of Fame for his success in television and philanthropic effort, including his *National Telethon*, which raised money to help ill and crippled children. In 2015, a street in New York was named after him, "Don Francisco Boulevard." He currently hosts the Sunday night show *Don Francisco Te Invita*, which airs on Telemundo.

Sources: Billboard.com, ABC News, *Forbes*

Figure 8.3 Don Francisco
Kathy Hutchins/Shutterstock

Telenovela Star

William Levy

William Levy was born in Cuba in 1980. He is most known for being an actor, producer, and a model—and has been called "The Latin Brad Pitt" for his good looks. His modeling career led him to his first roles on *Dancing with the Stars*, *Isla de la Tentación* and *Protagonistas de Novela 2*. More recently, William Levy has starred in *Single Mom's Club*, *Resident Evil*: *The Final Chapter*, and *Addicted*.

Sources: Latina.com, People.com, William-Levy.net

Figure 8.4 William Levy
DFree/Shutterstock

America during the decade, but remained cost prohibitive for most consumers. Univision continued to export some of its more successful domestically-produced programs such as *Sabado Gigante* and *Cristina*.

The new millennium began on a positive note for U.S. Hispanics as a Latin Boom, akin to the Decade of the Hispanic, surged in the late 1990s with performers such as Ricky Martin, Jennifer Lopez, Marc Anthony, Christina Aguilera, and Shakira attracting new attention to Latin music. There was also renewed press interest in the economic power and political potential of Latinos, and it appeared that President George W. Bush and his Mexican counterpart Vicente Fox would address issues between the two countries, especially immigration. Then the September 11, 2001 attacks occurred, and attention and resources focused on fighting terrorism. In the background, NBC acquired Telemundo for $1.98 billion (plus $700 million in debt) in 2002, finally providing the stability and resources the network needed to compete effectively against Univision. A third competitor also entered the field as Televisión Azteca, the Mexican network emerging from a high-profile privatization in 1993, launched Azteca América in 2001. The network's planned station rollout faltered as Azteca's U.S. partner, Pappas Broadcasting, faced financial problems; nevertheless, the network reached 70% of Latino television households by 2006, the year it joined the Nielsen Hispanic ratings service.

Another development early in the new century intersected the Spanish-language radio and television industries, bringing them into the national political spotlight. In mid 2002, Univision announced plans to acquire Hispanic Broadcasting Corp. (HBC) the owner/operator of fifty-five Spanish-language radio stations. HBC reached 60% of Latino listeners nationwide, according to Castañeda (2003). The prospect of the merger, one of dozens occurring in media around the turn of the century, caused an uproar regarding **monopoly** control over broadcasting. By some estimates, the merged enterprise could control up to 70% of national Latino advertising revenues. The Federal Communications Commission delayed a decision on the controversial merger in early 2003, and by June received overwhelming bipartisan pushback on its plan to raise the limits on local broadcast station ownership by a single entity. By the proposed rules, a company could legally own up to eight radio stations, three TV stations, a daily newspaper, and a cable operator in a single large metropolitan market. Due to its timing and Spanish-language media's growing political weight, the proposed merger evolved into a partisan wedge issue with

Figure 8.5 Univision studios in Los Angeles, California.
Shutterstock

prominent Democrats in the Senate warning that conservatives were taking over the Spanish airwaves because Univision CEO A. Jerrold Perenchio and HBC CEO McHenry Tichnor contributed funds to Republican politicians. The CEOs' non-Latino ethnicity also stirred cultural tensions that had long lurked behind U.S. Spanish-language broadcasting (Wilkinson, 2002).

"Al Rojo Vivo"

María Celeste Arrarás

María Celeste Arrarás is a Puerto Rican journalist, author, and actress. During her career, she worked for both Univision and Telemundo. María Celeste's hard work in journalism has earned her several Emmy awards. Now, she is hosting and serving as the managing editor for a popular news program titled *Al Rojo Vivo* on Telemundo.

Sources: TVGuide.com, Telemundo.com, HuffingtonPost.com

Figure 8.6 María Celeste Arrarás
Debby Wong/Shutterstock

Spanish-language radio's political influence was revealed again in spring 2006 when some stations and disc jockeys rallied listeners to oppose the **Border Protection, Antiterrorism and Illegal Immigration Control Act (H.R. 4437)**, intended to reduce illegal immigration by bolstering immigration law enforcement and enhancing border security measures. In addition to helping mobilize millions of people who attended rallies nationwide between March and May 2006, some disc jockeys organized campaigns for listeners to write letters to legislators. Although other Spanish-language media also promoted and covered the rallies, radio played a central role in demonstrating the latent power of ethnic-oriented media and the influence of popular radio personalities such as Eddie "Piolín" Sotelo, whose show in Los Angeles reached forty-seven markets nationwide.

Technological developments became another key factor throughout the first decade of the new century. The internet began evolving into a mass medium in the mid 1990s, and by 2010 an estimated 65% of Latinos were online regularly. A number of Spanish-language internet portals launched in the years bracketing the turn of the century, only a few of which survived the bursting of the so-called **Tech Bubble** in 2000–2001. One such portal was Univision.com, launched in 1999 and purportedly the most heavily used by Spanish-speaking Latinos between 2000 and 2006. It was not until the latter part of the decade, however, that the three principal television networks had archived significant volumes of video online, and that substantial numbers of Latinos had broadband internet access at home. Mobile devices also became popular for streaming video at that time.

Univision changed hands in 2007, selling for $12.3 billion (recall the 1986 sales price of $600 million) to a group of private equity firms. Financing for the acquisition included significant debt, which became burdensome during the **Great Recession** (2007–2009). The principal investor in the new group was Haim Saban who earned huge profits from the Mighty Morphin' Power Rangers franchise and the sale of Fox Family Worldwide to Disney in 2001. The Univision sale engendered bad blood with Emilio Azcárraga Jean, Televisa's president and grandson of the entrepreneur largely responsible for launching the industry. Azcárraga Jean headed an unsuccessful rival bidding group for Univision. In 2005 Televisa had filed a lawsuit against Univision in the U.S. federal court, charging insufficient compensation for promotional airtime, and seeking the right to distribute its television programs via internet in the U.S. The suit was not settled until 2010, and in the intervening years had a dampening effect on new business due to uncertainty regarding its outcome. In an eleventh-hour settlement reached between the companies, Univision agreed to pay $46.5 million in compensation to Televisa for its lost revenues. A judge later ruled that the companies' television programming agreement included internet distribution, and forbade Televisa from streaming content to which Univision held rights under their long-term contract. Interestingly, Televisa later acquired a 5% interest in Univision, infusing much-needed cash into the highly leveraged company at a critical time.

The 2010 U.S. Census reported demographic shifts, signaling challenges for Spanish-language broadcasters. It counted 50.5 million Latinos, comprising 16.3% of the entire U.S. population. Significantly, the census showed that U.S. births had replaced immigration as the central contributing force to population growth. This shift also accelerated the youthful skew of Latinos (which had already attracted the attention of many marketers focusing on the young

Latina Journalist in English-Language TV

Soledad O'Brien

María de la Soledad Teresa O'Brien, known as Soledad O'Brien, is a well-known journalist of Cuban and Australian descent. O'Brien started her career working at WBZ-TV. She then went to work for multiple affiliates of both NBC and CNN. O'Brien has also won Emmys for her work, including her coverage of the earthquake in Haiti in 2011. She also produced a special program called "Latino in America," which aired on CNN. O'Brien is founder of media production company, Starfish Media Group.

Sources: CNN, HollywoodReporter.com, Starfish Media Group

Figure 8.7 Soledad O'Brien
Lev Radin/Shutterstock

consumers): more than one-third of Latinos were 18 or younger, and half were under 26 years old. For broadcasters, this indicated a gradual shift away from Spanish dominance toward English and bilingualism among many future listeners and viewers. Some shifts in program content reflected this change.

Code-switching and Diversification

Code-switching, the rapid shift between English and Spanish within a single sentence, had been common on radio stations along the U.S.–Mexico border and Southwestern cities long before the demographic turn reported in the 2010 Census. It is a linguistic manifestation of many listeners' (and DJs') bilingual and bicultural identity. Thus, in the early decades of the twenty-first century, the linguistic diversity heard on Latino-oriented radio nationwide reflected the dialects people were speaking. Television began moving in the same direction, but more slowly and reluctantly. With very few exceptions—such as the SíTV network (later becoming NuvoTV)—use of Spanish had been the defining characteristic of Latino-oriented television. That started changing in the 2010s.

In 2013 Fusion, an English-language channel targeting Hispanics launched as a partnership between Univision and Disney's ABC network. Univision purchased a controlling interest in *The Root*, an African-American-oriented website in 2015, and the following year took full ownership of Fusion, and acquired the racy blog site *Gawker* and the satirical newspaper/website *The Onion*. This **diversification** strategy aimed to attract younger bilingual and English-dominant audiences, the same goal Telemundo sought via partnerships within the NBCUniversal conglomerate, of which Comcast became the sole owner in 2013.

Given the projections of Latinos' steady population and purchasing power growth through mid-century, the future looks bright for Latino-oriented broadcasting in the U.S. As communication technology continues to evolve and increasing percentages of Latinos are born, educated, and socialized within the United States, we may expect to see an expanding array of distribution platforms and content options, as well as advertisers eager to reach the people who consume it.

Vocabulary Words

Border Protection, Antiterrorism and Illegal Immigration Control Act
Code-Switching
Deregulation
Direct-to-Home (DTH)
Diversification

Great Recession
Monopoly
Panamsat
Tech Bubble
Ultra High Frequency (UHF) Stations

Points to Remember

- With the creation of KCOR-AM by Raoul Cortez, Spanish-language stations began to operate more like their English counterparts.
- The Chicano and Farm Worker movements in the 1960s brought more public attention to the civil rights of Latino populations in the U.S.
- The 1980s were identified as the Decade of the Hispanic and the 1990s marked a period of rapid media industry growth. Latino populations began to receive attention from audience research companies and academic researchers.
- Univision's plan to merge with HBC caused political and ownership controversy. The company would control up to 70% of national Latino advertising revenues and the company's CEOs had funded politicians who favored restricting immigration.
- In a 2010 U.S. Census report, Latinos comprised 16.3% of the U.S. population, of whom more than one-third were 18 years or younger.

Names to Remember

Emilio Azcárraga Jean
Emilio Azcárraga Milmo
Emilio Azcárraga Vidaurreta
Gustavo Cisneros
Haim Saban
Henry Cisneros
Raoul Cortez
Rene Anselmo
Spanish International Communications Corp.

Practice Questions

1   Who established the first Spanish-language-owned radio and television station, and in what city? What group created the KWEX, KMEX, WXTV, and WLTV television stations and who were the owners?

2   Why were the original owners of the Spanish International stations forced to give them up? What was the outcome of the legal process?

3   During what time period did corporations begin to realize the profit potential represented by the Latino market? Name the city that became a strategic spot for the industry.

4   What radio station company did Univision announce that it was going to acquire and why was it controversial?

5   What website was the most widely used by Spanish-speaking U.S. Latinos in the early 2000s? What other devices did these audiences later use to stream content?

6 List the challenges that Spanish-language broadcasters are currently facing based on the demographic shifts among U.S. Latinos. What language preferences are new listeners and viewers likely to have in the future?

Activity

Network Research: Look up two recent (post-2010) Hispanic-oriented media services, and answer the following questions.

1 When and where were these new services established?
2 Who owns them?
3 What is the primary language utilized in their programming?
4 Do they have any sister organizations (i.e., stations, newspapers, blogs, etc.)?
5 Who are they marketing to?
6 What kind of programming do they offer?
7 How do these new services compare to the news networks that you learned about in this chapter?

Next, based on this information, list some differences that you think might give one media outlet advantage over the other. Finally, what are they doing to adjust to a rapidly changing media landscape?

Timeline

1946: Raoul Cortez founds KCOR-AM in San Antonio, the first full-time Spanish language radio station owned by a Latino.

1961: KCOR-AM is acquired by SICC and is renamed as KWEX-TV.

Later 1960s: The Brown Power and farmworkers' rights movement.

1976: A lawsuit is filed by two U.S. investors in the Spanish International station group against the company claiming unfair financial gains by SIN.

1980s: ("The Decade of the Hispanic") A boom in Latino population growth brings more media attention, increasing the group's perceived political, economic, and cultural influence.

1986: A federal judge rules that SICC stations must be sold. Hallmark Cards Corp. and First Capital of Chicago buy the stations and in 1988 the network, renamed Univision. Reliance Capital Corp. acquires John Blair & Co., which would later create Telemundo Network.

1992: Univision changes owners: Jerrold Perenchio, Emilio Azcárraga Milmo (Mexico), and Gustavo Cisneros (Venevision). Telemundo struggles financially.

Mid 1990s: Internet expansion to a commercial mass medium.

1996: Telecommunications Act of 1996 loosens broadcast station ownership restrictions.

2000: A boom in popularity of Latino music and culture accompanies the new millennium.

2001: September 11, 2001 terrorist attacks. NBC acquires Telemundo and Televisión Azteca enters the field.

2002: Univision announces its plan to acquire Hispanic Broadcasting Corp. (HBC)

2003: FCC delays its decision on a possible merge of Univision and HBC.

2005: Televisa files a lawsuit against Univision claiming insufficient compensation for promotional airtime, and seeking right to distribute television programs via internet in the U.S. Lawsuit is later settled in 2010.

2006: Border Protection, Antiterrorism and Illegal Immigration Control Act (H.R. 4437) is established.

2007: The beginning of the Great Recession, which lasted until 2010.

2010: About 65% of Latinos were using the internet regularly. Latino population births outnumbered immigration according to the U.S. census report.

Additional Resources

A.B. Albarran, "A History of Spanish-Language Radio in the United States," Arbitron Inc., The Center for Spanish Language Media, University of North Texas, 2009, www.arbitron.com/downloads/mcl_unt_history_spanish_radio.pdf.

F.F. Gutiérrez and J.R. Schement, *Spanish-Language Radio in the Southwestern United States* (Austin, TX: University of Texas, Center for Mexican American Studies, 1979).

L. Piñón and V. Rojas, "Language and Cultural Identity in the New Configuration of the US Latino TV Industry," *Global Media and Communication* 7, no. 2 (2011): 129–147.

América Rodriguez, "Creating an Audience and Remapping a Nation: A Brief History of US Spanish Language Broadcasting 1930–1980," *Quarterly Review of Film & Video* 16, no. 3–4 (1997): 357–374.

About the Author

Kenton T. Wilkinson, Ph.D. is Regents Professor and director of the Thomas Jay Harris Institute for Hispanic and International Communication in the College of Media and Communication at Texas Tech University. He holds a Ph.D. in Radio-TV-Film from the University of Texas at Austin and is editor of the International Journal of Hispanic Media. Wilkinson's research interests

Kenton T. Wilkinson

Photo courtesy of Kenton T. Wilkinson

include international communication and Hispanic-oriented media in the U.S. His book, *Spanish-Language Television in the United States: Fifty Years of Development*, was published by Routledge in 2016.

Wilkinson has recently collaborated with Latin American colleagues to conduct eye-tracking research as well as comparative studies of how and why millennial populations use their smartphones. He also participates in an interdisciplinary collaborative of researchers and creators at Texas Tech who engage with the landscapes of West Texas in unique ways. His current book project concerns language difference in electronic media, approaching the topic from a variety of vantage points.

References

Castañeda, M. "The Transformation of Spanish-Language Radio in the U.S." *Journal of Radio Studies* 10, no. 1 (2003): 5–16.

O'Guinn, T.C and Meyer, T.P. "Segmenting the Hispanic Market: The Use of Spanish-Language Radio." *Journal of Advertising Research* 23, no. 6 (1983/1984): 9–16.

Wilkinson, K.T. "Collective Situational Ethnicity and Latino Sub-Groups' Struggle for Influence in U.S. Spanish-Language Television." *Communication Quarterly* 50 (2002): 422–443.

Wilkinson, K.T. *Spanish-Language Television in the United States: Fifty Years of Development* (New York: Routledge, 2016).

9 Connecting with "*Mi Gente*"

Hispanic/LatinX Influencers, Entrepreneurs, and Consumers Online

Erica Rodríguez Kight, Ph.D.

Lecturer in Journalism, Radio-TV and Hispanic Media, University of Central Florida

In the early days of the internet and social networking, millions of Americans started to connect virtually through email, forums, chat rooms, online journals, and personal home pages that were known as **weblogs**. In the 1990s, during this rise of online social networking, about 22.4 million people who identified as Hispanic lived in the United States, with roots in more than thirty-three countries and residing in all fifty states throughout the nation.[1] Like millions of their fellow Americans, members of the Hispanic/LatinX community in the U.S. started to use early social media platforms—like America Online, LiveJournal, and MySpace—as a way to connect, communicate, and consume information. Fast-forward to 2017, and the U.S. Hispanic/LatinX community represented about 57.5 million people,[2] of which an estimated 84% used the internet and about 73% used Facebook.[3] According to surveys, Hispanic/LatinX internet users appear to have a preference for mobile technology and an affinity for streaming video content online.[4] In addition to representing a large segment of the new media audience, Hispanic/LatinX people in the U.S. also actively contribute to content and connections on a national and international scale.

Big Names and Big Dreams

Some of the most influential people on social media today identify as Hispanic, Latino/a, or LatinX with several millions of followers across platforms like Twitter, Facebook, and Instagram. These social media influencers range from already-popular celebrities to self-made entrepreneurs, as well as well-known politicians, journalists, and more. They often use their large networks of followers and extensive reach to communicate various types of messages, including marketing their businesses, sharing their creative work, connecting with followers, supporting political causes, and promoting philanthropic efforts.

Colombian-born pop star Shakira's Facebook page had more than 104 million "likes" and more than 98 million followers as of 2017. Shakira frequently uses social media platforms not only to share updates about her music career but also information about her foundation, called *Fundación Pies Descalzos*, or "Barefoot Foundation," which supports education for children in Colombia. In another example, celebrity chef José Ramón Andrés Puerta, better known as Chef José Andrés, used his social media reach of almost a million followers across Twitter and Facebook to spread awareness of the ongoing struggles in Puerto Rico during the aftermath of Hurricane Maria in 2017. For months, the Spanish-born chef and owner of several restaurants posted videos of his team preparing and distributing meals to families on the island, who endured months without power and other necessities.

Starting out small and working her way up over the years, beauty **vlogger** Dulce Candy Tejada Ruiz now reaches more than 2.2 million subscribers on YouTube with her bilingual makeup tutorials in English and Spanish, sharing her slogan "Be Confident. Be Beautiful. Be You."[5] With posts dating as far back as 2008, Dulce Candy and other Latina beauty vloggers produce messages that go beyond simple makeup tutorials. They frequently share messages of empowerment for Latinas, who often face conflicting standards of beauty within their own cultures and in American culture.[6] Dulce Candy also made headlines after posing an immigration question and sharing her Mexican border-crossing

Figure 9.1 Pop star Shakira uses social media to connect with her fans and promote her philanthropic projects.

Tinseltown/Shutterstock

story via Twitter during the 2016 Republican debate.[7] These are just a few examples of Hispanic/LatinX influencers using the power of social media to connect with people on both a personal level and on a large scale.

Connecting Over the Years

To date, Hispanic/LatinX internet users have formed an extensive reach with continuing influence in the digital world as a result of years of engagement, contribution, and entrepreneurship. One of the first and most popular Latino-focused social networking sites emerged in the early 2000s as MiGente.com. MiGente.com started out as a social media site in which people created home pages and communicated with others who had similar interests or who sought personal connections. At the height of its popularity in the early 2000s, MySpace also launched a Latino-targeted "bilingual destination" called MySpace Latino. Another popular social networking site called Friendster, which is known as the oldest of its kind, added Spanish to its available languages later in the 2000s.[8] Several traditional media companies—such as television networks, newspapers, and magazines, for example—followed suit and started to establish a Latino-targeted presence online with bilingual content. For example, traditional news outlets like CNN en Español and Fox News Latino have established active social media presence, with 11 million and 122,000 followers on Facebook respectively.

Over the years, Hispanic/LatinX internet users have also established their own popular online communities on the **blogosphere**, gravitated toward video-sharing sites such as YouTube, and formed personalized groups and Latino-targeted pages on Facebook.[9] For example, sites and pages like Remezcla, Fusion, Hispanics Be Like, Pero Like, We Are MiTu, News Taco, FLAMA, Undocumedia, and Being Latino have attracted several million followers and continuously posted news, commentary, videos, discussions, and other Latino-focused content like humorous **memes** about Hispanic/LatinX life and culture in the U.S.

Communicating Across Borders

Hispanics and Latinos in the U.S. often also turn to social networking sites and mobile applications, also known as **apps**, to connect with friends and family in their countries of origin. As of 2016, a messaging platform called WhatsApp reached 1 billion users—with most of its popularity coming from Europe and South America.[10] Experian Marketing Services estimated in 2014 that nearly half of all WhatsApp users were Hispanic.[11] In 2016, Wired.com called WhatsApp the "second-most popular app on Earth after the primary Facebook app."[12] Facebook acquired WhatsApp in 2014 for $22 billion.[13] Even Hispanics in countries with a long history of a wider **digital divide** and limited internet connectivity have found ways to connect using such applications and platforms in recent years.

For example, popular Cuban vlogger Alain Rodríguez, better known as "*El Paparazzi Cubano*," regularly uses Facebook Live to communicate information from Cuba to his followers in the U.S. and abroad. *El Paparazzi Cubano* started out posting videos from WiFi hotspots in Havana, Cuba. He walked around and shared images of everyday life on the island. His efforts evolved to connecting people in Cuba with people who he calls "*padrinos*," or godparents, abroad in countries like the U.S. and Spain. After watching Alain's videos about individuals' struggles in Cuba, the *padrinos* send donations to Alain who distributes the goods to the families on the island. Similar bridges have formed via social media throughout the world and continue to connect Hispanics living in various countries. The internet has also facilitated the flow of news and information from news organizations in Latin America to audiences in the U.S.

Hispanic/LatinX Entrepreneurs and Tech Leaders Online

From bloggers to web developers, and everything in between, Hispanic/LatinX youth continue to find ways to benefit socially and financially online. For instance, in late 2004, Mario Lavandeira Jr.—better known as Perez Hilton—started a notorious Hollywood gossip blog called PageSixSixSix.com. The site

Figure 9.2 Mario Lavandeira Jr., best known as Perez Hilton, is a social media pioneer and entreprenuer.

Kathy Hutchins/Shutterstock

eventually evolved into PerezHilton.com, which Lavandeira claimed generated millions of hits per day and sometimes per hour.[14] Sources estimated Lavandeira's net worth reached close to $30 million by 2017. This is just one example of the financial success that many Hispanic/LatinX entrepreneurs have found online.

Others include Guatemalan-born Matias de Tezanos, who founded the Spanish-language hotel reservation site Hoteles.com, among several other successful websites generating millions of dollars. In 2009, at the ripe age of 29, de Tezanos was named a Young Global Leader by the Economic World Forum.[15]

YouTuber Karina García also found internet success and fame through her videos about making slime—yes, slime! As of late-2017, García had more than 6.8 million followers on YouTube with up to 26 million views per video. She also produced her own "Make-Your-Own Slime Kit," sold exclusively at Target, as well as books like *Karina García's Must Try DIYs* and *DIY Slime.* In mid-2017, *The New York Times* reported that García was bringing in up to $200,000 per month from her slime-making videos and business. Her sister, Mayra García, also gained YouTube success with her makeup tutorial page called Mayra Touch of Glam. The two sisters collaborated to purchase a six-bedroom home for their family. "I've retired my parents," Karina García told *The New York Times.* "It's definitely really crazy. Even I can't believe it. I'm like, 'How is this happening?'"[16]

Similarly, Puerto Rican comedian and entrepreneur LeJuan James attracted more than 2.8 million followers on Facebook with his homemade, funny video clips and satirical interpretations of everyday life as a Latino in the U.S. In a video that went viral across various social media platforms, LeJuan James showed gratitude for his financial success, wore a "God is Good" t-shirt, and explained to his loyal followers why he felt compelled to repay his parents for their hard work and support. "I am forever indebted to them," he said.[17] LeJuan said his parents worked multiple jobs to support him over the years, so he surprised them in the video with their first home in Central Florida. "*Tienen casa* [you have a home]," he repeated through tears. His emotional video generated hundreds of thousands of "likes" and views, and it is an example of the unique, often shared experience of many Hispanics and Latinos living in the U.S.

Latinos also work behind the scenes in the tech world. Nicolás Garcia Belmonte graduated in 2007 from the Instituto Tecnológico de Buenos Aires in Argentina with a degree in computer engineering. Belmonte has since worked with multiple technology companies, including the French search engine Exalead, the American start-up Sencha, and the international social media networking site Twitter. Belmonte became the head of data visualization at the transportation company Uber in 2015.[18] In 2017, CNET en Español published a list of the most influential Latinos in tech. That list included: YouTube Vice President of Product Management Manuel Bronstein, Pandora Senior Director and Head of Research Òscar Celma, Microsoft Principal Art Director Alberto Cerriteño, Apple Director of Machine Learning Carlos Guestrin, Airbnb Engineering Manager Daniel Loreto, and Twitter Software

Engineering Manager for Mobile and Front-end Development Diana Macías, among others.

Still, the pipeline of U.S. Hispanics to this industry is slim, and there is a lot of work to be done to increase the presence of Latinos in Science, Technology, Engineering and Mathematics (STEM) fields. According to the U.S. Department of Education, as of 2010, only 8% of undergraduate STEM degrees were awarded to Hispanic students. Those numbers were even lower for graduate degrees, with Hispanics earning only 4% of all master's degrees and 3% of all doctorates awarded in STEM in 2010.[19]

Making "Media Moves"

Veronica Villafañe

Veronica Villafañe is an Argentinian-American journalist who launched a website called MediaMoves.com, which focuses on media-related news. She has worked as a producer, reporter, writer, and an anchor for multiple networks, including Univision and CNN en Español. Villafañe is also a former president of the National Association of Hispanic Journalists (NAHJ).

Sources: MediaMoves.com, VeronicaVillafane.com, Forbes.com

Fiugre 9.3 Veronica Villafañe
Photo courtesy of Veronica Villafañe

Blending Media and Streaming Video

Popular musicians have also found internet success and started to blend new media with traditional media through their work. For instance, Colombian reggaeton artist J. Balvin's hit song, named *"Snapchat"* for the popular mobile app, had more than 12 million views on YouTube by 2017. The song and music video are about the *reggaetonero*'s sexy communication with a woman on Snapchat, an app that the musician happens to use often in his everyday life to connect with his fans. J Balvin regularly posts **"snaps"** of his friends, family, and fans—as well as posts on other social media platforms like Instagram and Facebook. This kind of connection on social media can amplify fan identification, making followers feel like the celebrities are actually connecting with them on a personal level.[20] J Balvin's music and approach to connecting with his fans has paid off. Born Jose Alvaro Osorio Balvin, J Balvin reached up to 1.4 billion views of his most popular song on YouTube, "Ay Vamos," by 2017.

Similarly, Puerto Rican pop artist Luis Fonsi and reggaeton artist Daddy Yankee, born Ramón Luis Ayala Rodriguez, reached 4.4 billion views on YouTube for their international hit "Despacito," which was released in early 2017. The song met and broke records, including: becoming the first video on YouTube to reach 4 billion views, topping the Billboard Hot 100 chart at No. 1 for 16 weeks in a row, generating the most views within 24 hours in Vevo history with 54 million views, and racking up 4.6 billion streams in just six months.[21]

Figure 9.4 and 9.5 Singer Luis Fonsi and reggaetonero Daddy Yankee collaborated to produce the record-breaking hit Despacito, which was an international sensation.
Kathy Hutchins/Miguel Campos/Shutterstock

Afro-Latina Anchor's KKK Interview Goes Viral

Ilia Calderón

Colombian-born journalist Ilia Calderón made headlines in 2017 after her interview with a Ku Klux Klan leader in North Carolina. The KKK leader said Calderón was the first black person to step foot on his property in his 20 years of living there. Videos of their tense encounter, in both English and Spanish, went viral on social media platforms YouTube and Facebook with millions of views. Calderón is an anchor for Univision Network, has won an Emmy award, and was named one of the 100 Most Important Hispanic Journalists by the Hispanic Media 100 organization.

Sources: Univision, Facebook, YouTube, *Washington Post*

Figure 9.6 Ilia Calderón
Photo courtesy of Univision Network

As previously mentioned in this chapter, studies show Hispanics gravitate toward mobile media use and video streaming as preferred uses of media devices.[22] In the 2010s, products such as Sling, Roku, AppleTV, Netflix, and Hulu became more and more popular in American households.[23] Netflix, in particular, has produced highly popular original programs featuring Hispanic/LatinX actors. *Orange is the New Black*, for example, features LatinX actors in prominent roles, including Dascha Polanco as Daya, Elizabeth Rodriguez as Aleida, Selenis Leyva as Gloria, Jackie Cruz as Flaca, Diane Guerrero as Maritza, Jessica Pimentel as Maria, Laura Gomez as Blanca, and Berto Colon as Cesar.[24] *Narcos*, which focuses on the life of drug kingpin Pablo Escobar, is another popular series on Netflix starring Hispanic/LatinX actors. Netflix also streams international content, such as Spanish television series *Velvet* and Cuban miniseries *Four Seasons in Havana*.

It is not all fun and entertainment content that goes viral online, though. Hispanic journalists have also reached millions of viewers when reporting for digital platforms. Longtime Univision anchor Jorge Ramos, for example, garnered attention for his encounter with then-presidential candidate Donald Trump at a press conference in 2015. Trump had Ramos forcibly escorted out of the room after the reporter tried to ask questions about immigration during the press conference. Video of the encounter went viral, with more than 1 million views on the Univision YouTube page and countless more "tweets" and "shares" across various social media platforms.

Power in Numbers

The presence of such Hispanic/LatinX trailblazers online has also led to the formation of organizations and events that support and foster this kind of entrepreneurship. For example, the Hispanicize conference is an annual event held in Miami, Florida, aimed at serving as "a launchpad for creative endeavors, new products, technologies, marketing campaigns, films, books and more targeting Latinos in the U.S. and/or Puerto Rico."[25] Similarly, the #WeAllGrow Summit is a unique conference for Latina bloggers and entrepreneurs that creates an environment in which they can network and train.[26] Another event called LATISM, which stands for Latinos in Tech Innovation and Social Media, focuses on education and creating a pipeline of Hispanic/LatinX youth in tech and social media industries.[27]

Perhaps the most impactful example of power in numbers of Latinos online is the **DREAMers Movement**. Hispanic/LatinX youth have successfully used social networking to mobilize and unify in their efforts to rally and lobby against policy changes that would force many who arrived in the U.S. illegally as young children to return to their countries of origin. Using **hashtags** like #protectdreamers, #dreamers, #withdaca, #dreamactnow, and #amnesty, undocumented youth have turned to social media for support, collaboration, and outreach.

"Work hard. . . . Dig deep. . . . Don't quit."

One-on-one with CNN Correspondent Rosa Flores

Q: What is it about the online environment that appeals to you as a journalist?
A: It's fun! It allows journalists to find new and compelling ways to tell stories. Creativity is the limit.

Q: When you are reporting online, how do you approach it differently than when you are reporting for TV?
A: We have more time, space, and latitude to adapt our storytelling on digital. My latest documentary, "Beneath the Skin," is a perfect example. We didn't know it was going to be a documentary until the end. When my team and I were ready to write and edit, we realized we had material for three episodes. Because the product was supposed to publish online, it wasn't a problem. The online platform allows us to tell a story in the most compelling way possible with very few limitations. You are your only limitation on a digital platform.

Q: Studies show Hispanic audiences gravitate toward mobile and video content. As a Latina journalist, how do you feel this may impact your work?

Figure 9.7 Rosa Flores
Photo courtesy of CNN

A: As a TV network correspondent, digital provides an opportunity to bring stories to those who may not be watching CNN air. As a journalist who often covers issues that impact the Latino community, it's important to push my work to online audiences. I do more and more work online. My most recent work, "Beneath the Skin," a three-episode documentary about a mother's fight for justice, was produced for digital. While I did live shots on TV to drive viewers online, the documentary was produced for an online audience. On top of that, I'm working with CNN en Español on a Spanish-language version of the digital documentary.

Q: You traveled with Pope Francis on the official papal plane. How was that experience unique for you as a Latina journalist?
A: I talked to the first Latin American Pope in his native language. I didn't need a translator. That's what made my experience unique. When I met the Pope on the papal plane he was so humble. He was so personable. And, of course, we conversed in Spanish!

Figure 9.8 Rosa Flores interviews Pope Francis on the official papal plane.
Photo courtesy of Rosa Flores

Q: What kind of response did you get from followers online about your coverage of the Pope?

A: My social media reach shoots up every time I travel with Pope Francis. My followers love all the little behind the scenes details that we don't get to share on TV. By sharing photos and videos, I try my best to bring them along with me as I travel, gather news, work, and even eat on the papal plane.

Q: Do you have any advice for young Hispanic journalists who would one day like to see themselves in your shoes?

A: Work hard. There are no shortcuts in journalism. Dig deep. Shine light on stories that are not on the surface. Don't quit. Our profession is more important than ever.

In summary, as social media continues to evolve and the Hispanic/LatinX community continues to grow in the U.S., these are just a few examples of the ongoing efforts to continue to leave a mark on this fairly new digital age. Whether the glue is power in numbers or a shared cultural connection, surely the impact of the Hispanic/LatinX community on new media in the U.S. will continue to stick for decades to come.

Vocabulary Words

Apps	Memes
Blogosphere	*Reggaetonero*
Digital Divide	Snaps
DREAMers Movement	Vlogger
Hashtags	Weblogs

Points to Remember

- Some of the most influential people on social media today identify as Hispanic, Latino/a, or LatinX with several millions of followers across platforms such as Twitter, Facebook, and Instagram.
- Hispanic/LatinX internet users have formed an extensive reach with continuing influence in the digital world as a result of years of engagement, contribution, and entrepreneurship.
- From bloggers to web developers, and everything in between, Hispanic/LatinX youth continue to find ways to benefit socially and financially online.

- Puerto Rican pop artist Luis Fonsi and reggaeton artist Daddy Yankee reached 4.4 billion views on YouTube for their international hit "Despacito," which was released in early 2017.
- Hispanic/LatinX youth have successfully used social networking to mobilize and unify in their efforts to rally and lobby against policy changes that would force many who arrived in the U.S. illegally as young children to return to their countries of origin.

Names to Remember

Alain Rodriguez
Chef José Andrés
Dascha Polanco
Karina García
LeJuan James
Matias de Tezanos
Perez Hilton

Practice Questions

1   Name three early social networking platforms.
2   In the early days of social networking, MiGente.com was a popular site for Latinos. Why do you think a site like this would attract Hispanic/LatinX internet users? Why not just use mainstream social networking sites? What might be the benefits of Latino-targeted online spaces like this?
3   Which social media application mentioned in this chapter has the majority of its followers in Europe and South America? What is the percentage of Hispanic users of this app?
4   Name two Hispanic/LatinX celebrities who actively participate in social media. How do you think this practice benefits them? Does it benefit their audience or followers?
5   In this chapter, you read about low numbers of college degrees in STEM fields being awarded to Hispanic/LatinX graduates. How do you think these numbers can be improved?

Activity

Entrepreneurs online, such as Karina García and LeJuan James, have come up with unique ways to find financial success on social media. Brainstorm a few unique ways you could do the same. What topics do you like? What topics do you think would appeal to your target audience? Describe your target audience. What would it take to get started? Do you think your idea could go viral? If so, explain and support your anticipated results with outside sources.

Additional Resources

Hispanicize—www.hispanicizeevent.com
LATISM—www.latism.org

About the Author

Erica Rodríguez Kight

Photo courtesy of the
University of Central Florida

Erica Rodríguez Kight, Ph.D., teaches courses in journalism, radio-TV, and Hispanic media at the University of Central Florida Nicholson School of Communication. She is also part of the UCF NSC Hispanic Media Initiative. Kight previously worked as a newspaper reporter, TV news assignment editor, and TV news reporter. Kight completed her undergraduate studies in English Literature at Florida State University and later earned graduate degrees in Mass Communication from the University of Florida. As a journalist, she won several awards for her work, including recognitions from Florida AP Broadcasters, the Society of Professional Journalists, and the Florida Emergency Preparedness Association. In her free time, Kight enjoys traveling and spending time with her family.

Notes

1 "We asked . . . You Told Us: Hispanic Origin," *U.S. Department of Commerce Bureau of the Census*, October 1992, www.census.gov/prod/cen1990/cqc/cqc7.pdf.
2 "FFF: Hispanic Heritage Month 2017," *United States Census Bureau*, August 2017, www.census.gov/newsroom/facts-for-features/2017/hispanic-heritage.html.
3 Anna Brown, Gustavo Lopez, and Mark Hugo Lopez, "Internet Use Among Hispanics," *Pew Research Center*, July 20, 2016, www.pewhispanic.org/2016/07/20/1-internet-use-among-hispanics; Jens Manuel Krogstad, "Social Media Preferences Vary by Race and Ethnicity." *Pew Research Center*, February 3, 2015, www.pewresearch.org/fact-tank/2015/02/03/social-media-preferences-vary-by-race-and-ethnicity.
4 Monica Anderson, "Racial and Ethnic Differences in How People Use Mobile Technology," *Pew Research Center*, April 30, 2015, www.pewresearch.org/fact-tank/2015/04/30/racial-and-ethnic-differences-in-how-people-use-mobile-technology; "Always connected: US-based Hispanic Consumers Dominate Mobile, Entertainment, and Beyond," *PwC: PricewaterhouseCoopers*, 2016, www.pwc.com/us/en/industry/entertainment-media/publications/consumer-intelligence-series/assets/pwc-emc-hispanics-report.pdf.
5 "Dulce Candy," YouTube.com, 2017, www.youtube.com/user/DulceCandy87.
6 Rosie Molinary, *Hijas Americanas: Beauty, Body Image and Growing Up Latina* (Emeryville: Seal Press, 2007).
7 Cedar Attanasio, "Who is Dulce Candy? Meet the Mexican Immigrant, Veteran, YouTube Star Featured in GOP Debate," *Latin Times*, January 29, 2016, www.

latintimes.com/who-dulce-candy-meet-mexican-immigrant-veteran-youtube-star-featured-gop-debate-video-367014.

8 "Friendster At A Glance," *Friendster*, 2008, https://web.archive.org/web/20090731 052122/http://images.friendster.com/images/Friendster_At_A_Glance_September_2008.pdf.

9 Susanna Kohly Jacobson, "How Hispanic Consumers Engage with YouTube," *Think with Google*, August 2016, www.thinkwithgoogle.com/consumer-insights/hispanic-consumers-engage-youtube.

10 Cade Metz, "One Billion People Now Use WhatsApp," *Wired*, February 2016, www.wired.com/2016/02/one-billion-people-now-use-whatsapp.

11 "The $19 Billion Question: Who Uses WhatsApp And Why Are They So Important To Facebook?" *Experian Cross-Channel Marketing Team*, February 21, 2014, www.experian.com/blogs/marketing-forward/2014/02/21/the-19-billion-question-who-uses-whatsapp-and-why-are-they-so-important-to-facebook.

12 Cade Metz, "One Billion People Now Use WhatsApp," *Wired*, February 2016, www.wired.com/2016/02/one-billion-people-now-use-whatsapp.

13 Reuters Staff, "Facebook Takes the Next Step to Monetize WhatsApp: WSJ," *Reuters*, September 5, 2017, www.reuters.com/article/us-facebook-whatsapp/facebook-takes-the-next-step-to-monetize-whatsapp-wsj-idUSKCN1BG20N.

14 Tom Ward, "Perez Hilton: The OG Who's Still Killing It 14 Years Later," *Forbes*, October 24, 2017, www.forbes.com/sites/tomward/2017/10/24/perez-hilton-the-og-whos-still-killing-it-14-years-later/#376605950144.

15 "BrokersWeb Inc. Founder & CEO Matias de Tezanos Named Ernst & Young Entrepreneur of the Year," *PR Newswire*, May 18, 2011, www.prnewswire.com/news-releases/brokersweb-inc-founder--ceo-matias-de-tezanos-named-ernst--young-entrepreneur-of-the-year-2011-florida-award-finalist-122148794.html.

16 Claire Martin, "Feel the Noise: Homemade Slime Becomes Big Business," *New York Times*, June 23, 2017, www.nytimes.com/2017/06/23/business/smallbusiness/homemade-slime-becomes-big-business.html.

17 LeJuan James, "Surprising My Parents With a New Home #TeamLejuan," YouTube.com, August 1, 2017, www.youtube.com/watch?v=OXxrinLM8Cc.

18 *crunchbase*, "Nicolas Belmonte," 2017, www.crunchbase.com/person/nicolas-belmonte; Patricia Puntes, "Nicolás García Belmonte: Desmenuzando datos para Uber," *cnet*, September 22, 2016, www.cnet.com/es/noticias/nicolas-garcia-belmonte-uber-latinos-en-tecnologia-2016.

19 "Hispanics and STEM Education," *White House Initiative on Education Excellence for Hispanics*, www2.ed.gov/about/inits/list/hispanic-initiative/stem-factsheet.pdf.

20 Melissa A. Click, Hyunji Lee, and Holly Willson Holladay, "Making Monsters: Lady Gaga, Fan Identification, and Social Media," *Popular Music and Society* 36, no. 3 (2013): 360–379, doi: 10.1080/03007766.2013.798546.

21 Lars Brandle, "Luis Fonsi & Daddy Yankee's 'Despacito' is First Clip to Hit 4 Billion Views on YouTube," *Billboard*, September 11, 2017, www.billboard.com/articles/news/7997618/luis-fonsi-daddy-yankee-despacito-first-4-billion-views-youtube.

22 PwC, "Always Connected, US-based Hispanic Consumers Dominate Mobile, Entertainment, and Beyond," *PwC Consumer Intelligence Series*, September, 2016, http://hispanicad.com/sites/default/files/pwc-hispanics-9-2016.pdf.

23 Amber Hunt, "For Millions of Cord Cutters, Cable TV Fades to Black," *USA Today*, August 24, 2014, www.usatoday.com/story/money/personalfinance/2014/08/24/for-millions-of-cord-cutters-cable-tv-fades-to-black/14513495.

24 Carmery Trinidad, "Meet the 8 Latinos of Netflix's 'Orange is the New Black'," August 10, 2013, www.latina.com/entertainment/tv/orange-is-the-new-black-latina-characters.

25 *Hispanicize*, "General Info," http://hispanicizeevent.com/about/general-info.
26 *#WeAllGrow Latina Network*, "#WeAllGrow Summit," www.weallgrowlatina.com/
     summit.
27 Jennifer Lubrani, "LATISM Announces 8th Annual Conference in Orlando,"
     LATISM, May 3, 2016, http://latism.org/latism-announces-8th-annual-conference-
     in-orlando-florida-to-include-hackathon-and-s-t-e-a-m-fair.

Unit 4

Reaching Hispanic/ LatinX Audiences

10 The Hispanic/LatinX Audience

Mobile, Social, and Traditional Media Use

Jessica Mahone, Ph.D.

Research Associate for the Public Square Program, Democracy Fund

The Hispanic population in the United States topped 56 million in July 2015, making up nearly 18% of the United States population and representing the largest ethnic minority group in the country.[1] An increasing number of this growing demographic are U.S. born,[2] and roughly 60% are bilingual.[3] And they are younger than their non-Hispanic counterparts. The median age for American Hispanics in 2014 was 28, lower than the median age of 43 for non-Hispanic whites and 33 for blacks.[4] They differ from the general American media audience in how they consume media. Hispanics watch less TV, are more likely to listen to radio, and use mobile much more than other Americans.[5] As a young and growing group, this demographic is an increasingly lucrative part of the American media audience.

This chapter provides an overview of media use among Hispanics in the U.S., focusing heavily on news media use. It is divided into three parts: (1) traditional media use among American Hispanics; (2) digital, social, and mobile media use among American Hispanics; and (3) language differences in media use. The section on traditional media use will present facts, figures, and information about consumption and use of newspapers, television, and radio. The second portion, on social media, will examine use of social networking sites such as Facebook, Twitter, and Instagram. The final portion, on language preferences, will provide a brief overview of the role of language in the media choices of American Hispanics.

Traditional Media Use

Like other racial and ethnic groups, Hispanics in the U.S. are reading daily newspapers less often. However, weekly newspaper readership has held relatively steady. At the same time, television viewership patterns have begun to shift among this demographic, with Telemundo viewership slowly increasing and Univision viewership in steady decline. As with other groups, radio use remains high among American Hispanics.

Newspapers

Surveys and industry data both show a decline in newspaper use among American Hispanics over the past ten years. In a 2012 Pew Research Center survey,[6] 42% of Hispanics said they get their news from a print newspaper, a 16-point drop from 58% in 2006. Data about **circulation**, the number of copies distributed on an average day, for Hispanic daily newspapers shows a similar decline over the past three years. The three largest Hispanic daily newspapers in the U.S.—*El Nuevo Herald*, *La Opinión*, and *El Diario La Prensa*— have seen steady declines in their daily circulation since 2013. Between 2013 and 2014, the daily circulation of *La Opinión*, the largest Spanish-language newspaper in the U.S., saw a 10% decline in daily circulation.[7] This decline continued in 2015 with a 13% decline in Monday through Friday circulation from 2014. This is a steeper decline than the decline of all U.S. newspapers between 2014 and 2015, where the average decline was 6.7%.[8]

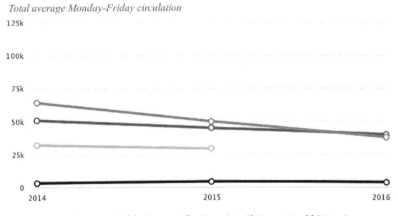

Hispanic daily newspaper circulation

Total average Monday-Friday circulation

Note: Numbers represent audited average circulation, if an audited statement is available for that year; if not, the most comparable publisher's statement was used if it exists. Circulation for La Opinión here is presented not including the average circulation for La Opinión Contigo, which is a free weekly insert. Sunday circulation is used for El Nuevo Heraldo.
Source: Alliance for Audited Media

Figure 10.1 Hispanic daily newspaper circulation.

Pew Research Center

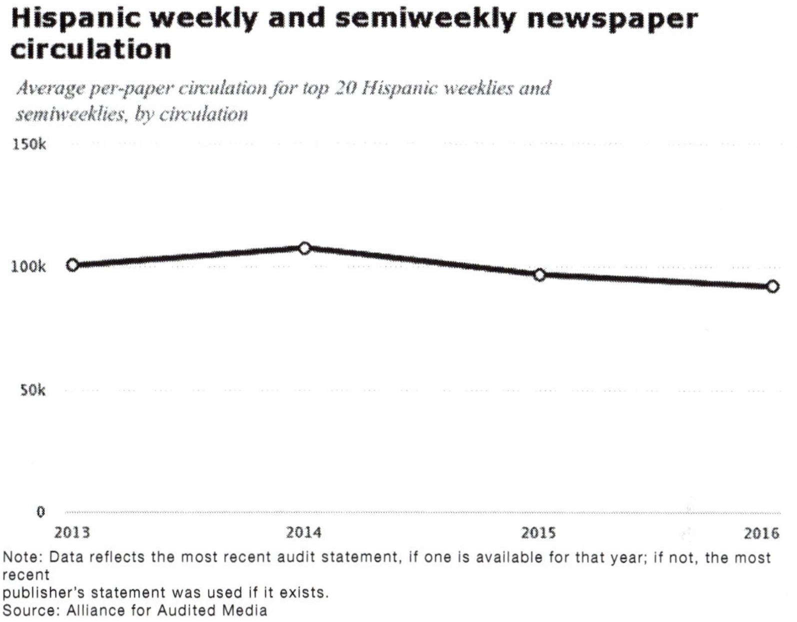

Hispanic weekly and semiweekly newspaper circulation

Average per-paper circulation for top 20 Hispanic weeklies and semiweeklies, by circulation

Note: Data reflects the most recent audit statement, if one is available for that year; if not, the most recent
publisher's statement was used if it exists.
Source: Alliance for Audited Media

Figure 10.2 Hispanic weekly and semiweekly newspaper circulation.

Pew Research Center

Overall, this demonstrates that newspaper circulation among Hispanics has fallen alongside newspaper circulation among Americans in general. However, daily newspaper circulation and **readership** estimates of how many people read a publication only tell part of the story of Hispanic media use. Weekly and semiweekly newspapers are a significant part of the Hispanic media landscape. And while Hispanic daily papers have seen a decline, Hispanic weeklies and semi-weeklies have held relatively steady. Combined circulation for twenty-five Hispanic weekly and semiweekly newspapers increased by 2% between 2014 and 2015.[9]

Television

Hispanic television has long been dominated by Univision, the Spanish-language news network launched in 1962. In 2013, Univision hit an important milestone in American network TV, finishing first in July **sweeps** with an average of 1.8 million viewers aged 18–49 between June 27 and July 24 of that year. The network's win is attributed in part to viewership of **telenovelas**, with new episodes airing during the summer sweeps period when the Big Four networks (ABC, NBC, CBS, and FOX) typically air fewer new episodes in favor of repeats.[10]

However, with the growth of competitor Spanish-language networks Telemundo and Azteca, Univision has had some decline in **viewership**—an estimate of how many people watch a program or network during an average specified time period—of some of its biggest news programs over the past several years. Viewership of *Noticiero Univision*, the network's flagship nightly news program, has decreased from an average weeknight audience of 2.05 million in 2013 to 1.79 million in 2016. In contrast, viewership of *Noticiero Telemundo*, the flagship nightly news program of rival Telemundo, has increased from 771,000 in 2013 to 962,000 in 2016. Viewership of Univision's other major news programs *Al Punto*, *Aquí y Ahora*, *Noticiero Univision: Edición Nocturna* and *Primer Impacto* have seen similar declines while Telemundo's *Al Rojo Vivo* and *Enfoque* had small increases over the same time period. As for Azteca, the network owned by Mexican media company TV Azteca and formerly known as Azteca America, has seen its total viewership reach over 21 million in the 2014–2015 season and currently holds 3% of the market share of the American Spanish-language audience.[11]

Local TV

According to Nielsen, the five largest Hispanic markets in the U.S. are Los Angeles, New York, Miami-Ft. Lauderdale, Houston, and Dallas-Ft. Worth.

Figure 10.3 Viewership between Univision and Telemundo has fluctuated over the years; while Univision's has increased, Telemundo's has decreased.

Blend Images/Shutterstock

Univision and Telemundo network news viewership by program

Average viewership of Univision and Telemundo news programs

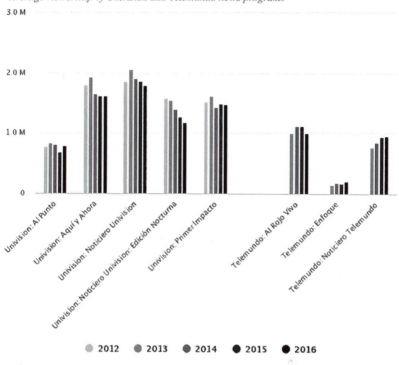

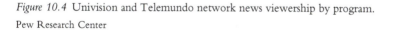

Note: Numbers represent the annual average for each show for each broadcast calendar year.
Data for Telemundo was first collected in 2013.
Source: Pew Research Center analysis of Nielsen Media Research data, used under license.

Figure 10.4 Univision and Telemundo network news viewership by program.
Pew Research Center

The Hispanic TV audience in these five markets alone equals more than 5.3 million. This represents about 36% of the total Hispanic TV audience in the U.S.[12] Local Hispanic TV is dominated by **affiliates** owned and operated by both Univision and Telemundo, and, much like their national counterparts, Univision affiliate viewership has declined over the past three years while Telemundo affiliate viewership has increased. Early evening news viewership on Univision stations has decreased from 1,654,000 in 2013 to 1,540,000 in 2015. Viewership for early evening news on Telemundo stations during the same time period has increased from 585,000 to 729,000.[13]

Univision and Telemundo local affiliates viewership, by time slot

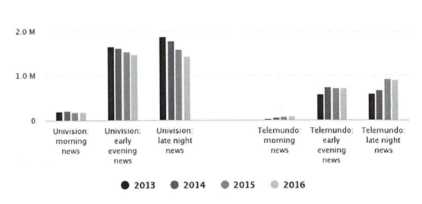

Average viewership for Univision and Telemundo affiliates, by time slot

Note: Numbers represent viewership for affiliates for the four sweeps – February, May, July, and November.
Time slots are morning news: 5-7a.m; early evening news: 5-7 p.m; late night news: 11-11:30 p.m
Source: Nielsen Media Research, used under licence.

Figure 10.5 Univision and Telemundo local affiliates viewership, by time slot.

Pew Research Center

Radio

Reflecting the overall increase in the number of Hispanics in the U.S., the Hispanic radio audience grew 11% between 2011 and 2016.[14] A full 97% of American Hispanics listen to the radio each week. However, while radio listenership is high among American Hispanics generally, radio use among this population is quite diverse. Fifteen million Hispanic millennials listen to the radio each week, more than twice the number of baby boomer Hispanics who do so. The size of the Hispanic millennial radio audience has propelled Mexican Regional to being the tenth most popular radio format in the United States, particularly among Hispanic millennial men, and the eighth most popular radio format among American millennials overall.[15] But despite the popularity of Mexican regional among Hispanic millennials,[16] the share of Hispanics aged 18–49 listening to this format is decreasing in favor of mainstream pop and Top 40 formats. Still, even as the Hispanic audience itself is growing, the amount of time American Hispanics spend listening to the radio each week is declining. In 2011, Hispanic radio listeners spent an average of almost 15 hours per week listening to the radio. In 2015, they spent an average of 13 hours listening to the radio.[17]

Social and Mobile Media Use

Internet and social media use among American Hispanics is generally similar to other racial and ethnic groups. However, there are some key distinctions in the social platforms American Hispanics use. American Hispanic internet users are more likely to use Instagram than white or black internet users, and Google+ use is considerably higher among American Hispanic teenagers than teens of other groups. American Hispanics also rely more on mobile media than other racial and ethnic groups.

Social Media

As of 2015, roughly 80% of Hispanic adults say they use the internet, a rate similar to the 85% of white Americans and 78% of black Americans who say they use the internet.[18] Social media use is generally even across racial and ethnic groups in the United States. Approximately 80% of Hispanic, black, and white internet users use at least one social media site, with Facebook being by far the most popular with approximately 70% of Hispanics, black, and white internet users.

However, American Hispanics stand out from their black and white counterparts in terms of their social media habits.[19] Fully 34% of American Hispanic internet users use Instagram, a share higher than that among all American internet users (26%) and noticeably higher than among white Americans (21%). In contrast, LinkedIn usage is generally higher among black and white internet users than among American Hispanics. Almost 30% of black and white Americans use the professional social network while not quite 20% of American Hispanic internet users use this platform. Perhaps most noteworthy is the popularity of Google+ among Hispanic teenagers. Almost half (48%) of Hispanic teenagers use the social network, higher than teens in general (33%), white teens (26%), and black teens (29%).[20]

Mobile Media Use

One of the most distinctive characteristics of Hispanic media use is a heavy reliance on mobile. American Hispanics use their phones to access apps, audio, video, and the web for more than 14 hours per week, and this continues in terms of talk time. American Hispanics spend almost 2 hours more talking on their mobile phones than other Americans.[21] This increased use of mobile has contributed to online media consumption among American Hispanics. In 2010, 15% of Hispanic adults connected to audio online. By 2014, that share had more than doubled to 32%. Online video consumption has followed a similar path. In 2010, 22% of Hispanic adults connected to video online. In 2014, just over half (51%) of Hispanic adults did so. It is also worth pointing out that, between 2006 and 2009, online consumption of video was behind that of audio. Between 2009 and 2010, the share of Hispanic adults watching video online more than quadrupled.[22]

Language Preferences

Language is an important though somewhat controversial aspect of Hispanic media use. The size of the Hispanic audience has frequently been measured by the use of Spanish-language media.[23] However, a growing number of American Hispanics are bilingual, an important factor that impacts on media habits within this audience. Spanish-language media is not dominant across all of the American Hispanic demographic, and media preferences in Hispanic households are shaped by the language primarily used at home. In addition, Spanish-language media are less popular among U.S.-born Hispanics than among foreign-born Hispanics.[24]

During the 2009–2010 TV season, Nielsen found that homes speaking Spanish primarily viewed nearly 80% of their TV content in Spanish while half of the TV content viewed in bilingual homes was in Spanish. Households where English is the primary language spent 3% of their viewing time watching Spanish-language TV.[25] Spanish-dominant Hispanics spend more time listening to radio each week than English-dominant Hispanics. Spanish-dominant radio listeners aged 18–49 devote just over 13 hours listening to the radio each week, compared to just under 12 hours for English-dominant radio listeners.[26]

Language also plays a role in the digital habits of American Hispanics. English-dominant Hispanics are more likely than either bilingual Hispanics or Spanish-dominant Hispanics to use social media platforms. When using social media, English is the most widely used language among American Hispanics. Among Hispanic social media users, 60% primarily use English, compared to 29% who use Spanish mostly and 11% who use both languages equally.[27]

Vocabulary Words

Affiliates	Sweeps
Circulation	Telenovelas
Readership	Viewership

Points to Remember

- Newspaper circulation and readership are declining among American Hispanics.
- Television viewing is becoming more diverse among Hispanic audiences with Telemundo and Azteca gaining in audience while Univision has seen slight declines.
- Hispanic millennials listen to radio more and are more likely to listen to mainstream formats than their older counterparts.

- Hispanic adults are heavier mobile users than other Americans, for app, web, audio, video, and talking.
- Hispanics use social media at similar rates to others but prefer Instagram to Pinterest and are less likely to use LinkedIn than other groups.

Names to Remember

Big Four Networks (ABC, NBC, CBS, and FOX)
Facebook
Instagram
Nielsen
Pew Research Center
Telemundo
TV Azteca
Twitter
Univision

Practice Questions

1   What is the relationship between local and network Hispanic TV viewership?
2   How does language influence media habits in American Hispanic households?
3   How are Hispanic millennials influencing both the Hispanic and general American radio landscape?
4   How is mobile use related to digital and social media use among American Hispanics?
5   Why is measuring the audience for Spanish-language media an inaccurate way to estimate the size of the Hispanic audience?

Activity

In groups of two or three, choose one of the top five Hispanic markets in the country. Then, look up demographic information about each city using American Factfinder (factfinder.census.gov). To do this, enter the name of a city into the search bar. When results come back, select "Origins and language" to the left to see information about race and ethnicity, place of origin, and language use. What percentage of that city is Hispanic or Latino? What proportion speaks primarily English at home? What proportion is foreign-born? Now, choose another one of these markets and look up the same information. What differences and similarities would you expect to find in media use among Hispanics in these two cities? For example, in which would Spanish-language media be expected to be more popular? In which city would we expect traditional Hispanic radio formats to be less popular?

Timeline

1962: Univision was established.

2010: 22% of Hispanic adults connected to video online and 15% to audio online.

2011: Hispanics spent approximately 15 hours listening to radio per week.

2013: Newspapers began to see a steady decline in readership nationally.

2014: *La Opinión* declined 10% in daily circulation from 2013. Hispanic adults connected to audio online increased to 32%.

2015: Hispanic population reached 56 million, accounting for 18% of the U.S. population. *La Opinión* declined 13% in circulation, more than the average 6.7% of other newspapers. Meanwhile, twenty-five Hispanic weeklies and semi-weeklies increased about 2% from 2014.

TV Azteca reaches a viewership of over 21 million from 2014. Univision viewership has decreased from 1,654,000 in 2013 to 1,540,000 in 2015. On the other hand, Telemundo viewership increased from 585,000 to 729,000.

Weekly radio listening among Hispanics increases to an average of 13 hours.

Approximately 80% of Hispanic adults said they used the internet, a similar statistic to other racial groups: white Americans (85%) and black Americans (78%).

2016: Hispanic radio audience grows by 11% from 2011.

Additional Resources

Alliance for Audited Media: http://auditedmedia.com/
Medialife Magazine: www.medialifemagazine.com/
The Nielsen Company, Reports: www.nielsen.com/us/en/insights.html
Pew Research Center, Hispanic Trends: www.pewhispanic.org/
Pew Research Center, Journalism & Media: www.journalism.org/

About the Author

Jessica Mahone, Ph.D., is the Research Associate for the Public Square Program at Democracy Fund, where she previously worked as a Research Fellow. Prior to rejoining Democracy Fund, she worked as a temporary Research Associate in journalism at Pew Research Center and as a research assistant for the News Measures Research Project at Duke University. Her primary research interests are

Jessica Mahone

Photo courtesy of Jessica Mahone

diversity in news media and the role of news and information in civic engagement. Her work has been published in *Mass Communication and Society*, *Newspaper Research Journal*, *Journal of Sports Media*, and the book *Presidential Campaigning and Social Media: An Analysis of the 2012 Campaign*. Jessica has a Ph.D. in mass communication, specializing in political communication, from the University of Florida, M.A.s in communication and sociology from East Tennessee State University, and a B.A. in religion from King College.

Notes

1 "American Fact Finder," *United States Census Bureau*, July 1, 2016, https://factfinder. census.gov/faces/nav/jsf/pages/index.xhtml.

2 Antonio Flores, "Statistical Portrait of Hispanics in the United States," *Pew Research Center, Hispanic Trends*, September 15, 2015, www.pewhispanic.org/2016/04/19/ statistical-portrait-of-hispanics-in-the-united-states-key-charts.

3 Jens Manuel Krogstad and Ana González-Barrera, "A Majority of English-Speaking Hispanics in the U.S. are Bilingual," *Pew Research Center, Fact Tank*, March 24, 2015, www.pewresearch.org/fact-tank/2015/03/24/a-majority-of-english-speaking-hispanics-in-the-u-s-are-bilingual.

4 Eileen Patten, "The Nation's Latino Population is Defined by its Youth," *Pew Research Center, Fact Tank*, April 20, 2016, www.pewhispanic.org/2016/04/20/the-nations-latino-population-is-defined-by-its-youth.

5 Editors of *Medialife Magazine*, "Truth is, Hispanics Use Media Very Differently," *Medialife Magazine*, July 20, 2016, www.medialifemagazine.com/hispanics-use-media-differently.

6 Mark Hugo López and Ana González-Barrera, "A Growing Share of Latinos Get Their News in English: IV. Watching, Reading, and Listening to the News," *Pew Research Center*, July 23, 2013, www.pewhispanic.org/2013/07/23/iv-watching-reading-and-listening-to-the-news/

7 "State of the News Media 2015," *Pew Research Center*, April 29, 2015, www. journalism.org/files/2015/04/FINAL-STATE-OF-THE-NEWS-MEDIA1.pdf.

8 "State of the News Media 2016. Hispanic Media Fact Sheet," *Pew Research Center*, June 15, 2016, www.journalism.org/2016/06/15/hispanic-media-fact-sheet.

9 Ibid.

10 Toni Fitzgerald, "A Surprise Winner in the July Sweeps," *Medialife Magazine*, July 29, 2013, www.medialifemagazine.com/a-surprise-winner-in-the-july-sweeps.

11 Anna Marie de la Fuente, "Azteca America Expands Programming Slate as Ratings Improve," *Variety*, April 12, 2016, http://variety.com/2016/tv/news/azteca-america-ratings-upfront-growth-ratings-1201751230.

12 "Local Television Market Universe Estimates: Hispanic or Latino TV Homes," *Nielsen*, September 26, 2015, www.nielsen.com/content/dam/corporate/us/en/ public%20factsheets/tv/2014-2015%20DMA%20RANKS%20Hispanic.pdf.

13 "State of the News Media 2016. Hispanic Media Fact Sheet."

14 "The Latino Listener: How do Hispanics Tune in to the Radio?" *Nielsen*, January 25, 2016, www.nielsen.com/us/en/insights/news/2016/the-latino-listener-how-do-hispanics-tune-in-to-the-radio.html.

15 "Tops of 2015: Audio," *Nielsen*, December 17, 2015, www.nielsen.com/us/en/ insights/news/2015/tops-of-2015-audio.html.

16 Lee Davis, "Think You Know What Hispanic Millennials Are Listening To? Think Again," November 4, 2015, https://corporate.univision.com/blog/demographics-

culture/2015/11/04/think-you-know-what-hispanic-millennials-are-listening-to-think-again.

17 "The Latino Listener: How do Hispanics Tune in to the Radio?"

18 Andrew Perrin and Maeve Duggan, "Americans' Internet Access: 2000–2015," *Pew Research Center*, June 26, 2015, www.pewinternet.org/2015/06/26/americans-internet-access-2000–2015/#internet-usage-by-raceethnicity.

19 Jens Manuel Krogstad, "Social Media Preferences Vary by Race and Ethnicity," *Pew Research Center, Fact Tank*, February 3, 2015, www.pewresearch.org/fact-tank/2015/02/03/social-media-preferences-vary-by-race-and-ethnicity.

20 Amanda Lenhart, "Mobile Access Shifts Social Media Use and Other Online Activities," *Pew Research Center*, April 9, 2015, www.pewinternet.org/2015/04/09/mobile-access-shifts-social-media-use-and-other-online-activities.

21 "U.S. Hispanics are Super Mobile, Super Consumers," *Nielsen*, September 14, 2015, www.nielsen.com/us/en/insights/news/2015/us-hispanics-are-super-mobile-super-consumers.html.

22 Ibid.

23 Jake Beniflah and Brian Hughes, "Is There a Better Way to Measure the U.S. Hispanic Television Audience?" *Mediapost*, September 15, 2015, www.mediapost.com/publications/article/258362/is-there-a-better-way-to-measure-the-us-hispanic.html.

24 Ibid.

25 "Three Things You Thought You Knew About U.S. Hispanics' Engagement with Media . . . and Why You May Be Wrong," *Nielsen*, April, 2011, www.nielsen.com/content/dam/corporate/us/en/newswire/uploads/2011/04/Nielsen-Hispanic-Media-US.pdf.

26 "Local Television Market Universe Estimates: Hispanic or Latino TV Homes."

27 "Closing the Digital Divide: Latinos and Technology Adoption, VI. Social Networking," *Pew Research Center*, March 7, 2013, www.pewhispanic.org/2013/03/07/vi-social-networking.

11 Tapping into Hispanic/ LatinX Buying Power

An Overview of Hispanic Marketing and Advertising in the U.S.

Sindy Chapa, Ph.D.

Director of the Center for Hispanic Marketing Communication, Florida State University

As the **buying power** of Hispanics in the U.S. continues to grow, the role of Hispanic marketing has become more visible and important for companies who want to connect with their consumers beyond demographics.[1] Marketers need to realize that strategic marketing communication is about creating customized campaigns that can facilitate the connection between brands and customers on an emotional level.[2] Data alone is not sufficient to inspire great ideas in Hispanic marketing communication. Cultural insights, on the other hand, and a deep understanding of the values shared by Hispanics can build emotional connections. This chapter provides a general overview of the Hispanic marketing industry and advertising in the U.S. It provides an introduction to the history of Hispanic marketing in the U.S., its market segments, and some concepts and examples of cultural values, meanings, and expressions recognized in Hispanic-targeted advertising. Finally, it provides some cases of culturally attuned campaigns, along with some recommendations for strategic planning.

Introduction to the Hispanic Marketing Industry

Marketing communication represents the voice of a brand and the means created by marketers to inform, educate, persuade, stimulate, and remind consumers as well as resonate with them.[3] The brand's positioning message, as well as its advertising format, appeal, design, and execution across communication platforms, should reflect the nature and culture of the consumers.[4] A clear understanding of the target market is extremely important in the selection of these basic aspects of marketing communication to elicit a positive and memorable response. Hispanic marketing in the U.S. was driven and developed by renowned individuals who were able to provide knowledge in practice, such as Felipe Korzenny, Tere Zubizarreta, Lionel Sosa, Roberto Orci, Ernest Bromley, Alex Lopez Negrete, Emilio Nicolas, and Rene Anselmo, among others.

In the late 1970s, Felipe Korzenny, who is originally from Mexico, began his doctoral studies at Michigan State University. This was the start of a lifelong quest for a better understanding of Hispanic consumers. With the unexpected Latino population growth in the 1980s, his research-based knowledge and real-world experience with the Hispanic consumer gained recognition. As a result, he was consulted by brands such as Procter & Gamble, General Foods, and other Fortune 1000 companies. The high demand for his expertise among America's corporations drove Korzenny to open the first Hispanic marketing research firm in 1984, called Hispanic Marketing Research. The firm later became the Hispanic & Asian Marketing Communication Research Co. in 1987. His trend-setting research, oriented to obtain insights specifically from Hispanic consumers, was the first of its kind in the marketing communication discipline. Through the firm's research process, meaningful knowledge, and insights based on culture were developed expressly to appeal to the Hispanic consumer. Based on this work, Korzenny was able to lead companies and advertising agencies to advance marketing strategies in this newly developed area of consumer practice. At the time, Korzenny referred to this discipline as "Hispanic marketing" in his publications. Today, his contributions are the foundation for the field. **Hispanic marketing** refers to the planning, development, and practice of marketing programs geared to connect with Hispanic markets by means of consumer insights. These insights are tied to their socio-psychographics and Hispanic cultural heritage—which includes social norms, manners, customs, myths, religion, interpersonal communication forms, social structures, and language.[5]

In 1999, Korzenny merged his company with Cheskin, a global strategic research and consulting firm, to provide integrated services in the U.S., as well as throughout Latin America and several Asian countries.[6] After a long and successful consulting career, Korzenny returned to academia in 2003 at Florida State University (FSU). In the same year, he finished his Hispanic marketing book *Hispanic Marketing: A Cultural Perspective*, co-authored with his wife Betty Ann Korzenny. His book became the first college-required book in multicultural and Hispanic-related courses, as well as for corporate training programs across the U.S. In 2004, Korzenny created the Center for Hispanic Marketing Communication at FSU, the first Center in the U.S. devoted to the study of Hispanic insight-driven strategies.[7]

Korzenny's contributions have served to define the practice of Hispanic marketing and also to underscore the importance of strategic insights in the dispute of localization versus **adaptation-standardization** in internal markets. His catchphrase, "all marketing is cultural,"[8] has served to explain the internal-localization approach of marketing strategies around the globe. The **internal-localization** approach deals with the idea of localization within markets, particularly among multi-diversified markets such as the U.S. The idea that any standardized campaign can produce the same results across all market segments is inconceivable. That is akin to saying that an English-language ad can simply be aired on Univision, a Spanish-language TV network, and produce similar results as those received by the same ad aired in the general market.

A Trailblazing Industry

While Korzenny's contributions defined the modern era of Hispanic marketing, the history of market adaptation and the Hispanic community within the U.S. dates back to the nineteenth century. Previously, the U.S. Hispanic marketing industry experienced several developmental phases rooted in the adoption of Spanish-language media. For instance, the first Spanish newspaper originated in 1808 with the establishment of *El Misisipí* in New Orleans, Louisiana.[9] The main purpose of this periodical was to inform the Hispanic community about political and legal issues such as identification documents for newcomers, and deportation cases, as well as job opportunities. The creation of *El Misisipí* was genuinely to serve the Latino community. However, over the years, selling space for advertising was needed to make the newspaper sustainable. This brought the newspaper from being simply a community resource to being one that more closely models the modern-day structure of media outlets, where the ad space sold is equally important as the news reported.

In the late 1920s, more than a century after the creation of the *Misisipí*, English-language radio stations also got in on the marketing of media ad space to Hispanics by starting to sell the "off hours" blocks of time to on-air brokers. The on-air brokers then used these times to air Spanish-language programing. The Spanish time slots were usually early in the mornings, between 4 and 6 a.m. As more and more listeners tuned in, the Spanish-language time turned out to be a prime-time slot. To cash in, enterprising companies such as Folgers, which became the first sponsor of Spanish radio programming, began to recognize the high impact of Spanish-language radio programming and the new opportunities it created. By the 1930s, Spanish-language radio blocks were transformed and their popularity bolstered as a way to communicate with Hispanic communities. As its popularity continued to grow, a few years later, in 1946, the first full-time Spanish-language radio station KCOR-AM was created in San Antonio, Texas.[10]

Following the establishment of the Spanish-language radio station was the first Spanish-language TV station KWEX-TV in San Antonio, Texas, in 1955. Emilio Nicolas, along with Rene Anselmo and Emilio Azcarraga of Mexico's Televisa, created the Spanish International Communication Corp (SICC), which, after several transformations, later became known as Univision.[11] With the proliferation of Spanish-language media, corporations and brands had a new thirst for connecting with Hispanics, but this presented new challenges as well. These challenges opened the doorway for the establishment of marketing agencies specializing in the Hispanic market.

The first Hispanic-owned advertising agency was established in Miami. Tere Zubizarreta, a Cuban refugee, founded Zubi Advertising in 1976. Simultaneously, other Hispanics began to stand out and make significant contributions to the field along with Zubizarreta, but it was not until few years later that some of them were able to follow her example and operate independently. One of these new pioneers was George San Jose who, in 1981, founded The San Jose Group (SJG) in Chicago, the second Hispanic-owned advertising agency in the U.S. To further this trend, in Texas, both Hispanic and non-Hispanic entrepreneurs made great efforts during the 1980s to establish more Hispanic-focused advertising shops. Certainly the most prominent among these were Sosa & Associates, founded by Lionel Sosa, and Bromley Communications, established by Ernest Bromley, both based in San Antonio. Meanwhile, on the east side of Texas was Alex Lopez Negrete, who founded Lopez Negrete Communication in his native Houston in 1985.

Finally, on the west coast, Roberto Orci founded La Agencia de Orcí in Los Angeles in 1986, which became the perfect counterpart for the agencies in Miami, Chicago, and Texas. While the industry was fairly new and growing, the establishment in 1996 of the Association of Hispanic Advertising Agencies (AHAA), also founded by Orci, cemented Hispanic marketing as a permanent component of the communications industry. The purpose of this association was to strengthen the efforts of advertising agencies and other associates who cater their services to Hispanic consumers. With the establishment of this trade organization, it became apparent that appealing to the Hispanic market was a necessity, not a passing trend.[12]

As Hispanic marketing grew in prominence, mainstream U.S. culture began to recognize the contributions of this trailblazing industry. In 2015, the Smithsonian National Museum of American History added the collection "Hispanic Advertising History," featuring the pioneering work of the first

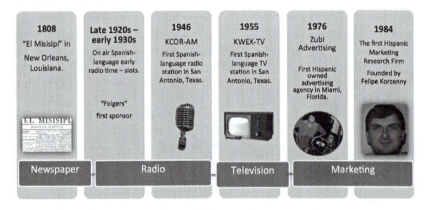

Figure 11.1 The rise of Hispanic media from 1808 to 1984.

Sindy Chapa

Hispanic advertising agencies in the U.S. Books, too, are recognizing the historical contributions of these agencies, including Felipe Korzenny's latest Hispanic marketing book, *Hispanic Marketing: The Power of the New Latino Consumer*, which is used in many marketing programs throughout the U.S., and where the author provides both a history of the industry and a comprehensive list of today's advertising agencies focusing on Hispanics. It is important to mention that most of these agencies are members of the AHAA and a similar list can be found in its website, www.ahaa.org.

Hispanic Market Segmentation

Successful marketing communication strategies must be based on market segmentation.[13] Although Hispanic consumers share some cultural values and a language, they are not part of a homogenous market. They comprise a diverse group of immigrants and U.S.-born Hispanics whose ancestry can be traced to many different countries of origin, each with a unique migration history, varied education levels, shopping patterns, and language proficiencies and preferences. Therefore, the approach to Hispanic segmentation must go beyond one-size-fits-all socio-psycho-demographics. The segmentation must also include consumer characteristics related to their culture of origin, language, acculturation, and their whole American experience.[14]

Labels and Identities

The identification of Hispanic or Latino can be subjective.[15] What is important is to understand how consumers feel about themselves. Some labels used by the consumer can be traced to their country of origin, such as Puerto Rican, Mexican, Colombian, Cuban, and other Hispanic nationalities. If born in the U.S., they might add their heritage to the American label, such as Mexican-American, Cuban-American, or simply identify with the Hispanic or Latino label. These nationality-based self-descriptors seem to indicate that the individual using them feels the people of that country are his or her closest cultural reference group. Still, other labels used by Hispanics were created out of political movements, pride, or trends such as Chicanos, Nuyorican, Tex-Mex, and Floridians.

Chicano, for instance, can be used by someone whose primary reference group is that of Mexican origin but who feels they are not Mexican or American, but have a new identity born from both.[16] The label was introduced during the 1960s Chicano civil movement, which favored equality and unification of Mexican-origin individuals.[17] Mexican-Americans make up over 10% of the entire U.S. population, with over 31 million members. They are the largest Hispanic group, representing 70% of the Hispanics in the U.S.[18] However, because of the political and sometimes hostile atmosphere of the Chicano movement, not all Mexican-Americans feel connected with this label.[19]

Nuyorican is a term that refers to Americans of Puerto Rican ancestry who settled primarily in New York, but have now dispersed throughout America. Some who do not feel connected with the term Nuyorican like to be called *Boricuas*.[20] Regardless of their labels, Puerto Ricans are the second largest Hispanic group in the United States, with an estimated 5.37 million people in 2015. They represent 9.5% of the Hispanic market and 1.7% of the U.S. population (excluding the island Puerto Rico).[21]

Tejanos (Texans in Spanish) historically has been a term used to refer to Mexicans living in Texas. In the 1990s, the term was reborn with the internationalization of Tex-Mex food and Tejano music.[22] The proliferation of the Tejano culture brought the Mexican-American community a sense of pride. In addition, the tragic death of the singer Selena in 1995, with the subsequent outpouring of mainstream media coverage and eventually a Hollywood film about her life, added to a sense of unity.[23] It is within this context that Mexican descendants living in Texas formed the new identity tied to Tex-Mex culture. It is important to acknowledge here that, even though this group shares cultural commonalities with Chicanos in California and/or Chicanos in Chicago or elsewhere, Chicanos in Texas feel they are not the same. Some of these Texan Hispanics might not even like to be called Chicanos, but Tejanos.[24]

Floridian Hispanics are the most diverse group of Hispanics. Approximately 29% of all Hispanics in Florida are of Cuban descent, and they are primarily found around south Florida in the Miami to Tampa geographical area.[25] The second largest group with the most influence in Florida is Puerto Ricans. In the last century, a large group of Puerto Ricans migrated from their home territory to New York City, New Jersey, Chicago, Philadelphia, and Boston in the U.S. Nowadays, Florida has become the new destination for many Puerto Ricans, making this shift the fastest growing population in the U.S.[26] Finally, the third group in terms of magnitude in Florida is of Mexican descent. This populace is followed by a diverse (37%) mix of people from other Hispanic countries in Central America and South America. Florida is an interesting case in terms of marketing. Because of its heterogeneity, marketing messages attuned to Mexican culture, for instance, do not necessarily resonate with all Floridian Hispanics.

For marketing communication purposes, in fact, Korzenny advises that marketers should focus on what a label means to each consumer. He suggests that, if the consumer takes great pride in a label, such as being Hispanic or Tejano, then using the term in marketing communications may be emotionally evocative and, therefore, more effective. In many cases, however, Korzenny claims "the label should not be used at all because there is more of a risk to alienate individuals who do not feel the label is accurate or appropriate."[27] He says that what matters are the symbols and cultural manifestations that are used as references to the group. When the consumer makes purchase decisions these conscious and subconscious indicators may have a greater impact than the label one has attached to their culture or themselves. Therefore, recognizing all the nuances and lifestyle characteristics tied to each group is important, but the use of labels is not.

Language Preference and Acculturation Levels

In addition to the socio-psycho-demographics and the attributes related to a country or origin or label, language proficiency and acculturation are other approaches utilized by marketers for Hispanic segmentation. Korzenny's framework suggests one approach, **linear segmentation**, which is based on the language of preference and works by identifying consumers as Spanish-dominant, transitional, and English-dominant. While language can be a very important communication consideration, in addition to this there are other factors that influence how people behave. Specifically, it is paramount to also look at Hispanics' level of acculturation.

Korzenny defines acculturation as the process of "how groups and individuals orient themselves to and deal with the new culture contact and change."[28] From the acculturation process, two outcomes are expected: either assimilation

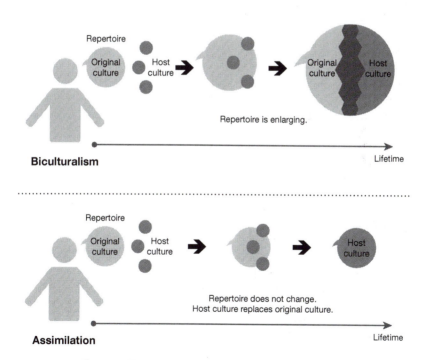

Figure 11.2 Difference of biculturalism and assimilation and its effect on the identity of an individual.

Sindy Chapa

with the new culture or conversion to biculturalism. Assimilation means that an individual absorbs the new culture and incorporates him or herself into it, losing his/her attachment to their original culture, and, therefore, adopting the values of the host culture.[29] **Biculturalism**, on the other hand, means that an individual's values attached to their country of origin are not lost, but his or her repertoire of values, attitudes, and traditions is enlarged to integrate their original culture and their host culture. As displayed in Figure 11.2, biculturalism brings both cultures together, creating at this intersection a new bicultural identity in the individual. Here, Hispanics could keep their original culture, while adding elements of the second culture to their repertoire. Assimilation, on the other hand, would mean abandoning their original culture in favor of the second culture, or claiming a new label, as was discussed at the beginning of this section.

Culture and Advertising

Once the target market has been clearly identified and consumer insights attained, marketers must explore the best way to connect. According to Marieke de Mooij,[30] researcher and author of several publications on advertising and culture, there are three facets of the message that should be considered in light of cultural influences: (1) the core values and motivational drivers used in the advertising appeal; (2) the basic advertising form guided by a low-context or high-context communication style; and (3) the execution of the ad in relation to language and the implementation elements of the culture.

Core Values as Motivators

Values can be defined as deeper internal guides that mediate the relationship between the person and the world in the social context.[31] These values provide insights with regard to consumer beliefs and attitudes that, in turn, help marketers to differentiate between Hispanics and other groups of consumers. The following discussion emphasizes Hispanic-focused values, beliefs, perceptions, and orientations that may impact advertising.

Collectivist orientation—Studies show Hispanic societies lean toward **collectivism**, which is why family and the group as a whole are considered more important in the consumer's decision-making process than the sole individual.[32] Advertising appeals that include the product or brand benefits that apply to the whole group can be more motivational to Hispanics in general than those enhancing the benefits for a single person. For instance, the 2015 Wells Fargo Souvenir TV commercial uses as its main message "You work hard for more than just you. Working together we'll help you save for her (the main character's daughter) future biology degree—Wells Fargo together we'll go far."[33] Here, the main emphasis is to educate the consumer on how families as a whole can benefit from the services provided by the company. Whereas a

Landing the Dream Job

by Eduardo Lowe
Graphic Artist

It's a beautiful Florida morning in September 2015. "It's time for a change," I said to myself after working 10 years in Tampa. The inner hunger that one day you awaken with, a feeling of believing in yourself and re-prioritizing what makes you happy in life. To me, passion has been always in editorial (magazines), aviation, and traveling. I didn't mind if I had to move out of Tampa and sell my house and most of my belongings. That is how committed I was.

So I began an online search in larger U.S. cities for an Art Director job. I couldn't believe my eyes. An opening for a Bilingual Art Director at American Airlines NEXOS magazine was available in Miami. You have to understand that when I was in my teens, living in Panama (Central America) and came to Tampa, Florida, to visit my grandma and aunt on vacations every year, we would always fly American Airlines. So it was natural for me to grab all the magazine in the front pocket of my seat and read them. I fell in love with NEXOS ever since, and I remember saying: "One day, I will work here!"

Yes, I applied . . . and, after a very intense and long interview process, I became the Art Director at NEXOS. I wouldn't have gotten the job if it weren't for my family values, passion, education, and an impeccable professional experience. This comes to a more profound level than any other job I've had. It was my dream job.

Figure 11.3 Eduardo Lowe
Photo by Mark DeLong

more mainstream U.S. commercial may focus on helping the individual reach their personal financial goals, this approach appeals to the nature of the Hispanic consumer whose satisfaction is typically derived from being able to contribute to the financial security of the whole group, or in this case, their family. Other companies use similar appeals. For instance, a more explicit or tangible approach is the one used by AT&T, which focuses on the *family share plan*. In this case, AT&T makes it evident that the company is tailoring their services for family benefits. Although this plan is available marketwide, this approach would be one that Hispanics may find particularly appealing based on their cultural characteristics.

Masculine orientation—In masculine-oriented cultures, males are dominant and a significant portion of the power structure in society tends to be dedicated to and controlled by males. As a result, the orientation of the community is predominantly characterized by masculine traits such as the desire for competition and accomplishment. Feminine-oriented cultures are expected to be more modest and nurturing, aspects typically associated with the idea of femininity. Hispanic communities (countries) rank medium to high in their masculine tendencies.[34] Therefore, culturally, Hispanics are more drawn to messages that communicate success, competition, and achievements. The TECATE series of TV ads, *"Por lo Que Quieren Mas"* (For those who want more), for example, appeals to these masculine traits among Hispanics. The ads, using a humorous appeal, showcase a series of challenges, obstacles, and funny creative solutions, which suggest that use of the product can successfully prolong the

Figure 11.4 The 2015 Wells Fargo Souvenir TV commercial featured a father saving for his daughter's education.

Photo courtesy of actor Ariel Suarez

consumers' good times. The focus in these spots is on portraying a masculine hero, a "man's man," who not only reinforces his and the consumer's masculinity by use of the product, but also connects the U.S. Hispanic consumer to his Mexican roots.

Power distance and social status-oriented—The level of **power distance** in most Hispanic countries is medium/high. This means the members of the culture perceive a social class differentiation.[35] Hispanics are highly aware of their social class status. This information can be used to accentuate the desire to be part of a higher social class or reinforce positively viewed class standing. A good example of a message that takes advantage of high power distance is that of Dos Equis Beer with their "The Most Interesting Man" campaign. This campaign, while humorously tongue-in-cheek, still appeals to aspirational traits such as elegance, distinction, attractiveness, and sophistication. It connects social class and status with the consumption of the product, adding value to the brand through consumers' desire to be like the main character.

Indulgence and instant gratification—Hispanic countries' level of indulgence is regularly higher than the level reported in the U.S. Unlike the Puritan vein that runs through much of mainstream U.S. culture, wherein "work now, play later" is more of the norm, Hispanics prefer to engage in enjoyment and fun more immediately. This trait arises from Hispanics' perception that God controls their destiny and that the future is not in their hands. This, therefore, drives them to enjoy life in the moment, not counting on future rewards. Based on this, messages of instant access to enjoyment and pleasure appeal to Hispanics.

Fatalism and Spirituality—As previously mentioned, Hispanics share a strong belief in the supernatural and tend to accept that God controls everything.[36] Therefore, they are likely to attribute everything to destiny. This being the case, marketers should not highlight product benefits that suggest the consumer ultimately can control all of life's events,[37] but instead use arguments that focus on family, success, status, and enjoyment. State Farm's "For Every One of Those Moments" series of ads, for instance, focuses on accidents that can happen to any consumer. The English-language version of the ads ends with the tagline "*To Help Life Go Right.*" The tagline of the Spanish-language ads, on the other hand, is "*Aqui Para Ayudar a Que Te Vaya bien en la Vida*" (helping life go well). Generally, Hispanics do not believe in accidents, but in destiny. They often accept that bad things happen and believe that they are supposed to happen. Therefore, they are not looking for anyone to blame nor have a need "to make it right." Instead, when dealing with unfortunate events, a message of solidarity and support appeals perfectly.

Culture and a High-Context Communication Form

Beyond the cultural values that a target populace holds, de Mooij suggests that advertising forms can be guided by understanding the role of low-context and high-context communication styles. Edward Hall, in his book *Beyond Culture*,[38] indicates that **low-context communication** specifies explicit forms of communication—everything is clear, either verbally or in writing, and non-members of the community can easily understand the message. In **high-context communication** cultures—which are believed to be mostly Asian, Arab, and Hispanic cultures—it is posited that individuals place most of their communicational meaning within context. This means that the communication form can be either explicit or implicit, and that it is mostly hard to decode or interpret by the non-members of the community. The connotation, for example, of cultural nuances, symbols, and traditions can produce a high effect on consumers who can understand the message, but might prove almost impossible to interpret by a non-member of the community. For example, a TECATE beer ad geared to Mexican-Americans used the regional phrase *"Por Los Que No Se Rajan."* *Rajan* (plural) in Spanish can literally mean to cut or speak badly of a person. However, in this context it means "for the brave ones." This message, therefore, has little meaning or resonance with non-Mexican-Americans or non-Hispanic groups. Because of their traits of communication, Hispanics gravitate to stories in context with explicit or implicit elements. Korzenny calls these elements intangible and tangible manifestations of culture.

Execution of Advertising

Examples of explicit or tangible manifestations of the Hispanic culture are also found in the language, music, food, customary attire (folklore, quinceañeras, mariachi), and religious artifacts, among others. Some intangible but implicit manifestations of culture are apparent in elements related to the core values discussed earlier, such as masculinity, status, and spirituality. Coupled with this are the social manners, customs, and myths unknown by non-Hispanics. According to Korzenny, the reason these elements of culture, whether explicit or implicit, are still important even once they are no longer functionally necessary is that they continue to have emotional value for a long time. This can be readily seen in the positive reception of **Spanglish**, or code-switching, in advertising. Whereas many Hispanics fully understand and fluently speak English, the use of the Spanish language connects with consumers to an emotional level. Spanish is no longer required by the consumer, but it is desired.

A good example of a campaign that employs explicit and implicit manifestations of cultures to activate and engage young Hispanics is the FORD Fantastical Adventure digital series. The campaign, called *"Las Fantasticas Aventuras del Focus 2015,"* was created by Zubi Advertising. It consisted of a series of digital videos, along with user-generated content. Here, the purpose was to connect with younger Hispanic Millennials, in the 18–24 age range, in an entertaining and interactive way using new media (Tumblr, Facebook, Twitter, Univision, Hulu, and more). The strategy was to inspire the audience to create stories for FORD. The stories, produced in collaboration with the audience, focused on traditional and familiar Hispanic cues (e.g., *piñatas,*

Inspired by My Roots

by Veronica Garrote
Fashion Stylist

When you live in a city that is painted so beautifully with lush tropical foliage, pastel art deco buildings, and gorgeous aqua waters, it's difficult not to get inspired when working in fashion. The visual aspects of living in Miami are quite captivating, but it's the culture and heartbeat of the Hispanic community that truly runs through my veins after living in this city for over 30 years. My career as a fashion stylist has been molded and influenced directly by my Cuban heritage and the lifestyle that has surrounded me from a young age.

Opening my portfolio, you will see a wide array of photo shoots and videos I have worked on. Through these images, you get a sense of my style; colorful bracelets stacked to mid arm, the layered gold jewelry, and a love of color, all show a piece of me that is influenced by my environment, heritage, and interests. My background influences my work and aesthetic, but these are not the only things that are taken into account when styling for a shoot. Yes, it's important as a stylist to put your personal style into your work, but it's also important to listen to the client's needs and help make a vision become reality through clothing,

Figure 11.5 Veronica Garrote
Photo courtesy of Veronica Garrote

shoes, and accessories. Working as a fashion stylist you must have the ability to help create a story. This is something a stylist does not only do when working on fashion editorials for magazines, but also when styling actors and models for advertising campaigns and commercial shoots.

Fashion editorials incorporate current trends and a lot of creativity to tell a story. For example, an editorial I styled for a magazine wanted the clothing to match graffiti art that decorated the walls of the Miami Marine Stadium. When pulling the wardrobe, I had to reference the artists' work and tie in color, shapes, and texture to match the art, in addition to having clothing on trend, in season, and able to fit the model's body. You also have to incorporate what will translate well on camera and when the pictures are all side by side, the images should be able to tell a story. During that shoot, it was not only the art that inspired me, but also the historic Miami Marine Stadium, a staple in my city.

When working on advertising campaigns, catalogs, or commercial shoots, fashion can be used to sell a dream or certain lifestyle. When working as a stylist for a major beverage company that was gearing a soccer-themed advertisement toward Latin America, I was required to dress the talent in extreme soccer fan gear. The client wanted the talent to look like they were hardcore soccer fans having the best time at their favorite sporting event, all while drinking the advertised beverage. The wardrobe needed to convey that these were devoted soccer enthusiasts from Latin America. I had to incorporate appropriate clothing styles, certain team colors, sports fan accessories, such as colored wigs, beaded necklaces, flags, and colored jewelry to get that message across. It was helpful that living in Miami I have seen this type of style worn during events that showcase the soccer culture of Latin America.

It doesn't matter what kind of shoot a stylist is working on, their personal style and aesthetic always influences their work. The best part about being a stylist is being able to take a little bit of who I am and transcend that into different photo shoots. No matter how big or small the project, as a stylist you always need to find a way to tell a story.

quinceañera, *machos*, *luchadores*, drama queens, etc.) and implicit manifestations of the Hispanic values, such as loyalty, spirituality, and masculinity. Through this collaborative effort and the marketing team's understanding of the power of explicit and implicit cultural artifacts, the campaign connected in a more personal and relevant way with young Hispanic Millennials. Therefore, the campaign was able to "cut through the noise" of so many brands in the media landscape trying to grab the attention of this particular audience.

The Spanish-language media landscape and the media behaviors of Hispanics have evolved rapidly. The FORD interactive campaign in 2015 is just one example of how this transformation can inspire marketers to try new means of product placement, sponsorship, consumer engagement, and advertising. The increased number of bilingual and English-dominant Hispanics has also changed the conversation around how to reach Hispanics. In many cases, appealing to Hispanics requires more than solely Spanish-language media, a mainstay of past Hispanic marketing. In the FORD *"Las Fantasticas Aventuras del Focus 2015"* campaign, both English- and Spanish-language platforms were utilized. Here one can clearly observe that it is not the utilitarian aspect of Spanish that makes the use of the language important. It is the emotional value that makes the difference. The context can guide the marketer to decide which language to use and/or how.

In a further example, the Nestlé Nescafé Case Study illustrates the executions of traditional and non-traditional advertising focusing on cultural values communicated in context—explicitly and implicitly.

Nescafé *"Make the Moment Happen"* Case Study

The Nescafé brand wanted to create an experiential campaign for digital and social media that appealed to Latinos. Representatives from the Nescafé brand hit the busy streets of Miami, Florida, with an odd yet simple question, "Would you share a coffee with a stranger?" Stopping everyone they could, they asked this question over and over again looking for answers. To no one's surprise the overwhelming response was "no." While these replies were nothing out the ordinary there were a few brave souls who replied "yes" to this question. These participants were then led to a secluded area and asked to have a seat and await the mysterious stranger they had agreed to share a cup of coffee with. Suddenly the stranger was revealed and to every participant's surprise, the stranger was Ricky Martin! Elated and shocked participants greeted Martin with hugs, handshakes, and stunned expressions on their faces. Nescafé had cups showcasing the company name holding freshly prepared Nescafé coffee for the participants and Martin to sip as they enjoyed each other's company.

Obviously the goal of this experiential marketing tactic was to draw in the target audience by using a celebrity endorsement. Ricky Martin was selected because of his popularity as a successful crossover artist in both the Hispanic and mainstream American market. This campaign gave Nescafé the opportunity to become directly involved with the community and make its presence known. Although the footage of the participants interacting with Ricky Martin added fodder for the ads Nescafé was looking to create, they also came to find out they would receive so much more. While interacting with the participants, Martin agreed to take pictures that appeared on several of the participants' social media accounts. The brand gained digital recognition across multiple social channels immediately and continued to launch original content over the

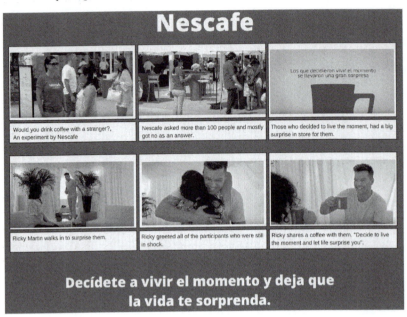

Figure 11.6 Nescafe's *Make the Moment Happen* campaign with Ricky Martin, 2014. Nescafe multicultural COE, Nestle USA. Casanova/McCann Agency

next weeks. Pictures, videos, and posts were circling the internet plugging the Nescafé brand, allowing them to reach an audience that was beyond the streets of Miami and beyond the Hispanic market Nescafé had intended to reach. The impact of the now viral campaign was huge. Choosing the right celebrity with the right amount of personality and charisma both on screen and in person was a crucial factor in this experimental advertising campaign and ultimately helped the brand to do more than they planned. Nescafé successfully utilized this experiential advertising campaign to strengthen their community presence and directly engage with their target market. The main proposition of the message is to " live life to the fullest by taking these great opportunities and seeing what comes out of them. Choose to make great moments happen!"[39]—all of these can happen when you drink Nescafé. These messages are connected with the Hispanic core values of achievement and collectivism, need for social sharing, and high indulgence for enjoyment. The high tendency of Hispanics to share on social media added a positive outcome to this campaign.[40]

Conclusion

The Hispanic marketing industry has its roots in the work of scholars and business leaders, such as Felipe Korzenny, as well as in corporate America. This was a result of the proliferation over time of the Spanish-language media in the U.S. This has made the work of Korzenny, Zubizarreta, Orci, and others essential for any company that hopes to succeed in the current and developing U.S. market as more and more Hispanic influence is felt.

For those companies seeking success, a comprehensive segmentation process for Hispanic markets is essential. Understanding cultural values is a necessity to recognize the homogeneity among varied Hispanic groups. Nevertheless, even within the populace, there is a certain amount of heterogeneity as well, and therefore, group differences are important to understand as well. Marketers must learn the significance of the context in which the message is distributed and understand the consequences of how the message is delivered.

Hispanics are more attuned to messages that can connect to them on an emotional level, yet are executed in a culturally relevant context. Hispanics' communication style allows marketers to connect through both explicit and implicit means, but a clear understanding of the culture is needed to avoid a backlash from poor or uninformed communication choices. Marketers should explore the subjectivity of the intangible elements of the Hispanic culture within segments. This exploration, in turn, will reveal Hispanics' core values, beliefs, attitudes, and perceptions, allowing communications professionals to create effective advertising appeals and executions. It is only through a thorough understanding of this diverse market that companies can ultimately "buy in" to the buying power of the Hispanic consumer.

Vocabulary Words

Adaptation-Standardization
Biculturalism
Buying Power
Collectivism
High-Context Communication
Hispanic Marketing

Internal-Localization
Linear Segmentation
Low-Context Communication
Power Distance
Spanglish
Strategic Marketing Communication

Points to Remember

- In 1984, Felipe Korzenny opened a Hispanic marketing research firm that provided unique insights about Hispanic consumers. It was the first firm to launch within the marketing communication discipline.
- In 2003, Korzenny publishes his book, *Hispanic Marketing: A Cultural Perspective*, which becomes a required text in many college multicultural and Hispanic courses and corporate training programs in the U.S.
- The Association of Hispanic Advertising Agencies (AHAA) emphasized the importance of creating advertising and providing services geared toward Hispanic consumers as it became more of a necessity rather than a trend.

- Mexicans and Puerto Ricans are the largest Hispanic groups in the U.S., accounting for 70% and 9.5% of Hispanics, respectively.
- Scholar Marieke de Mooij points out three things that should be considered in order to create more effective messages for people from different cultures: (1) core values as motivators; (2) level of communication context; and (3) execution of advertising.

Names to Remember

Alex Lopez Negrete
Emilio Nicolas
Ernest Bromley
Felipe Korzenny
Lionel Sosa
Marieke de Mooij
Roberto Orci
Tere Zubizarreta

Practice Questions

1   Who is Felipe Korzenny? Explain the kind of company that he established in 1984 and how it changed the marketing communication field.
2   What are the roots of Hispanic marketing based on? What strategy can be used to effectively target and communicate with the Hispanic market?
3   What are the labels or identities used to refer to some of the Hispanics born in the U.S.? Why were some of these labels created?
4   Explain the difference between explicit and implicit manifestations of culture.
5   How can Hispanic markets be segmented?
6   What are the core values of Hispanics and how do they influence advertising?

Activity

Advertising Research: Based on the information that you have read about Hispanic marketing and advertising, find a video advertisement that you believe is targeting a particular Hispanic market segment. When conducting your analysis, think about the different Hispanic groups you have read about in this chapter and answer the following questions:

1   Who are they trying to communicate with?
2   What is this group's country of origin?
3   Do they have any labels? If so, where did this/these label(s) originate?

Next, examine and discuss the different elements that you observed from the ad and determine the strategies used to appeal to their target audience. Do you think the brand is effective at getting their message across? What is it telling you about the brand? Did you respond positively or negatively to this ad? Explain why. Lastly, what could they have done better?

Timeline

1808: The first Hispanic newspaper, *El Misisipí*, is created.

1920s: English-language stations begin to offer off-hour blocks to on-air brokers that contain Spanish-language programming.

1946: The first Spanish-language radio, KCOR-AM, is created in San Antonio, Texas.

1976: Tere Zubizarreta establishes the first Hispanic-owned advertising agency, called Zubi Advertising, in Miami, Florida.

1981: George San Jose founds the second Hispanic-owned advertising agency, called The San Jose Group, in Chicago, Illinois.

1984: Felipe Korzenny opens the first Hispanic marketing research firm.

1985: Alex Lopez Negrete founds *Negrete Communication* in Houston, Texas.

1986: Roberto Orci founds *La Agencia de Orcí* in Los Angeles, California.

1996: The Association of Hispanic Advertising Agencies (AHAA) is created by Orci.

1999: Korzenny merges with global strategic research and consulting firm, Cheskin.

2003: Korzenny returns to academia at Florida State University (FSU) and publishes *Hispanic Marketing: A Cultural Perspective*.

2004: The Center for Hispanic Marketing Communication is created at FSU by Korzenny.

2015: A collection called *Hispanic Advertising History* is added to the Smithsonian National Museum of American History. Puerto Ricans become the second largest Hispanic group in the U.S., with approximately 5.37 million people.

Additional Resources

Matthew Harris, "Marketing to Hispanics: Why It's Not Just About Speaking Spanish," *Entrepreneur*, June 6, 2017, www.entrepreneur.com/article/295296

Felipe Korzenny, Sindy Chapa, and Betty Ann Korzenny, *Hispanic Marketing: The Power of the New Latino Consumer* (New York: Taylor & Francis, 2017).

Francisco J. Valle and Judy M. Mandel, *How to Win the Hispanic Gold Rush: Critical Cultural, Demographic, Marketing and Motivational Factors* (Lincoln, NE: iUniverse, 2003).

About the Author

Sindy Chapa, Ph.D., is the Director of the Center for Hispanic Marketing Communication at Florida State University, and co-founder/ member of the Association for Latino Media and Marketing Communication Research. Chapa has established a reputation as a scholar with an expertise in Hispanic Marketing Communication. She co-authored with Felipe and Betty Ann Korzenny the new edition of the book *Hispanic Marketing: The Power of the New Latino Consumer*. She has published numerous articles in recognized journal publications such as *Journal of Advertising Research, International Journal of Advertising, Journal of Marketing Communication*, and others. Chapa teaches courses on Hispanic marketing, advertising, and marketing communication. She thanks Liz Vidal and Carlos Galindo, who contributed to the content and development of these lines, and the Center for Hispanic Marketing Communication Advisory Board whose guidance is reflected in the cases and illustrations shared in this chapter. Finally, she thanks her husband and sons for their support.

Sindy Chapa

Photo courtesy of Sindy Chapa

Notes

1 Keith Reinhard, Chairman Emeritu at DDB Global Advertising at the Ahha Conference in Chicago in 2017.
2 Alan Cooper, Leslie Butterfield, Merry Baskin, Paul Feldwick, and Rita Clifton, *How to Plan Advertising* (Hampshire, UK: Cengage Learning EMEA, 2011).
3 "Definition of Marketing," *AMA*, June 28, 2017, www.ama.org/AboutAMA/Pages/Definition-of-Marketing.aspx.
4 Marieke de Mooij, *Global Marketing and Advertising: Understanding Cultural Paradoxes* (Los Angeles, CA: Sage, 2014).
5 Felipe Korzenny and Betty A. Korzenny, *Hispanic Marketing: Connecting with the New Latino Consumer* (New York: Routledge, 2012).
6 *Felipe Korzenny Hispanic Qualitative Research & Consulting*, "Dr. Felipe Korzenny's Bio," https://korzenny.com/?page_id=42.
7 "Center for Hispanic Marketing Communication: Home," *Florida State University Libraries: Research Guides*, http://guides.lib.fsu.edu/chmc.
8 Felipe Korzenny, Sindy Chapa, and Betty Ann Korzenny, *Hispanic Marketing: The Power of the New Latino Consumer* (Abingdon, UK: Routledge, 2017), 180.
9 Edna Negron, "The New South's Spanish Language Press Upholds Legacy of *El Misisipí*," *International Journal of Spanish Language Media*, paper presented at Latino Media and Marketing Conference, Florida State University, February 21, 2015.
10 Alan B. Albarran and Brian Hutton, "A History of Spanish Language Radio in the United States," *The Center for Spanish Language Media: The University of North Texas*, 2009, www.arbitron.com/downloads/mcl_unt_history_spanish_radio.pdf.

11 Kenton T. Wilkinson, *Spanish-Language Television in the United States: Fifty Years of Development* (New York: Routledge, 2015).

12 *AHAA*, "About AHAA," www.ahaa.org/About.

13 Kevin Lane Keller, "Building Strong Brands in a Modern Marketing Communications Environment," *Journal of Marketing Communications* 15, (2009): 139–155.

14 Felipe Korzenny and Betty Ann Korzenny, *Hispanic Marketing: A Cultural Perspective* (Burlington, MA: Elsevier/Butterworth-Heinemann, 2005).

15 Ibid.

16 Ibid.

17 Maritza De La Trinidad, "Chicano Movement," in Steven L. Danver, *Encyclopedia of Politics of the American West* (Washington, DC: Sage, 2013), 235–236.

18 Edward Telles and Vilma Ortiz, *Generations of Exclusion: Mexican Americans, Assimilation, and Race* (New York: Russell Sage Foundation, 2008).

19 Sharon R. Ennis, Merarys Rios-Vargas, and Nora G. Albert, "The Hispanic Population: 2010," *U.S. Census Bureau*, May 2011, www.census.gov/prod/cen2010/briefs/c2010br-04.pdf.

20 Regina Bernard-Carreño, *Nuyorganics: Organic Intellectualism, the Search for Racial Identity, and Nuyorican Thought* (New York: Peter Lang, 2010).

21 Ana Brown and Eileen Patten, "Hispanics of Puerto Rican Origin in the United States, 2011," *Pew Hispanic Center*, June 19, 2013, www.pewhispanic.org/2013/06/19/hispanics-of-puerto-rican-origin-in-the-united-states-2011/.

22 Catherine A. Ragland, *Voz del Pueblo Tejano*, in Juan Tejada and Avelardo Valdez, *Puro Conjunto: An Album in Words and Pictures* (Austin, TX: University of Texas, 2001), 211–228.

23 Frances R. Aparicio, "Jennifer as Selena: Rethinking Latinidad in Media and Popular Culture," *Latino Studies* 1, no. 1 (2003): 90–105.

24 Korzenny and Korzenny, *Hispanic Marketing*.

25 Jeanne Batalova and Jie Zong, "Cuban Immigrants in the United States," *Migration Policy Institute*, November 9, 2017, www.migrationpolicy.org/article/cuban-immigrants-united-states.

26 Korzenny and Korzenny, *Hispanic Marketing*, 95.

27 Ibid., 163.

28 "Florida's Puerto Rican Population Surpasses 1 Million, Rivaling New York," *Pew Research Center*, October 30, 2015, www.pewresearch.org/fact-tank/2015/10/30/in-a-shift-away-from-new-york-more-puerto-ricans-head-to-florida/ft_15-10-27_puertorico.

29 John W. Berry, Jean S. Phinney, David L. Sam, and Paul Vedder, "Immigrant Youth: Acculturation, Identity and Adaptation," *Applied Psychology* 55, no. 3 (2006): 303–332.

30 de Mooij, *Global Marketing and Advertising*.

31 Edward S. Reed, Elliot Turiel, and Terrance Brown (eds), *Values and Knowledge* (Mahwah, NJ: Lawrence Erlbaum Associates, 2013), 1.

32 Geert Hofstede, *Culture's Consequences: National Differences in Thinking and Organizing* (Beverly Hills, CA: Sage, 1980).

33 *iSpot.tv*, "Wells Fargo Commercial: Souvenir," www.ispot.tv/ad/7hAe/wells-fargo-souvenir.

34 Geert Hofstede and Gert Jan Hofstede, *Culture and Organizations. Intercultural Cooperation and its Importance for Survival, Software of the Mind* (New York: McGraw-Hill, 2005).

35 Ibid.

36 Korzenny and Korzenny, *Hispanic Marketing*.

37   Julian B. Rotter, "Generalized Expectancies for Internal Versus External Control of Reinforcement," *Psychological Monographs: General and Applied* 80, no. 1 (1966): 1.
38   Edward T. Hall, *Beyond Culture* (New York: Anchor, 1989).
39   Maribel Lackey, Account Manager. Casanova Pendrill, Advertising Agency.
40   Nescafé Latino, "Nescafé Clásico: ¿Te tomarías un café con un desconocido?" YouTube.com, www.youtube.com/watch?v=k63vXSJI7-Y.

12 Don't Forget the *Brasileiros*

Reaching the Brazilian Audience

Sabrina Habib, Ph.D.

Assistant Professor of Mass Communication,
Winthrop University

Many might think of Brazil as the land of samba, soccer, and beaches. Although it rings true, this oversimplified view undermines its cultural nuances. Brazil is larger than the continental U.S., and likewise, it presents vast and diverse cultures, subcultures, and landscapes. In 2016, the Olympic and Paralympic games were hosted in Rio de Janeiro, turning the world's attention to Brazil as an important country. This spotlight also reminded the world of Brazil's contrasts: troubled economy, political corruption, and inequality; but also rich culture, beautiful places, hospitality, and abundant resources.

Unlike the rest of Central and South America, the national language of Brazil is Portuguese. Although influence from Portugal is distinct, African music, religion, cuisine, and dances are just as influential in Brazilian culture as in other parts of Latin America. The south of the country received more European immigrants, and Asian immigrants are concentrated in the State of São Paulo, which is also the country's business hub. Most of the country's population lives in urban centers near the coast.[1]

Brazil is the world's seventh-largest economy and the United States' tenth-largest trading partner.[2] In 2014, 336,000 Brazilian immigrants lived in the United States, representing 1% of immigrants in the country. Compared to the total foreign-born population, Brazilian immigrants have higher educational attainment and income, have lower poverty rates, and are less likely to have limited English proficiency.[3]

Latino, Hispanic, or Other?

The terms "**Hispanic**" and "**Latino**" originated in organizations such as U.S. government agencies in their efforts to classify people of Spanish-speaking origin.[4] Many Brazilian immigrants and U.S.-born descendants of Brazilians do not self-identify as Hispanic. U.S.-based television networks such as Univision, Telemundo, UniMas, and MundoMax do not include Portuguese-language content, but they air Brazilian soap operas (telenovelas), which are always dubbed in Spanish.

Figure 12.1 Brazil is the only country in Latin America where Portuguese is the official language.

Tatiana53/Shutterstock

> Brazilians are officially defined as both non-Hispanic (as of 1980) and non-Latino (as of 2000) on the U.S. census . . . However, these official definitions do not always mesh with U.S. natives' views of Brazilians, or even with some of Brazilians' own self-conceptions.[5]

There are three key reasons for considering the label of Latino for Brazilians: the first is that Portuguese is a language of Latin origin, like Spanish. The second is the geographical location (Figure 12.1)—it is part of Latin America. The last is the mixed racial heritage, which is similar to other South and Central American countries. Despite the differences between the two terms, one referring to language, and the other to geographical location, they are used interchangeably and often cause confusion in regard to Brazilians.[6]

Brazilian Media

Between 1964 and 1985, Brazil was under a military **dictatorship**. When it ended, the **democratization** and freedom of the press raised questions about the role of journalists in the country. One of the most significant events was the media support for direct presidential elections toward the end of the military regime in 1984. Journalists were accused of corruption against the first president elected post-dictatorship, Jose Sarney, but they played a key role in the impeachment of the next president, Fernando Collor, in 1992.[7] Ultimately, journalism found its own voice. A survey comparing Brazilian and American journalists showed that "[Brazilians] perceived themselves first as disseminators (77.6%) then as interpreters (66.2%) of information . . . Americans, on the other hand, perceived themselves first as interpreters (62.9%) and then as disseminators (51%) of information."[8]

Scholars contributed to the establishment of a journalistic identity in Brazil. Having a college degree in Mass Communication was required for all Brazilian journalists, a decree from 1970 that is still rather controversial. On the one side, media companies advocated for the end of the requirement, while on the other educators and professionals stood by it. Congress denied attempts to ban the decree in 2005 and then again in 2007.[9] However, in 2009, the Brazilian federal court decided that a degree in journalism was no longer a requirement, which was viewed by many as a lack of appreciation for the profession. This decision has been challenged almost every year since and was nearly reversed in 2014 on the premise that new media (digital) needs professionals with higher education knowledge.[10] The growth of students enrolled in Mass Communication programs in Brazil has been increasing steadily since 2000, despite controversies.[11]

Broadcast and radio are far more popular than print in Brazil. At first, this was partly attributed to a large part of the population being illiterate, but even after illiteracy rates diminished,[12] the cultural habits remained. Cable and streaming services such as Netflix are available in Brazil; however, they come with a cost that many cannot afford. Only 10% of the Brazilian population watches paid TV. The cultural habits of watching telenovelas (novelas, as they are known in Brazil) at primetime are dominant across all income levels and demographics. The most popular telenovelas are produced and aired by Rede Globo, the largest television network in Latin America and the second-largest television network in annual revenue worldwide, just behind the American ABC television network. Although Globo is the largest producer of telenovelas,[13] other channels such as TV Record also produce telenovelas, but have a drastically smaller **market share**.

Globo's reach in Brazil includes radio stations and newspapers, and they provide entertainment and journalism nationwide. Through its network, the broadcaster covers 98.6% of Brazil's territory. Well known for its high standards in production, Globo has already been awarded fifteen International Emmys. The international operations of Globo include seven pay-per-view television channels and a division that distributes Brazilian sports and entertainment content to more than 190 countries around the world.

Globo TV reaches 99.5% of prospective audiences, which is virtually the entire Brazilian population, with 122 broadcasting stations that deliver programming to more than 183 million viewers. The network has been responsible for the twenty most-watched TV programs broadcast on Brazilian television, including *Avenida Brasil*, a 2012 record-breaking telenovela that reached 50 million viewers and was sold to 130 countries.[14] Primetime news is also highly regarded:

> The [Globo] nightly newscast, shown between two prime-time TV soap operas, is among the programs with the largest audience. In the 1970s and 1980s, when the TV newscast lasted half an hour, the audience ratings were impressive, reaching 70 points. In the beginning of the 1990s, with competition from another station which stood out in the group of networks, the SBT of Silvio Santos, Globo saw its larger audience threatened: thus, the newscast began to present a large number of investigative items and increased its duration to 50 minutes. Today, with an average of 40 points daily, the Jornal Nacional is still the TV newscast with the highest audience rating in Brazilian television.[15]

Secondary broadcast channels fall far behind Rede Globo, which has about 40% of the viewership at **primetime**, while other channels have around or below 10% of the shares. In order of popularity, Globo, Rede Record (which is run by the Universal Church of the Kingdom of God), SBT (Sistema Brasileiro de Televisao), Bandeirantes, RedeTV!, and TV Cultura comprise the main providers of Brazilian media. It is also noteworthy as a reflection of the culture that at least one out of every twenty radio stations in Brazil belongs to the Catholic Church.[16]

In terms of digital, in 2016 there were over 100 million internet users in Brazil, which is the fourth most connected country in the world. However, only about half have internet at home; others access it through mobile or family and friends' homes. The sales of computers are rising steadily and it is expected that the number of users and people with internet at home will too. The clear majority of internet users focus their time on product and service reviews.[17]

Lastly, the Brazilian film industry was not thriving prior to the 1990s. In 1990, it basically disappeared because President Fernando Collor cut federal funds previously available through EMBRAFILME, a federal enterprise that he ended. Five years later, new tax incentives saw a revival of the Brazilian film industry, which has been steadily growing since,[18] with a peak in 2016.[19] Films such as *City of God* (2002), *Midnight* (1998), *News of a Personal War* (1999), *Chico Xavier* (2010), and others had a large international viewership. Most recently, the series *3%* (2016, 2018) a Netflix exclusive, has gained even more attention.

Brazilian Media in the U.S.

In the U.S., Globo International is the main source of news and entertainment for Brazilian immigrants. Mariana Castro is a public relations professional who serves as a freelancer for Globo International and is based in New York. Castro is from Brazil and has a degree from New York University in Media Studies.

She stated that the U.S. LatinX/Hispanic population is the largest minority segment in the country, one that continues to grow. This demographic has attracted attention from companies, advertisers, and the media overall. She believes it is imperative to pay attention to this segment, and to learn its cultural nuances and its differences. Castro said that, when she writes to Brazilians in the U.S., her approach is different since they have ties with both cultures. Mariana Castro described her role with Globo:

> Besides its strong presence in Brazil, Globo has also an international presence in two fronts, which are the areas my work is focused on: First, Globo currently has seven international channels, which are the first national channels of the genre to be broadcast for Brazilians and Portuguese speakers who live abroad. They are present in all continents, with over 3 million subscribers. In the U.S., I work to publicize the network's international programming to Brazilian publications that cater to the Brazilian communities around the country. They are small-scale media publications, which are mostly written in Portuguese.
>
> Second, through its international business arm, Globo licenses telenovelas, series, documentaries, and special programs to television companies around the world . . . though in a smaller scale, I am also involved with this account, which is B2B focused, where we work with international TV trade publications, to publicize the company's catalog and its licensing business.[20]

Figure 12.2 Mariana Castro
Photo courtesy of Mariana Castro

DIRECTV Beams Latin America

by Luiz Duarte, Ph.D.
International Media Marketing Consultant

In 1996, only two years after its initial days in the U.S., the pioneer direct broadcast satellite system DIRECTV launched operations in Latin America, reaching mostly all the region with dedicated satellite television feeds aimed at small dishes installed even in the most remote distant parts of the continent. It was one of the most complex TV network deployments in the world, with hundreds of channels collected in multiple broadcast centers and sent to a single satellite that distributed it all to households with varying levels of access conditioned by sophisticated technology.

The company needed to expand fast and contacted American universities for students with both technical and language/cultural skills. Two of us were pulled from classrooms to get started right away and in the early days I was able to move from Engineering to Customer Loyalty and Marketing rather fast, learning different topics along the way. I created standard procedures for new engineers, managed millions of dollars in marketing research, and implemented company-wide software platforms to help manage workflows.

Even at a low ranking in the largest pay TV company in the world, I could get the feeling of ownership for so many different projects. However I still had to finish my doctoral dissertation, so I took advantage of my position to also study the unique moment in time when all those American

Figure 12.3 Luiz Duarte
Photo courtesy of Luiz Duarte

TV networks started to enter Latin America for the first time and what strategies they were adopting to woo audiences. Every day, the DIRECTV Programming department would receive pitches for a variety of new networks just created and every day we learned that many of these new players never made it.

Beyond the obvious factors, such as funding from a strong studio, some patterns of success started to show. It seemed like networks best able to adapt to the local culture were doing better than those that simply delivered their original American packages. This matched the theoretical expectations of my academic mentor, Joseph Straubhaar, who predicted international audiences would gravitate toward programming culturally closer to their own.

In observing the programming strategies of the networks, the Sony Channel became a template example of success in negotiating the local appeal of its standard slate of reruns for American sitcoms. First, it recognized that Brazil required Portuguese subtitles faster than others that continued to run Spanish content for Brazilian audiences. Second, it identified that Spanish didn't work equally in all countries and adopted the more neutral Colombian accent to avoid the mutual disdain other local accents have. It repackaged *Friends* with promotional interstitials in which the stars talked directly to the local audiences in each country, many times after they actually toured the region to promote the show.

The Latin American media industry is one of the most interesting and challenging in the world, representing significant advertising markets, ahead of many European nations, and understanding how to operate there may be key to reaching their fellow countrymen in the U.S.

Aside from Globo, there are many small publications in the U.S. that cater to Brazilian immigrants. One example is *BrasilBest Media*, an award-winning publication based in California. The objective of *BrasilBest* is to promote and spread Brazilian culture, as well as provide useful information for Brazilians through content such as art, interviews, photographs, humor, recipes, health, music, literature, and discussion of legal and immigration issues. They offer a print newspaper and online articles. In an interview with the editor, Celso Braz, he stated that "even though there are similarities, Brazilian audiences are significantly different from the Spanish-speaking ones. Because of the language difference, colonization history and other cultural aspects." Braz also mentioned that ethical/regulatory and communication styles are different in Brazilian and American journalism practices.[21]

There are other targeted publications like *BrasilBest*, such as the newspaper *Brasileiros e Brasileiras*, a publication that started as print only and available to the Brazilian community living in the Orlando, Florida, area but that now has online subscribers from all fifty states. Some online publications available to Brazilians in the U.S. are *Achei USA, Gazeta Brazilian News, Brazilian Times, Brazilian Voice, A Semana, Brazilian Press, Acontece Magazine,* and *Nossa Gente,* among others.

Advertising to Brazilian Audiences

Brazil has a worldwide reputation for creating some of the world's most creative advertising.[22] Most of the recognizable multinational agencies have offices in Brazil, but many local agencies enjoy distinctive awards as well, placing them among the top creative agencies worldwide. One interesting cultural aspect is that nightly telenovelas reach nearly 90% of the nation's households, giving advertisers a prime **spot** for advertising and product placement. Following telenovelas, a wide reach can be found in televised soccer games and carnivals.

Many cultural overlaps and values have been classified as "shared Hispanic values"[23] since differentiating between each country's cultural nuance (e.g., Cuban-Americans, Dominican-Americans, etc.) presented a challenge for media markets. Appealing to Hispanics and Latinos as a single market has many advantages, but at the cost of neglecting complex identities and cultures. One cultural aspect that stands out in Brazilian advertising and its TV content is sexuality; O'Barr stated that "one of the first things that foreigners notice in Brazil is the extraordinary focus on nearly nude bodies, sensual clothing, and overt expressions of sex."[24] He also stated that, in contrast, there is little violence in advertising because social problems are not entertainment, and advertising is embraced and accepted as such in Brazil.

While the literature regarding the advertising industry in Brazil is vast, there are few studies focused on advertising to the Brazilian audience in the U.S. To understand this void, an interview with a Brazilian advertising professional was conducted. Quim Gil leads the strategic planning practice at Richards/Lerma in Dallas, TX, a full-service advertising agency with offices in Dallas, Mexico, and Buenos Aires. Their clients include Anheuser-Busch, Doctor Pepper, Snapple Group, and MetroPCS among many others. Gil said:

> While obviously interesting and different in terms of culture and mindset vs. other ethnicities, there are less than 400,000 Brazilians officially living in the U.S. For most companies, it would not be efficient to invest on dedicated communication efforts for such a small audience . . . The main barrier is size and ROI [return on investment]. If the audience was interesting in terms of potential returns, the industry (advertising, media, social, etc.) would find ways around the language difference. They [Brazilians] are simply not considered. Hispanic marketers are focused on Hispanics. Smarter Hispanic marketers are focused on the growing influence of Hispanics in the mainstream. Hispanics are a driving cultural and social force in the U.S.[25]

Despite Brazil's position as a creative leader in advertising, the Brazilian population is too small in the U.S. to be targeted outside of small publications in specific venues. Although Brazilians are not included in the Hispanic market, some of the "shared Hispanic values" resonate with that audience. If Brazilian immigrants become a larger group in the U.S. and fall under a significant consumer group, we might start seeing ads in Portuguese. Until then, they will remain a small part of the Hispanic/Latino/Other groups.

Brazilian Artist Makes His Mark

Romero Britto

Romero Britto is a Brazilian-born artist whose work is known internationally. His work features bold, colorful patterns and imagery that can be seen in museums and galleries located in over 100 countries around the world. Romero Britto is also known for his contributions to charity, as he has donated to over 250 different charities worldwide. He currently has an art gallery located in Miami Beach, Florida.

Sources: Britto.com, Artbios.net, AmericanFineArtGallery.com

Figure 12.4 Rio de Janeiro, February 19, 2012. The painter Romero Britto parades at the Renascer Samba school in Jacarepaguá during the Carnival of Rio de Janeiro, considered the biggest carnival in the world.

A.PAES/Shutterstock

Conclusion

Despite growth of the Hispanic market, Brazilians are not part of that demographic due to language differences, and therefore enjoy prolific small publications rather than national content. While Brazilians do not have enough numbers in the U.S. to attract media attention, neither would most other Hispanic countries in isolation. However, Brazilians living in the U.S. can watch Globo via satellite and cable as well as other channels online.

English-Language Journalist Has Brazilian and Puerto Rican Roots

Natalie Morales

Natalie Leticia Morales-Rhodes, known as Natalie Morales, is an American journalist of Brazilian and Puerto Rican descent. Morales is best known for her work on NBC as a host for the *Today Show*. Morales has also been named as one of the "Fifty Most Beautiful People" by the *People en Español* magazine.

Sources: Today.com, NBC News

Figure 12.5 Natalie Morales
Kathy Hutchins/Shutterstock

Vocabulary Words

Democratization   Market Share
Dictatorship   Primetime
Hispanic   Spot
Latino

Points to Remember

- Brazil's national language is Portuguese.
- Brazil has the largest media market in Latin America.
- Brazil is the largest Latin exporter of broadcast content, especially tele-novelas.
- The Brazilian audience in the U.S. is not significant on its own.
- The terms Hispanic and Latino have mixed results when referring to Brazilians.

Names to Remember

Celso Braz
Fernando Collor
Jose Sarney
Mariana Castro
Quim Gil

Practice Questions

1   What type of productions is the Brazilian media best known for? What network company contributes to this success?
2   Do you believe that a college/university degree in Mass Communication should be required in the U.S.? Would the American media environment be different if this was a requirement enforced by law? How?
3   Why are broadcast and radio more popular than print in Brazil?
4   What is the best way to reach the Brazilian audience in the U.S.? What network can reach this audience?

Activity

Look at the top headlines of today's main American news sources, get into groups and discuss how you would write the same story/stories for an American publication in Brazil. Would your approach be different from the way it is presented in the U.S.? How? Why/why not? When answering these questions, be sure to provide examples that support your answer.

Timeline

1985: Military dictatorship that began in 1964 ends.
1992: President Fernando Collor is impeached.
1995: Tax incentives cause the Brazilian film industry to grow.
2009: Mass Communication degree requirement for all journalists, established in 1970, comes to an end.
2014: Brazilian immigrants in the U.S. represent 1%.
2016: Olympic and Paralympic games were hosted in Rio de Janeiro, Brazil. Over 100 million internet users in Brazil.

Additional Resources

Brazil News: http://brasilbest.com
Globo TV: redeglobo.globo.com and www.globotvinternational.com
Hispanic vs. Latino: www.diffen.com/difference/Hispanic_vs_Latino

About the Author

Sabrina Habib
Photo courtesy of Sabrina Habib

Sabrina Habib is a Brazilian scholar living in the U.S. She joined Winthrop University in 2015 as Mass Communication faculty to teach Integrated Marketing Communication courses. She holds a BFA in Photography (2000), an MFA in Electronic Media (2003), and a Ph.D. in Advertising from the University of Florida (2013). Prior to her academic experience, she owned a production studio in Gainesville, Florida, to service advertising clients, local businesses, and individuals. Most of Habib's academic research has focused on the creative process and creative education; however, she has also performed studies on science communication and culture.

Notes

1 "Instituto Brasileiro de Geografia e Estatistica," *IBGE*, www.ibge.gov.br/home.
2 "Censo da Educação Superior," *INEP*, October 20, 2015, http://portal.inep.gov.br/web/censo-da-educacao-superior.
3 Jie Zong and Jeanne Batalova, "Brazilian Immigrants in the United States," *Migration Policy Institute*, July 13, 2016, www.migrationpolicy.org/article/brazilian-immigrants-united-states.
4 Anthony LaPastina, "Telenovela," *Museum of Broadcast Communication*, www.museum.tv/eotv/telenovela.htm.
5 Helen Marrow, "To Be or Not to Be (Hispanic or Latino): Brazilian Racial and Ethnic Identity in the United States," *Ethnicities* 3, no. 4 (2003): 427–464.

6 Ibid.
7 Heloiza G. Herscovitz, "Brazilian Journalists' Perceptions of Media Roles, Ethics and Foreign Influences on Brazilian Journalism," *Journalism Studies* 5, no. 1 (2004): 71–86.
8 Ibid., 96.
9 Sonia Virgiania Moreira and Carla Leal Helal, "Notes on Media, Journalism Education and News Organizations in Brazil," *Journalism* 10, no. 1 (2009): 91–107.
10 "Conselho de Comunicação aprova exigência do diploma de jornalista," *Camara dos Deputados*, June 8, 2014, www2.camara.leg.br/camaranoticias/noticias/COMUNICACAO/472526-CONSELHO-DE-COMUNICACAO-APROVA-EXIGENCIA-DO-DIPLOMA-DE-JORNALISTA.html; Brasilia, "Câmara Deve Discutir Diploma para Lornalistas," March 6, 2015, www1.folha.uol.com.br/poder/2015/03/1599104-camara-deve-discutir-diploma-para-jornalistas.shtml
11 "Censo da Educação Superior."
12 "Literacy Rate, Adult Total (% of People Ages 15 and Above)," *The World Bank*, 2017, https://data.worldbank.org/indicator/SE.ADT.LITR.ZS.
13 LaPastina, "Telenovela."
14 Marrow, "To Be or Not to Be (Hispanic or Latino) Brazilian Racial and Ethnic Identity in the United States."
15 Moreira and Helal, "Notes on Media, Journalism Education and News Organizations in Brazil," 101.
16 Zong and Batalova, "Brazilian Immigrants in the United States."
17 "Dados, Estatísticas e Projeções sobre a Internet no Brasil," *To Be Guarany*, http://tobeguarany.com/internet-no-brasil/.
18 Cacilda M. Rêgo, "Brazilian Cinema: Its Fall, Rise, and Renewal (1990–2003)," *New Cinemas: Journal of Contemporary Film* 3, no. 2 (2005): 85–100.
19 Paulo Virgilio, "Apesar da Crise, Cinema Teve Maior Crescimento dos últimos 5 Anos no Brasil," *Vol*, January 26, 2016, http://cinema.uol.com.br/noticias/redacao/2016/01/26/apesar-da-crise-cinema-teve-maior-crescimento-dos-ultimos-5-anos-no-brasil.htm.
20 Mariana Castro, interview by Sabrina Habib, phone interview, September 22, 2016.
21 Celso Braz, interview by Sabrina Habib, phone interview, September 7, 2016.
22 William M. O'Barr, "Advertising in Brazil," *Advertising & Society Review* 9, no. 2 (2008), http://muse.jhu.edu/article/241036.
23 Marye Tharp, *Transcultural Marketing: Building Customer Relationships in Multicultural America* (Armonk, NY: M.E. Sharpe, 2014).
24 O'Barr, "Advertising in Brazil."
25 Quim Gil, interview by Sabrina Habib, phone interview, October 12, 2016.

Unit 5

Management, Diversity, and Language

13 Behind the Scenes

Decision-makers in the Growing Hispanic/LatinX Media Market

Katidia Barbara Coronado, M.A.

Associate Instructor of Journalism, Radio-TV, and
Hispanic Media, University of Central Florida

Selena Gomez, Lin-Manuel Miranda, and Shakira are just some of the more popular Hispanic/LatinX faces that you probably see often in newspapers or magazine covers, as the Hispanic/LatinX population in the U.S. continues to grow. It is also more common for a website to have an "*en español*" tab and a for a television show or movie to have "produced or directed by" a Hispanic or LatinX last name in the credits. More and more, we also continue to see media outlets branching out with Hispanic-targeted content, programming, and social media pages. However, for these examples to continue popping up, leadership in these media industries should also continue to diversify. Research shows that, in order to produce successful efforts of diversity and inclusion, while leading a multicultural staff, it helps when the people spearheading these efforts possess the background and education that facilitates well-informed decision making to best serve this growing community.[1]

Despite recent organizational efforts to reach the growing Hispanic/LatinX audience, there is still much work to be done to increase diversity and representation across all platforms and levels in the media industry. It is important to note that there are limited studies on the number of Hispanic/LatinX media managers in the U.S. The available research shows the demographics of the people working behind the scenes in American media companies, especially in upper-level management positions, rarely reflect the audiences they serve. The U.S. Census reports 55.4 million Hispanics living in the United States in 2014.[2] But, as explained below, there are few Hispanic/LatinX media managers at the top making decisions about how to reach those millions of viewers, readers, and consumers.

As a result, this lack of diversity in media management can create a trickle-down effect through hiring decisions and promotion practices within the organizations that fail to prioritize diversity and inclusion. These deficiencies are present across the board and throughout the U.S.—from small-town news organizations to multibillion dollar corporations and everything in between.[3] Still, several Hispanic/LatinX media professionals have worked their way up into management positions despite these challenges. Professional organizations have also launched initiatives to support Latinos to obtain management roles, encourage better job placement, foster professional growth, and create mentorship opportunities.

TV Executive Worked His Way Up

Cesar Conde

Cesar Conde is a television network executive, of Peruvian and Cuban descent, who is well-known for his roles at multiple news organizations. He had once worked for Univision, holding many positions, including interim president of Univision Interactive Media. He has also worked for NBCUniversal as an executive vice president. His work led him to be named one of the "Top 25 most powerful Hispanics" in the *Hispanics Magazine*. Most recently, Cesar Conde was appointed as chairman of the NBCUniversal International Group and NBCUniversal/Telemundo Enterprises.

Sources: Bloomberg.com, Comcast.com, NBCuni.com

Figure 13.1 Cesar Conde
Cesar Conde/Shutterstock

The Low Numbers

Radio

A recent study by Radio Television Digital News Association (RTDNA) shows the number of Hispanic/Latino radio news directors in the U.S. was at 2.4% in 2016. Overall, minority news directors were much more likely to be in the biggest markets and at stand-alone stations. Meanwhile, the number of minority radio managers, which includes Hispanics/LatinX, was at 3.6% in 2016. Overall, Hispanic news directors were most often found in top twenty-five markets, newsrooms of under thirty-one employees, and other commercial and non-commercial stations.[4]

Meanwhile, Hispanic/LatinX-targeted media projects are becoming more prevalent in major media markets. For example, in 2016, Cox Media Group launched a Spanish-language FM contemporary format radio station called 107.3 Solo Exitos. While most of the upper management at the station is not of Hispanic/LatinX background, the on-air team and Hispanic/LatinX account executives lead the station efforts.[5]

Television

In the television industry, the same RTDNA study shows only 3% of television general managers throughout the U.S. were Hispanic/LatinX in 2016.

Figure 13.2 José Díaz-Balart
Photo courtesy of Telemundo Network

Serving the Hispanic/LatinX Community in English-Language News

by Matt Parcell
News Director, WFTV, Orlando, Florida

The impact of Hurricane Maria has ramifications that stretch far beyond Puerto Rico. The destruction and human tragedy left behind is a story unto itself and has wide interest to Central Florida's Puerto Rican community. Our area now has the largest concentration of Puerto Ricans in the United States. So, events on the island have direct and indirect impacts on a large segment of our population.

But the utter devastation from the storm has created far greater implications for Central Floridians. To this point, 200,000 people have fled Puerto Rico for Florida. The majority have come to Orange and Osceola Counties. This is creating shifts in population, adding pressure to social service organizations, and increasing school populations. As the influx continues, the region will see fundamental changes to its culture. The growth of the Latino population is accelerating at a far more rapid pace than predicted. The flood of Puerto Ricans to the area is likely to shift political power as well.

It's critical for news organizations to do more than simply cover the day's events. We have to look ahead at potential issues and potential

Figure 13.3 Matt Parcell
Photo courtesty of WFTV Channel 9

changes to our communities and help put them into perspective. Our role is to inform the citizenry as to the breadth and scope of these potential changes. Furthermore, we must press elected officials and leaders to see if they are staying ahead of the changes and creating plans for dealing with the issues.

There are not many events, natural or man-made, that have the potential to so fundamentally change a region. Our aggressive reporting on the issue is designed to help the community understand what is happening and prepare for the adjustments that will be necessary.

The number of Hispanic/LatinX television news directors rose slightly from 6% in 2015 to 8.8% in that year. Meanwhile, Hispanic/LatinX representation at non-Hispanic TV stations rose from 5.9% in 2015 to 6.7% in 2016. Those numbers are much higher at Hispanic/LatinX TV news stations. Overall, 98.1% of those managers are Hispanic/LatinX. But representation of Hispanic/LatinX managers in television management in English-language stations was lower than in Spanish-language stations.[6] However in some cases, television companies have started to make small strides toward increasing diversity on air. For instance, in 2016, NBCUniversal announced that, in a historic move, long-time Telemundo anchor José Díaz-Balart would make a major crossover from Spanish-language network news to English-language news. He is the first anchor in the U.S. to broadcast on two major broadcast networks in two languages.[7]

Print and Online Journalism

Meanwhile, the same 2015 numbers from the American Society of News Editors (ASNE) found that minority journalists make up 12.8% of newsroom employees at daily newspapers, while Hispanics/LatinX journalists make up 4.2% of that total. The study did not specify the number of Hispanics/LatinX in print journalism management.[8] A previous study published by *The Communicator*, the magazine of the Radio-Television News Directors Association, shows that, although the 2001 percentage of minorities in TV news was 24.6%, an all-time high, just about 9% of newspaper newsroom managers were minorities during that time frame. The study shows that most of the respondents held mid-level managerial positions.[9]

Media General is one example of a key player in the multimedia industry that launched a print and online publication targeting the Hispanic/LatinX community. The company, based out of Richmond, Virginia, partnered with experts in the Hispanic/LatinX media market of Tampa, Florida, to meet the community's news and information needs. In 2005, Media General executives hired Orlando Nieves, an award-winning Hispanic advertising expert, to launch

CentroTampa.com. The editor-in-chief of the Spanish-language publication was Manuel Ballagas, a seasoned journalist who had previously worked at the *Wall Street Journal*.[10] Nieves made history with Cuban-born Ballagas in one of the largest Hispanic media markets in the U.S. By hiring managers who understood the product and audience needs, the print publication and website's early stages allowed for a successful outcome that, despite market changes, has maintained its reputation in that community.

Calling the Shots and Making History in Hollywood

Hispanic/LatinX leadership in the film industry is also scarce. In their study, Smith, Choueiti, and Pieper found that between 2007–2014, Hispanic or LatinX directors were not represented in any of the top 100 films. They also attribute a large part of the lack of on-screen representation to the lack of diversity in film leadership.[11] Despite that lack of diversity in film leadership, Hispanic/LatinX directors and producers continue to prove their abilities through box office hits and award-winning work. The film *Instructions Not Included* (2013), directed by Mexican actor-director Eugenio Derbez, was the highest-grossing Spanish-language film of all time in the U.S., taking $44.5 million at the box office.[12] Other successful Hollywood film directors include Alfonso Cuarón (*Gravity* (2013), *Y Tu Mamá También* (2001), *Children of Men* (2006))[13] and Alejandro González Iñárritu (*Birdman* (2014), *The Revenant* (2015), *21 Grams* (2003)), who have won multiple Oscars for best film and best director.[14] Meanwhile, Mexican-born Salma Hayek continues to break gender barriers as well. Some of her most recognized work includes producing *Frida* in 2002. The Emmy Award winner and Oscar nominee also served as executive producer of the hit television series *Ugly Betty*, which was based on the hit Colombian telenovela *Yo Soy Betty La Fea*. The series ran from 2006 to 2010.[15]

Why Diversity Behind the Scenes Matters

A historic example of one of the top selling Spanish-language magazines is *People en Español*. Weeks after the Tejano singer's death in 1995, *People* magazine released a commemorative issue in honor of Selena. There were two versions of the magazine printed, one in English and one in Spanish. Within days of its release, the Spanish version had been sold out everywhere. In the end, *People* would have to go through six more reprint sessions of the Spanish-language issue to meet demand.[16] After its sixth reprint, magazine executives decided to create a permanent Spanish-language edition of their magazine, which is owned by Time Inc. Currently, the magazine reaches 7 million people. It was due to Selena's death that *People en Español* came to be.[17]

Whether it relates to the allocation of resources or being a part of the team that helps oversee the creative process involved in the content, the people making decisions have some form of influence over the message. A 1999 study

Vergara Starts Firm for Hispanic Talent

Latin World Entertainment

Latin World Entertainment, also known as Latin WE, is a 100% Hispanic-owned firm that was founded in 1994. The firm focuses on Hispanic Talent Management and Entertainment Marketing. The founders, Sofía Vergara and Luis Balaguer, created Latin World Entertainment when Vergara realized that there had to be managers in place to represent the growing population of Hispanic talent. Now, it is the number one Hispanic talent agency in the United States.

Sources: LinkedIn, Latinwe.com, *ABC News*

Figure 13.4 Sofía Vergara arriving at *New Year's Eve* world premiere on December 5, 2011 in Hollywood, California.

DFree/Shutterstock

conducted at the Unity Convention, explored minority electronic and print media journalists, as well as other media professionals' perceptions about the ability of minority executives to influence news coverage of minorities and how career satisfaction relates to these perceptions. The findings suggest that, regardless of ethnicity, occupation, or years in the business, minority journalists believe that a minority executive can make a difference in the content. Respondents expressed concerns in several key areas, including a news operation's sensitivity

Figure 13.5 Hugo Balta is the Senior Director for Multicultural Content for ESPN and
strives to expand the breadth of the network's content to reflect its diverse
audience.

Photo courtesy of Hugo Balta

to racism and how minority issues are covered. The researchers found that most
journalists of color agreed that a minority at the head of a news operation would
improve the media coverage of minorities.[18]

Training, Support, and Mentorship

Academics are also contributing to the making of Hispanic/LatinX media leaders. California State University Fullerton's Latino Communications Institute,[19]
University of Texas at Arlington's UTA Noticias en Español,[20] and the University of Central Florida's Hispanic Media Initiative,[21] which launched the state
of Florida's first Hispanic/Latino Media Certificate, are some key examples of
these efforts.

Exposure of different perspectives and professional ties will help create
more opportunities for future media executives to lead teams that create and
produce diverse content. Participation in specialized training programs such as
the National Hispanic Media Coalition's (NHMC) Writers program and the

Managing Spanish-Language Media

by Laura Santos
Former TV News Executive

Managing a Spanish-language television, radio, or general-market station in a small market is similar to running a small business—the manager should have an overall knowledge of the business, from sales, to news, to traffic, and should be prepared to play the role of teacher and mentor.

That's because most Spanish-language stations are located in small markets (this trend will continue for the foreseeable future, since most Latinos congregate in a few states and a handful of cities within those states), and the majority of their incomes will come from local advertisers, who cannot afford the higher advertising fees paid by national, or regional, advertisers. In the Spanish-language media world, only those stations located in the top 15–20 Nielsen-rated market can expect to be part of the most-buy promotions strategy of national/regional advertisers. Without healthy national, or Spot sales, the station will not bring in enough national/regional income to afford the luxury of hiring experienced employees and to purchase the necessary equipment to effectively compete with other stations in the market.

The pool of possible employees available will be mostly inexperienced, or fresh out of college. These employees will have to be trained and that is where the expertise of the manager comes into play.

Figure 13.6 Laura Santos
Photo courtesy of Laura Santos

During my more-than-30-year career in media, I managed several Spanish-language television and radio stations. These stations were located in 20-something markets in Florida. Although the markets were not extremely small, they were past the cut-off, must-buy criteria and therefore we had to fight for every Spot sales dollar available for the rest of the country.

To win, our sales force had to be not only better trained but creative, since a simple Spot schedule would not do. In order to get in front of the media buyers, our proposals had to go the extra mile and offer enough incentives to win over the buyer. And by incentive I don't mean just throwing in some more spots at no charge. No, the proposal had to include strategies that would convince the advertiser that it would generate sales.

Take IHOP. After more than six months of trying to get in front of the client, we were finally given the opportunity to make a presentation for the Orlando market. We knew a simple Spot schedule would not work. So we came up with a plan that would guarantee traffic to the stores. First we researched the location of every IHOP store within our DMA as well as our viewing area, which by the way extended from Osceola County to St. Johns County in northern Florida.

We decided to hold a no-purchase-necessary contest in which the winner would win an all-expenses paid trip for two to a beach. The station would cover the expenses (we had made trade deals with a hotel and airline, and the only real expense was to cover meals).

We walked out with a very profitable contract in our hands, beating the competition. Our elation was soon dampened by the realization that we had a lot of work ahead of us and little time to do it.

We had to purchase hundreds of boxes that would collect the entries and design the entry form. Then we had to deliver the boxes and forms to each store, meet the manager and employees, and explain what the rules of the contest were. It took several days to deliver the boxes to all the stores.

The flight worked, increasing store traffic beyond our expectations. Latinos loved the promotion and we ended up winning a new Spot client.

Every Spot client we signed took great effort and thinking outside the box. As the manager I had to be involved in every aspect of the planning, from training people who had never worked in television and knew nothing of the business, to encouraging their creativity and supporting each employee in every endeavor.

In addition to the regular managing and training duties, the manager of a Spanish-language station needs to spend a good portion of his/her time in public relations. Latinos believe in a handshake and prefer to do business with those they know and with whom they have developed a relationship. When you call on a client, you first ask how their family is doing, by name if possible, before you ever dare to get into the reason for the visit.

This approach works not only with Latino businesses, but with general-market clients as well. Being involved in community organizations is not only an excellent way to position your station top-of-mind among potential clients, but affords you the opportunity to establish close relationships with those businesses. Not only are you contributing to the well-being of the community you serve, but you are also opening lines of communication with potential clients. More than 90% of our local clients were the result of community involvement.

So the ideal manager of a Spanish-language or small general-market television station should have management experience, knowledge of sales, public relations expertise or prior involvement with the community, and, if possible, news experience.

As the world becomes a village, people crave more local involvement. A focus on local issues will become ever more important. Local news, community affairs programs, and local events are the link that connects a station to its viewers. Without that connection, one that reassures viewers that the station has his/her back, the station will have a hard time attracting viewers. And increased viewership translates to more advertisers and higher Spot prices.

National Association of Hispanic Journalists (NAHJ) Parity Project will undoubtedly play a role in future numbers reflecting Hispanic/LatinX media managers in the U.S.[22] Also, future leaders in print media can find support in the American Society of News Editors' Emerging Leaders Institute. The institute launched in 2012 with the goal of training minority journalists to become leaders in their organizations and to prepare them to drive change.

As the U.S. Hispanic/LatinX population continues to grow, it is vital to maintain a vision of the community's needs. Part of the plan for continued growth and development should include the mentoring of leaders that can provide that multicultural point of view to produce content of importance to that population. It is also important to note that minorities in leadership positions also have a responsibility to not just open doors but to hold those doors open for those who follow. And as the Spanish-language saying goes, "*Pa'lante.*"

Points to Remember

- Exposure of different perspectives and professional ties will help create more opportunities for future media executives to lead teams that create and produce diverse content.
- Between 2007 and 2014, Hispanic or LatinX directors were not represented in any of the top 100 films.
- A recent study by Radio Television Digital News Association (RTDNA) shows that the number of Hispanics/Latino radio news directors was at 2.4% in 2016.
- In the television industry, the same RTDNA study shows that only 3% of television general managers throughout the U.S. were Hispanic/LatinX in 2016.

Names to Remember

Eugenio Derbez
Jose Diaz-Balart
Radio Television Digital News Association
Salma Hayak

Practice Questions

1   The author mentions the importance of Hispanic/LatinX media managers. What does the research show to support this?
2   Name some of the organizations mentioned that will help train and mentor future Hispanic/LatinX media leaders in the U.S.
3   What hit television series did Salma Hayek executive produce? The show was based on an original hit series from Colombia. What was it called?
4   How did journalist José Díaz-Balart make history on television news in the U.S.?
5   What is the current Hispanic/LatinX U.S. population? How does this relate to media management in the U.S.?

Activities

The chapter mentioned Media General and Cox as American-owned companies with primarily English language content products. Research the topic, find and name another company following those footsteps.

If you were a media manager (non-Hispanic/LatinX) hiring a team of five Spanish-speaking reporters, how would you recruit your team? Find and name three strategies you would implement for talent recruitment.

How should a radio station manager choose their programming? What information should they know about their audience? And where will they find that data? Call at least two of those organizations and ask for the latest audience breakdown in your media market. Provide their contact information and their responses.

Call one of the organizations listed in this chapter. Find out what services they offer in your media market. List how you could get involved.

Additional Resources

National Association of Hispanic Journalists (NAHJ): www.nahj.org/
National Hispanic Media Coalition (NHMC): www.nhmc.org/
Radio Television Digital News Association (RTDNA): www.rtdna.org/

About the Author

Katidia Barbara Coronado

Photo courtesy of the University of Central Florida

Katie Barbara Coronado is a journalist and associate instructor of broadcast journalism, radio-television, and Hispanic Media. After working in both English- and Spanish-language media for more than 13 years, NSC appointed her to the instructor position in 2011. She currently teaches news writing as well as on-air delivery. As part of her commitment to educating the next generation of journalists, she launched the university's first Spanish-language course, Knightly Latino, which offers students an outlet through which to cover issues of interest to the Latino community in both English and Spanish. She has helped pave the way with the School's Hispanic Media Initiative, which includes the first Hispanic/Latino Media Certificate to help introduce students to work on air and behind the scenes in a multicultural environment.

She continues to work as a bilingual freelance reporter, which helps her bring real-world experience into the classroom. During her free time she enjoys being with her family and traveling to new places.

Notes

1   Maggie Rivas-Rodriguez, Federico A. Subervi-Velez, Sharon Bramlett-Solomon, and Don Heider, "Minority Journalists' Perceptions of the Impact of Minority Executives," *Howard Journal of Communications* 15, no. 1 (2004): 39–55.

2   "FFF: Hispanic Heritage Month," *United States Census Bureau*, September 14, 2015, www.census.gov/newsroom/facts-for-features/2015/cb15-ff18.html.

3   Bob Papper, "RTDNA Research: Women and Minorities in Newsrooms," *Radio Television Digital News Association*, July 11, 2016, www.rtdna.org/article/rtdna_research_women_and_minorities_in_newsrooms.

4   Ibid.

5   "CMG Orlando Launches 107.3 Solo Éxitos," *Cox Media Group*, February 22, 2016, www.coxmediagroup.com/cmg-orlando-launches-107-3-solo-exitos.

6   Papper, "RTDNA Research: Women and Minorities in Newsrooms."

7   "José Díaz-Balart Named Anchor of Saturday 'NBC Nightly News'," *NBC Universal*, July 13, 2016, www.nbcuniversal.com/press-release/jos%C3%A9-d%C3%ADaz-balart-named-anchor-saturday-%E2%80%9Cnbc-nightly-news%E2%80%9D.

8   Papper, "RTDNA Research: Women and Minorities in Newsrooms."

9   Gina Barton, "Is Diversity Making a Difference?" *Society of Professional Journalists: Quil*, March 5, 2002, www.spj.org/quill_issue.asp?ref=260.

10 Nancy Ayala, "'Centro' Newspaper Launches in Tampa Bay Area in October," *Editor & Publisher*, September 7, 2005, www.editorandpublisher.com/news/centro-newspaper-launches-in-tampa-bay-area-in-october.

11 S.L. Smith, M. Choueiti, and K. Pieper, "Gender Inequality in Popular Films: Examining On Screen Portrayals and Behind-the-Scenes Employment Patterns in Motion Pictures Released Between 2007–2014," *Media, Diversity, & Social Change Initiative, USC Annenberg*, 2014, http://annenberg.usc.edu/sites/default/files/MDSCI_Gender_Inequality_in_600_films.pdf.

12 Anna Marie De La Fuenta, "Release Ever With 'How to Be a Latin Lover' (Exclusive)," *Variety*, March 9, 2017, http://variety.com/2017/film/global/pantelion-release-eugenio-derbez-latin-lover-1202005272.

13 A&E Television Network, "Alfonso Cuarón," *Biography.com*, April 2, 2017, www.biography.com/people/alfonso-cuar%C3%B3n-21377605 .

14 A&E Television Network, "González Iñárritu," *Biography.com*, April 17, 2016, www.biography.com/people/alejandro-gonzalez-inarritu-212151.

15 A&E Television Network, "Salma Hayek," *Biography.com*, April 27, 2017, www.biography.com/people/salma-hayek-14514423.

16 "Selena, Biography," *IMDb*, www.imdb.com/name/nm0702373/bio.

17 "Still Missing Selena: Here Are 6 Reasons Why," *NBC News*, March 31, 2014, www.nbcnews.com/news/latino/still-missing-selena-here-are-6-reasons-why-n66031.

18 Rodriguez, Subervi-Velez, Bramlett-Solomon, and Heider, "Minority Journalists' Perceptions of the Impact of Minority Executives."

19 "Latino Communications Institute," *California State University, Fullerton*, 2017, http://communications.fullerton.edu/studentlife/lci.

20 "UTA Noticias en Español," *University of Texas Arlington, Department of Communication*, www.uta.edu/communication/organizations/utane.php.

21 "Communication Professor Lead Hispanic Media Initiative," *University of Central Florida, COS News*, October 14, 2016, https://sciences.ucf.edu/news/communication-professors-lead-hispanic-media-initiative.

22 "Home Page, National Hispanic Media Coalition," *NHMC*, 2017, www.nhmc.org; Pam Johnson, "From Diversity to Parity," *Poynter*, May 3, 2004, www.poynter.org/news/diversity-parity.

14 Representations of "La Raza"

Stereotypes, Gender Issues, and the Impact of Images in Media

Jennifer A. Sandoval, Ph.D.

Associate Professor of Communication,
University of Central Florida

Always partial and often problematic, representation is an important component of media creation, consumption, and critique. It is often said that you cannot be what you cannot see. For many communities outside of the dominant culture in the United States, the little representation that has occurred in various media outlets has relied upon **stereotypes** and the conflation of the diversity of Hispanic and LatinX identity into one limited caricature. While Hispanic and LatinX individuals make up the largest minority in the U.S., this is not reflected in most programming available in mainstream media. At the same time, there has been an explosion of Spanish-language television programming, with Univision being rated higher than all other networks in July of 2014.[1] While some of these changes have been positive we are still far from seeing a representation of the diversity of Hispanic and LatinX cultures, traditions, and origins in the U.S. media landscape.

Hispanic, Latino/a, or LatinX?

For the purposes of this chapter, the terms *Hispanic* and *LatinX* are used in concert to broadly encompass the variety of identities that include both Spanish-speaking communities, as well as the diversity of ethnicities that share origins in Latin America. It is important to note the socially constructed ethnicity of Hispanic in the United States. This term is not without controversy and many continue to disagree about the usage of a term that references the colonizing forces of Spain. In the U.S., there was strategic decision making about how to refer to the exploding population in the West and Southwest region in the 1970s. Flores-Hughes explains the term originates as a collaboration between the Office of Education and activists at the time who were attempting to define issues for Hispanic and Native American students. An "Ad Hoc Committee on

Racial and Ethnic Definitions"[2] was created to consider a range of terms for demographic purposes. The debates continued throughout the 1970s and 1980s, with various groups weighing in regarding the more expansive term "Latino." Many agreed that there was no singular term that was inclusive enough to honor indigenous heritage and that practicality would be a final factor. In 1975, the Census Bureau came to an agreement with the activists for the use of the term Hispanic. The media then became an important partner in efforts to popularize the term.[3]

What is Representation?

According to Hall, Evans, and Nixon, **representation** "is an essential part of the process by which a meaning is produced and exchanged between members of a culture."[4] Meanings are in people and are co-constructed, but the symbols that make up the words and images being interpreted are the building blocks of understanding. As we reflect upon symbols the objects interplay within our own worldviews. Representation is complicated by a number of issues, not the least of which is who has decision-making power about programming, editing, and funding of media. U.S. media has a long tradition of "**racializing**" the other. That is, whiteness is not racialized, but rather the presence of something other than whiteness is often labeled and portrayed in a negative light.

"Latin Looks"

When we ask, importantly, what does a Latino look like the media answers with a uniform portrayal that reinforces negative stereotypes.[5] Historically, Hispanic and LatinX representation has centered around negative stereotypes portraying both men and women as unethical, lazy, unintelligent, oversexualized, and even criminal.[6] These depictions have had lasting effects on social attitudes toward Hispanic and LatinX communities in the U.S. Furthermore, the reliance on these limited images in popular media influences the interpretations of news and reporting on Hispanic and LatinX topics, most notably that of immigration. Media has been a driving force in advancing **gendered** and racial stereotypes. There are many paradoxes in the contemporary media landscape where representations can be outdated and also progressive.

What's on Primetime

In a foundational contemporary study of representation in primetime television, Mastro and Greenberg found that Hispanic and LatinX characters were vastly **underrepresented**, constituting only 3% of characters and roles.[7] A decade later Monk-Turner and colleagues replicated the study and the updated findings are mixed. Hispanic presence only increased to 5%.[8] While a majority of

Did You Know?

In recent years there has been an increased fascination with identifying actors and other famous people who are not commonly known as Hispanic. The online outlets of *Huffington Post*, *Cosmopolitan*, *Latina Magazine*, and even CNN have created numerous lists of these individuals. Here are a few examples:

- Cameron Diaz's father is of Cuban descent.
- Nicole "Snooki" Polizzi was born in Chile and later adopted by Italian-American parents.
- David Blaine is of Puerto Rican descent.
- Vanna White's biological father was Puerto Rican.
- Rita Hayworth's father was from Spain.
- Nicole Richie's biological father is of Mexican descent.
- Raquel Welch's father was from Bolivia.
- Carmelo Anthony is of Puerto Rican descent.
- Anthony Quinn has Mexican roots.
- Alexis Bledel was born to Argentinian parents.
- Bella Thorne's father is Cuban.
- Kat Von D was born in Mexico and is of Argentine and Spanish descent.
- Sara Paxton's mother is from Monterrey, Mexico.
- Kid Cudi's father is Mexican.
- Reggie Jackson's father was half Puerto Rican.
- Fabolous is half Dominican.
- Lynda Carter is of Mexican descent.

Figure 14.1 Kat Von D
Photo Works/Shutterstock

Hispanic and LatinX characters did have main roles in the new study, unlike the findings in 2000 that saw LatinX roles as "the least ridiculed and most respected," the roles were plagued by negative stereotypes and a lack of respect. Additionally, "unlike Mastro and Greenberg, we found that black and Latino characters were significantly more likely to be shown as being less intelligent compared to whites."[9] In the replication study the group represented as least intelligent was in fact LatinX.

Featured in Film

Similarly, Ramírez Berg had identified six primary stereotypical depictions of Hispanic and LatinX people in U.S. films. He found that *el bandido, the harlot, the male buffoon, the female clown, the Latin lover,* and *the dark lady* images were "consistent over a century and still evident today."[10] *El bandido* was the typical dishonest criminal who spoke broken English and was "dirty and unkempt, usually displaying an unshaven face, missing teeth, and disheveled, oily hair."[11] The harlot was a woman with a temper who openly expressed sexuality. The male buffoon and the female clown were the comic relief and offered a contrast to the white characters with their foolish antics and often dumb comments. The Latin lover and dark lady are the dangerous sexual individuals. While they are often portrayed as more intelligent than the other stereotypes, they are predatory.

Indigenous groups, Native populations, and American Indians have not fared any better in the media landscape. Rollins and O'Connor argue that Native Americans "are not only trapped by history, but are forever trapped in the history of film."[12] From the noble savage to the bloodthirsty warrior, Native Americans have been reduced to the basest stereotypes and their entire history has been reconstructed to fit the dominant culture's narrative of the settling of the West. Similarly troubling is the tradition of white actors playing native roles in film and television.

In the News

There are serious implications from the poor representation that reduces women and people of color to these negative stereotypes. Audiences develop their understanding of issues via the framing of those issues by media outlets.[13] Hispanic and LatinX groups have been virtually absent from coverage in English-language news for decades. When they were present they were frequently not portrayed as subjects with agency, but rather as objects to be commented on.[14] Viewers can internalize prejudice and have not only an unfair self-assessment but problematic perspectives on their own community. Sui and Paul found that Hispanic and LatinX people are still severely underrepresented in local daily newspapers.[15] They noted that when coverage is present it focuses on crime or immigration. In spite of the actual presence of Hispanic

Afro-Latina Journalist Encourages Mentorship

Cloe Cabrera

Cloe Cabrera was one of the first Spanish-speaking female reporters at the *Tampa Tribune*. The newspaper hired her to make inroads in the Hispanic/LatinX community, which had not been previously covered in that area. She became the reporter who interviewed Latinos and gave them a voice in the newspaper for the first time. She covered stories dealing with immigration, Cuba, and Puerto Rico, as well as education, which were always among her beats. Cabrera would make sure to feature Spanish speakers in her stories. Through her work, she encouraged other reporters from the community to become aware of the Spanish speakers so that their voices would be included. Part of her work allowed her to create a list of Spanish speakers and Latinos so that all the reporters could utilize them for their stories, and Cabrera would offer to help if they needed assistance for their stories.

Cabrera's *¿Qué Pasa?* column was a spotlight on positive things Hispanic/Latinos were doing in the community. Cabrera encourages students who are passionate about working in media and journalism in particular not to give up. For her, "as a triple minority woman, black and Hispanic, it is harder." Cabrera recommends looking for mentors. One of Cabrera's mentors was Sylvia Rodriguez Campbell, the first Latina county commissioner. She said they had many conversations about her culture and race that helped her realize "what a powerful position she was in to be able to tell stories and give voices to those that had been denied."

Figure 14.2 Cloe Cabrera
Photo courtesy of Cloe Cabrera

and LatinX communities in the U.S. the representation remains problematic and incomplete.

Gender and Sexuality Issues in Representation

Representation of Hispanic and LatinX people does not improve when examining top films. Smith, Choueiti, and Pieper found no change in demography for the top 100 films each year from 2007 to 2014. Hispanic characters were only 4.9% of the total. In that same time frame zero films in the top 100 had Hispanic or LatinX directors.[16] Smith and colleagues have also tracked gender representation in the same context. They found the ratio of males to females in the films was 2.3:1. Only twenty-one of the films featured a female lead or co-lead and of those twenty-one, three were from underrepresented racial/ethnic groups. They attribute a large part of the problem to lack of diversity in film leadership. In 2014, of the top 100 films, two had female directors, less than 12% of the writers and less than 20% of the producers were female.[17] Many have pointed to this as contributing to the increased **sexualization** of women and girls.[18] In the same study Smith and company found that girls aged 13–20 were just as likely to be shown in sexualized attire and/or with some nudity as women aged 21–39. Additionally, most women characters were depicted in stereotypical roles of caregivers and other domestic positions.

Recognition of the many gendered issues in media is not a new phenomenon. In 1985 cartoonist and comedienne Alison Bechdel wrote about a "test" in her comic *Dykes to Watch Out For*. The test was simple. She would only see a film if it met three requirements: (1) there has to be at least two women in it; (2) they have to talk to each other; (3) the topic of conversation cannot be a man. The joke was that the last movie she was able to see was *Alien*. Feminist scholars and pop-culture critics have popularized the "Bechdel Test" as a way to gauge how male-dominated the film industry is. Bechdel has also publicly given credit for the idea to her friend Liz Wallace.[19]

Representation of lesbian, gay, bisexual, transgender, and queer (LGBTQ) characters is also lacking across the entire U.S. media landscape. In Spanish-language television, LGBTQ people were deemed "nearly invisible" by GLAAD in 2016. The first ever report on this matter examined Spanish-language primetime television from July 2015 through June 2016 on major networks. The analysis showed that a mere 3% of characters were LGBTQ, and many of these were auxiliary to the main plot, filling the role of the "gay best friend" or used for comic relief. The little representation that was observed was primarily found in telenovelas, and the characters were based on limited stereotypes. LGBTQ characters are not necessarily new in telenovelas and, while there have been some historic moments, such as a gay wedding on the Univision novela *Amores Verdaderos*, there is considerable work to do to increase the complexity and diversity of these images.[20]

"Mami, cumplí."

by Victoria Moll
Bilingual Television News Producer

I was born in the neighborhood of Little Havana in Miami, Florida. My mother is Honduran, and my father was Cuban. By the time I was 8 years old my mom was on her own raising my brother and me. My mom was a certified nursing assistant, but she was also that lady who gave out food samples at a local supermarket. She even wore a sandwich board for a while and passed out flyers on the street to save up for my *quinceañera* party. No job was below her, because nothing was greater than her love for us. She always knew the key to a better life was something she didn't have—an education.

In our home, going to college wasn't optional. My mom worked three jobs to put us through private school and constantly told us the biggest disappointment we could give her in life was not graduating college. Many times she told us that if she were to pass away before we finished college the day we finally graduated we were to go to her grave and say, *"Mami, cumplí."* (Mom, I did it.) You don't realize how powerful those words are until you're an adult.

Figure 14.3 Victoria Moll
Photo courtesy of Victoria Moll

My family doesn't care about my résumé consisting of working in the Orlando market during the Casey Anthony trial, or my being the only person from my college (UCF) to ever be accepted into one of the most prestigious programs at NBC, or having worked at CNN, or having also worked for the first anchor to broadcast daily in both English and Spanish. That's all irrelevant to them. Visiting Honduras and comparing it to the luxuries we have here is a reminder of the real world and that is a narrative I bring to the newsroom every day.

My mother is the daughter of an illiterate spitfire named María Victoria, aka Doña Toya. Having conversations with my grandmother makes me think of how to simplify things without making her feel less than, because she's not. No one is. She makes me a better communicator. That's the importance of having a diverse background. I know what it's like to have someone who is important to me not read or write. I know what it's like to go home and have a parent who doesn't speak English. I know what it's like to have your only parent not know how she's going to make ends meet. I know what it's like to depend on student loans, scholarships, financial aid, and your job at the mall to get through college.

I read and write in two languages, yet I go home to Honduras and have a grandmother who will never know what it's like to read a birthday card from a granddaughter named after her. I have a mother who will never fully understand the articles, segments, and stories I write for national newscasts watched by thousands, if not millions, of people every day. That makes me a better human and a better journalist. In the end what society considers the odds stacked against me have actually worked out in my favor.

Conclusion

Representation in media has many gendered and raced components. Media can contribute to the normalization of violence and oversexualizing of women and girls. It can also erase the experiences and thus the very identities of groups on the margins. Rodríguez rightly asserts that "The future is brown, is my thesis; is as brown as the tarnished past."[21] As the Hispanic and LatinX demographics of the U.S. continue to increase it is important to critique bias that is present against specific groups. There are tangible and material impacts to the lived experiences of everyday people. Consumers of media should interrogate the production and their own consumption of all mediated messages. Media representation may always be partial, but it can be inclusive, fair, and truly representative when diversity is valued not only on screen and in print, but in the board rooms and editing offices of major conglomerates.

Vocabulary Words

Gendered

Racializing

Representation

Sexualization

Stereotype

Underrepresented

Points to Remember

- This term Hispanic is not without controversy and many continue to disagree about the usage of a term that references the colonizing forces of Spain.
- Meanings are in people and are co-constructed, but the symbols that make up the words and images being interpreted are the building blocks of understanding.
- Historically, Hispanic and LatinX representation has centered around negative stereotypes portraying both men and women as unethical, lazy, unintelligent, oversexualized, and even criminal.
- Media representation may always be partial, but it can be inclusive, fair, and truly representative when diversity is valued not only on screen and in print, but in the board rooms and editing offices of major conglomerates.

Names to Remember

Alison Bechdel

Practice Questions

1   What is the difference between the terms Hispanic, Latino, and LatinX? How did these terms originate?

2   What does the X in LatinX stand for?

3   What are your thoughts about these labels (Hispanic, Latino, and LatinX) for an ethnicity with roots in so many countries representing people of so many races?

4   Why is representation in media important?

5   Give an example of a recent representation of Hispanics that you saw on screen (either TV, film, or online). What do you think the impact of that representation might be?

Activity

Representation: Write down three examples of representations of Hispanics/LatinX people that you have seen in media. These can be representations from entertainment, news, or any type of content online, on television, or in film, etc. Describe each of those representations. Do you think they are positive or negative? If you could recreate a character or a depiction from one of your examples, how would you frame that representation? Explain your reasons.

Additional Resources

Catherine A. Luther, Carolyn Ringer Lepre, and Naeemah Clark, *Diversity in US mass media* (Hoboken, N. J.: John Wiley & Sons, 2017).

Charles Ramírez Berg, *Latino images in film: Stereotypes, subversion, and resistance* (Austin, TX: University of Texas Press, 2002).

Dana E. Mastro and Elizabeth Behm-Morawitz, "Latino representation on primetime television," *Journalism & Mass Communication Quarterly* 82, no. 1 (2005): 110–130.

Ediberto Roman, "Who exactly is living la vida loca: The legal and political consequences of Latino-Latina ethnic and racial stereotypes in film and other media," *J. Gender Race & Just*, no. 4 (2000): 37.

About the Author

Jennifer A. Sandoval
Photo courtesy of the University of
Central Florida

Jennifer Sandoval, Ph.D., is an Associate Professor at the Nicholson School of Communication at the University of Central Florida. She has a Ph.D. in Communication and Culture from the University of New Mexico and a Master's of Dispute Resolution from Pepperdine School of Law. Dr. Sandoval brings her experience as a mediator, project manager, trainer, and consultant to the classroom and her research program at UCF. She is interested in the communication of marginalized identity in various contexts. Her research focuses on the communicative elements involved in the intersection of identity, the body, and health. Additionally, she examines the rhetoric of choice and Assistive Reproductive Technology, as well as looking at reproductive health access for the LGBT community. Dr. Sandoval also continues to work with community-based participatory research projects focusing on health intervention in underserved and underrepresented populations.

Notes

1 Kenton T. Wilkinson, *Spanish-Language Television in the United States: Fifty Years of Development* (New York: Routledge, 2015).
2 Grace Flores-Hughes, "The Origin of the Term 'Hispanic'," *Harvard Journal of Hispanic Policy* 18, (2006): 81–84.

3 G. Cristina Mora, *Making Hispanics: How Activists, Bureaucrats, and Media Constructed a New American* (Chicago, IL: University of Chicago Press, 2014).

4 Stuart Hall, Jessica Evans, and Sean Nixon, *Representation*, 2nd Ed. (London: Sage, 2013), 1.

5 Clara E. Rodríguez, *Latin Looks: Images of Latinas and Latinos in the U.S. Media* (Boulder, CO: Westview Books, 1997), 21.

6 Dana Mastro and Bradley Greenberg, "The Portrayal of Racial Minorities on Prime Time Television," *Journal of Broadcasting & Electronic Media* 44, no. 4 (2000): 690–703. doi:10.1207/s15506878jobem4404-10; Dana Mastro, Elizabeth Behm-Morawitz, and Michelle Ortiz, "The Cultivation of Social Perceptions of Latinos: A Mental Models Approach, *Media Psychology* 9, no. 2 (2007): 347–365, doi:10.1080/15213260701286106; Charles Ramírez Berg, *Latino Images in Film: Stereotypes, Subversion, and Resistance* (Austin, TX: University of Texas Press, 2002); Rodríguez, *Latin Looks: Images of Latinas and Latinos in the U.S. Media.*

7 Mastro and Greenberg, "The Portrayal of Racial Minorities on Prime Time Television."

8 Elizabeth Monk-Turner, Mary Heiserman, Crystle Johnson, Vanity Cotton, and Manny Jackson, "The Portrayal of Racial Minorities on Prime Time Television: A Replication of the Mastro and Greenberg Study a Decade Later," *Studies in Popular Culture* 32, no. 2 (2010): 101–114.

9 Ibid., 109.

10 Ramírez Berg, *Latino Images in Film: Stereotypes, Subversion, and Resistance*, 66.

11 Ibid., 68.

12 Peter C. Rollins and John E. O'Connor, *Hollywood's Indian: The Portrayal of the Native American in Film* (Lexington, KY: University Press of Kentucky, 2003), 6.

13 Mingxiao Sui and Newly Paul, "Latino Portrayals in Local News Media: Under-representation, Negative Stereotypes, and Institutional Predictors of Coverage," *Journal of Intercultural Communication Research* 46, no. 3 (2017): 273–294, doi:10.1080/17475759.2017.1322124.

14 L. Navarrette and C. Kamasaki, *Out of the Picture: Hispanics in the Media* (Washington, DC: National Council of La Raza, 1994); C. Luther, C. Lepre, and N. Clark, *Diversity in U.S. Mass Media* (Malden, MA: Wiley-Blackwell, 2012).

15 Sui and Paul, "Latino Portrayals in Local News Media: Underrepresentation, Negative Stereotypes, and Institutional Predictors of Coverage."

16 Stacy L. Smith, Marc Choueiti, and Katherine Pieper, "Gender Inequality in Popular Films: Examining On Screen Portrayals and Behind-the-Scenes Employment Patterns in Motion Pictures Released Between 2007–2014," *Media, Diversity, & Social Change Initiative, USC Annenberg*, 2014, http://annenberg.usc.edu/sites/default/files/MDSCI _Gender_Inequality_in_600_films.pdf.

17 Ibid.

18 Ibid.

19 Megan Garber, "Call It the 'Bechdel-Wallace Test'," *The Atlantic*, August 25, 2015, www.theatlantic.com/entertainment/archive/2015/08/call-it-the-bechdel-wallace-test/402259.

20 GLAAD, "Nearly Invisible: LGBTQ Representation on Spanish-Language Television in the United States," November 2016, www.glaad.org/files/SLMR/SPA Report2016.pdf.

21 R. Rodríguez, *Brown: The Last Discovery of America* (New York: Penguin Books, 2002), 35.

15 Linguistic Diversity in Hispanic/LatinX Media

Leveraging Your Skills

Laura Gonzales, Ph.D.

Assistant Professor of Rhetoric and Writing Studies, University of Texas at El Paso

The presence of Hispanic communities in the United States is only increasing, expected to encompass 20% of the U.S. population by the year 2020.[1] According to Alcance Media Group, Hispanics in the U.S. have an annual purchasing power of $1.5 trillion, meaning that an increasing number of broadcasters, marketers, and advertisers are focusing their attention on the U.S. Hispanic market.[2] In short, being able to reach Hispanic audiences through media is an increasingly valuable asset.

Bilingual individuals who speak Spanish and English in the U.S. are able to communicate with a wide range of individuals from multiple countries, cultures, and contexts. Indeed, according to the United States Census Bureau, "Hispanics" in the U.S. include individuals from multiple South and Central American nations, including Mexico, Puerto Rico, Cuba, El Salvador, and many others.[3]

The term Hispanic was originally developed by the U.S. government during the 1970 Census (referring to individuals from Mexico, Puerto Rico, or South America). Accordingly, the concept of "Hispanic" can mean a wide variety of things and can describe a wide variety of people, all of whom have distinct cultures, backgrounds, languages, and experiences. As Rodríguez explains, the term "Hispanic" was (and still often is) used to "denationalize" or disconnect LatinX people from their home countries (e.g., Cuba, Ecuador, Colombia) and to "re-nationalize" or re-establish them as U.S. Hispanics.[4] To be Hispanic, in turn, means to be a person from a Latin American country who lives in the U.S.

So, what does this mean for people working in media industries in the United States? First, preparing yourself to reach a Hispanic audience can mean developing strategies for addressing people from multiple different countries and nations, often simultaneously. Language is a critical component of these differences, since individuals from different Spanish-speaking places use different words, accents, and intonations. Just as there are different types of English, there are different forms of Spanish, and it is a broadcaster's responsibility to embrace, value, and address these differences as we provide valuable information to our audiences.

This chapter provides some background and strategies for understanding, preparing, and addressing language differences as media professionals working to reach Hispanic audiences in both Spanish and English. The three sections outlined below will provide you with some introductory understanding of what it means to use and develop your languages as strengths in Hispanic media communication.

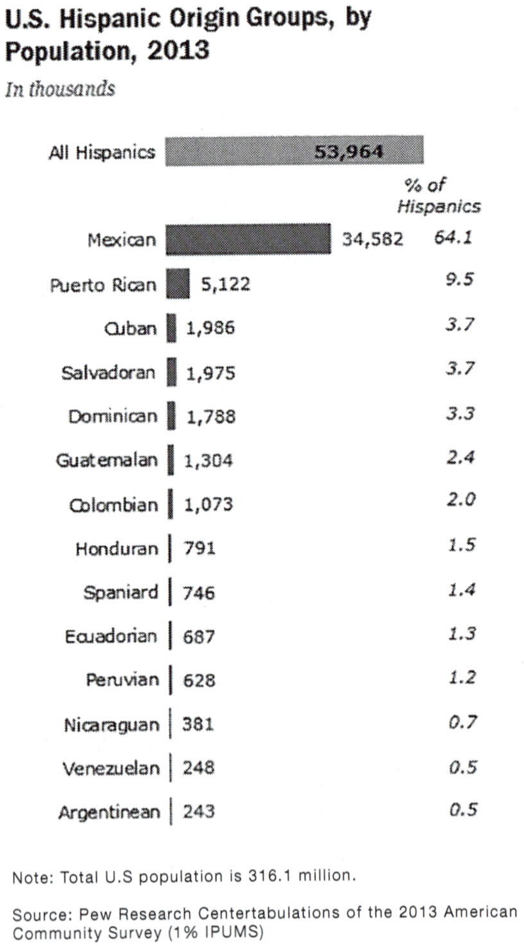

U.S. Hispanic Origin Groups, by Population, 2013

In thousands

		% of Hispanics
All Hispanics	53,964	
Mexican	34,582	64.1
Puerto Rican	5,122	9.5
Cuban	1,986	3.7
Salvadoran	1,975	3.7
Dominican	1,788	3.3
Guatemalan	1,304	2.4
Colombian	1,073	2.0
Honduran	791	1.5
Spaniard	746	1.4
Ecuadorian	687	1.3
Peruvian	628	1.2
Nicaraguan	381	0.7
Venezuelan	248	0.5
Argentinean	243	0.5

Note: Total U.S population is 316.1 million.

Source: Pew Research Centertabulations of the 2013 American Community Survey (1% IPUMS)

Figure 15.1 Bar graphs of Hispanic origin groups in 2013.

Courtesy of Pew Hispanic Center

Understand Your History

Growing up speaking Spanish does not necessarily mean that you feel confident speaking Spanish in all contexts. Some people who grew up speaking Spanish were encouraged to assimilate in an English-speaking world, often resulting in the loss of some Spanish proficiency. For example, during an anonymous interview with a student we will refer to as "Ana," a communication college student working in a bilingual news broadcasting organization, she reflected on her experiences growing up speaking both Spanish and English. She explained:

> I was raised speaking Spanish, but the [education] system was designed to, instead of helping me embrace my first language, to tell me "no, we don't do that here, we don't speak that language here." I was not allowed to speak Spanish at school, so I lost a lot of my Spanish as I learned English.[5]

As she continued her interview, Ana shared that when she thought of Spanish at a young age, "all I could hear is 'No, we don't do that here.'"[6] When she would try to speak Spanish in her classroom or to use Spanish when words in English were not readily available, Ana's teachers would reprimand her, telling her "no, *that* language is not acceptable *here*."[7] For this reason, now that she is in college, Ana does not feel as comfortable communicating in Spanish as she does in English, primarily because she worked so hard to "get rid of" her Spanish as a child. In turn, Ana decided to join the bilingual news broadcasting organization in college as a way to re-learn her Spanish, and to reconnect with the history she was forced to leave behind early on. As she becomes more involved with the news broadcasting organization, Ana has to practice using Spanish, even though this was her first language.

A Bilingual TV Show Before Its Time

¿QuéPasa, USA?

¿QuéPasa, USA?, which translates to "What's Happening, America?," was a comedy series that appeared on PBS from 1977 to 1980. This series is America's first bilingual comedy, as well as the very first sitcom that was produced for PBS. The series focused on a Cuban-American family living in Little Havana, a predominately Cuban community in Miami, Florida. The show is still popular and sold on DVD.

Source: QuePasaUSA.org

As people train to be bilingual news broadcasters, it is important they explore and understand their own histories, learning and using both Spanish and English. Knowing this history can help them understand why they might struggle and how others struggle, too. Since they are Spanish speakers communicating with other Hispanics in the U.S., many of their own struggles with the language can resonate with the experiences of the audience. In turn, being honest about their journey may help guide the audience toward their own understanding.

There Is No "Right" Language

Since Spanish speakers come from so many backgrounds and cultures, providing one news broadcast that can be understood by all is a tough challenge. For this reason, bilingual news agencies may encourage you to adopt a "**neutral**" or "standard" version of Spanish as a news broadcaster. The "neutral" or "standard" version of Spanish is to help broadcasters reach the widest possible range of Spanish-speaking audiences. These linguistic standards require that broadcasters avoid jargon or country/culture-specific language that may be inaccessible to some viewers or listeners.[8] Training and using perceivably standard varieties of Spanish has helped bilingual news broadcasters and networks to communicate with their target audiences.

Institutions such as Real Academia Española (www.rae.es) provide standards for what is considered "generalized," "neutral," or "standard" Spanish. In particular, Real Academia Española was established to both establish and preserve the Spanish language, providing dictionaries, commentaries, and other relevant information that has come to set the standard for Spanish speakers in many nations.[9]

That being said, all language-based organizations are centered in a specific culture, country, or institution. For example, Real Academia Española is based in Spain and has focused on preserving the integrity of Castilian Spanish.[10] Language is power, which means that individuals who have added resources (e.g., education, money) often maintain the power to set standards in what is considered neutral or appropriate language.

As bilingual news broadcasters, it is important to always have an understanding about the audience. In some cases, adopting "standard" varieties of Spanish such as those sanctioned by Real Academia Española may be the most appropriate option for successfully conveying our message. At other times, however, we may need to target specific varieties of Spanish in order to reach a more specific population. When communicating health messages and other critical information, we may want to research the specific area where our broadcasts will be shared, and then alter our language to meet the specific conventions of this population. This is what some language and communication scholars refer to as localization, which is the process of tailoring information and designs to the specific needs and conventions of a local audience.[11] When we localize, we research our audience and their specific terminology, and we alter our words to reach that audience more directly.

Covering the LatinX Community in Local News

by Nancy Alvarez
News Anchor for WFTV Channel 9 Orlando, Florida

The day after the mass shooting at Pulse nightclub in Orlando, my co-anchor, Jamie Homes, and I were live on the air for 8 hours of continuous coverage. It was over the course of those hours that many of the victims' names were released. That is when the realization began to sink in—most of the victims were Hispanic.

I work for the ABC affiliate in Central Florida, an English-speaking station where Latino names that pop up on our teleprompter are always delivered with the "Americanized" pronunciation. This morning should have been no different. But it was. Split-second decisions on what to say during breaking news are not uncommon on the anchor desk and they're usually based on knowledge of the situation or the area. My decision on how to pronounce the names was based solely on my experience of growing up Latina.

I had heard all these names before . . . *Angel, Juan Ramon, Javier, Alejandro* . . . they're common names in Hispanic communities. But on this particular morning these names were tied to an unimaginable tragedy for their families and our community. I did not know these victims personally but I felt a connection to them just by learning their names. So, as I explained on the air, I decided to pronounce their names "the way their *mamis* and *abuelas* would pronounce them. The way they probably heard their names at home all their lives."

It was my own small, personal way of honoring who they were. I didn't think much of it at the time but the response from viewers both inside *and outside* the Hispanic community was overwhelmingly positive. Some saw it as a sign of respect. Others called it comforting. For me, it was a learning experience. I made an editorial decision based on my history, my upbringing, my culture, and my knowledge of what the heart of my community looks and sounds like. I took a risk based on instinct. And it was okay.

That instinct served me again one year later when covering the aftermath of Hurricane Maria in Puerto Rico. I landed in San Juan shortly after the storm to report for my English-language station on an island where the predominant language is, of course, Spanish. I discovered that, even among Puerto Ricans who spoke perfect English, describing the storm, the damage, and the heartbreak was more natural and more cathartic in their native tongue. Bottom line—the sound bite was always better in Spanish.

So, for the most part, Spanish it was. My content for our social platforms as well as for our on-air newscasts was woven with both languages, with me translating along the way.

After countless stories aired and thousands commenting on social media, here's the verdict on the language aspect of my coverage: no one noticed. Or no one cared. I don't think I heard a single complaint about so much Spanish on an English-language channel. I had initially worried it could be a distraction but it actually made the stories more authentic.

I also used language as a reporting tool. In stories related to the migration of Puerto Ricans to Florida, I made a concerted effort to find islanders who spoke English. This helped me send a message home to places such as Orlando and Kissimmee that are seeing a huge influx: your new neighbors, coworkers, and classmates are not foreigners from a faraway land. They are Americans. Don't believe me? Just listen to them speak.

In the end, the experiences of the Puerto Rican people during and after Hurricane Maria transcended culture and language. And, I'm proud to say, so did the journalism.

Figure 15.2 Nancy Alvarez
Photo courtesy of WFTV Channel 9

Be Creative: Language is More than Words

Bilingual news broadcasters will likely encounter difficulties communicating with the audience at some point. This is part of the process for all media production, but it is especially applicable when working in bi- or multilingual contexts. For example, during an interview, one might encounter some difficulty communicating with the interviewee, especially if she or he comes from a different country or culture than the one(s) the reporter has been trained in. When these situations arise, it is time to be creative and use any of the other available resources to communicate.

During an anonymous interview with another communication student we will refer to as "Natalie," she explained,

> When I struggle to understand what someone is telling me during an interview, or when I can't think of a way to phrase what I want to say, I use my hands or arms to point or gesture, or I even draw or sketch something, or look something up that might help me and my interviewee understand each other.[12]

As Natalie suggests, struggles with communication are almost unavoidable, especially when you are sharing information with Spanish-speaking individuals from so many different backgrounds. Fortunately, however, one's experiences as a bilingual learner position you favorably to overcome these types of discrepancies, turning them into assets rather than detriments to the communication.

Research has shown that being bilingual changes the architecture of the brain. Sometimes, this restructuring causes the languages that a person knows to compete, as he or she transforms his/her understanding of a concept or idea into a word in a specific language. Many bilingual people experience moments where they cannot think of how to say something in Spanish rather than English, or vice versa.[13] In these cases, we might have to pause to think of exactly how we want to voice our thoughts or ideas, deciding among the various options that we might have within the different languages we speak. Over time, however, as we practice switching between languages, our brains become trained to not only communicate more quickly, but also to come up with more creative options for describing our thoughts. For instance, while a monolingual learner might only have one or two ways to describe a concept or idea, a bi- or multilingual learner, especially one who has practiced switching between languages, may have ten or twenty ways for describing that same concept.

As a media professional, this might mean coming up with several creative solutions for communicating with a wider range of audiences. In these cases, rather than limiting you, the languages you speak help you transform ideas across contexts and cultures, helping you and your audience to better understand the information being presented. For this reason, as you practice moving between Spanish and English, and as you gain experience communicating with

Hispanic audiences from different backgrounds, it is important not to limit yourself. Use your resources—your ideas, your body, your stories—to share the important information that you have to deliver. You know a lot more than you have been trained to acknowledge.

Tips and Next Steps

The suggestions and descriptions listed above are just a starting point for helping you to understand and exercise the value of your linguistic abilities.

Bilingual Actress Defies Stereotypes

Karla Souza

Born in Mexico, Karla Souza is a television and film actress of Chilean and Mexican descent. Her breakout role was in a Mexican telenovela titled *Verano de amor*. She also stars in the incredibly popular show *How to Get Away with Murder*, in which she plays a smart law student. She told Variety.com: "Audiences are very happy to see a Latina represented without being sexualized or being part of a drug cartel. She's sort of opening the way for other storylines."

Sources: Latina.com, KarlaSouza.org, Variety.com

Figure 15.3 Karla Souza
s_bukley/Shutterstock

Understanding our language differences as assets rather than deficits is an important part of supporting our Latino and Hispanic community. At the same time, part of our role as communicators, particularly in bilingual media, is to continuously adjust our language and communication skills to meet the needs of increasingly diverse audiences. As you continue your training in bilingual news broadcasting, you might find it helpful to study Hispanic culture, gaining a better understanding of Latino communities that might be very different from your own. Listening to Spanish-language radio or watching Spanish-language television from various networks might also help you grasp the cultural and linguistic transitions that you may interact with through your work. Follow along, training your voice, gestures, and expressions to be increasingly flexible and to move across languages.

Although imitating accents may be unproductive, listening and following along to different types of Spanish might provide you with more options for conveying information. Keep track of these options, making lists of words, phrases, or expressions that you might encounter in your interactions with people from specific regions or countries. The more you know how to read your audience, and the more you train your ear to listen across languages, the more valuable you will be, both to your potential employers and to the communities you aim to reach through your work.

Points to Remember

- By 2020, Hispanics will account for approximately 20% of the U.S. population.
- The broad term Hispanic is utilized to describe people from a variety of cultural backgrounds.
- Broadcasters must communicate in "neutral" Spanish in order to reach a wide range of Spanish-speaking audiences.
- The Real Academia Española sets standards for Spanish speakers in many nations.

Names to Remember

Real Academia Española

Practice Questions

1   Who developed the term Hispanic? According to Rodríguez, what was the purpose of creating such term to describe these populations in the U.S.?
2   Explain why is it important for a bilingual broadcaster to remember where she/he came from? How can it help new professionals in the field of broadcasting?

3   What is the purpose of communicating in standard or neutral Spanish? What are some implications of failing to do so?

4   What is the Real Academia Española? How is it being used by news broad-casters?

5   What are some advantages of being bilingual according to the text?

Activity

News Story Language Analysis: Think about a time that you read or watched a particular news report and had difficulty understanding the scope of the story due to a language barrier. In a few sentences, explain what you remember about the story and describe how the story was narrated or written. Did the story have jargon language? If so, do you think it was trying to reach a specific target audience? Or was it inadvertent use of language? Did it change the meaning of the story?

Additional Resources

Real Academia Espanola: www.rae.es/
1970 Census addition of the term "Hispanic" www.pewsocialtrends.org/2010/03/03/census-history-counting-hispanics-2/

Laura Gonzales

Photo courtesy of Laura Gonzales

About the Author

Laura Gonzales, Ph.D., is an Assistant Professor of Rhetoric and Writing Studies at the University of Texas at El Paso. Her work focuses on highlighting the value of linguistic diversity in professional and academic spaces. Her monograph, *Sites of Translation: What Multilinguals Can Teach Us About Digital Rhetoric and Writing*, was awarded the 2016 Sweetland/UM Press Digital Rhetoric Collaborative Book Prize.

Notes

1   J. Piñón and V. Rojas, "Language and Cultural Identity in the New Configuration of the US Latino TV Industry," *Global Media and Communication* 7, no. 2 (2011): 129–147.

2   Alcance Media Group, 2015. www.alcancemg.com/en/home/

3   "Hispanic Heritage Month," *United States Census Bureau*, www.census.gov/eeo/special_emphasis_programs/hispanic_heritage.html.

4 America Rodríguez, *Making Latino News: Race, Language, Class* (Thousand Oaks, CA: Sage, 1999).

5 Interview with Ana.

6 Ibid.

7 Ibid.

8 Alan R. Stephenson, David E. Reese, and Mary E. Beadle, *Broadcast Announcing Worktext: Performing for Radio, Television, and Cable* (Abingdon, UK: Taylor & Francis, 2005).

9 "What is Neutral Spanish," *Globalization Partners International*, June 17, 2011, http://blog.globalizationpartners.com/what-is-neutral-spanish.aspx

10 Ibid.

11 L. Gonzales and R. Zantjer, "Translation as a User-Localization Practice," *Technical Communication* 62, no. 4 (2015): 271–284.

12 Interview with Natalie.

13 F. Fabbro, "The Bilingual Brain: Cerebral Representation of Languages," *Brain and Language* 79, no. 2 (2001): 211–222.

Glossary

Acculturation   Cultural modification of an individual, group, or people by adapting to or borrowing traits from another culture.

Adaptation-Standardization   The process of making things of the same type have the same basic features.

Affiliates   Local broadcast stations with an agreement to carry network programming exclusively.

Anglo-American Society   North Americans whose native language is English, especially those whose culture or ethnic background is of European origin.

App   Short for application. A program (such as a word processor or a spreadsheet) that performs a particular task or set of tasks.

Appropriation   The action of taking something for one's own use, typically without the owner's permission.

Assimilation   In anthropology and sociology, the process whereby individuals or groups of differing ethnic heritage are absorbed into the dominant culture of a society.

Bachata   A genre of popular song and dance of the Dominican Republic performed with guitars and percussion.

Bajo Sexto   A twelve-string guitar found throughout Northern Mexico.

Bandido   The Spanish word for "bandit." The *bandido*, a villainous character usually of Mexican ethnicity, was often used in early motion-picture westerns; the *bandido* was the villain to the hero Anglo cowboy.

Biculturalism   Having or combining the cultural attitudes and customs of two nations, peoples, or ethnic groups.

Blackface   A form of theatrical makeup applied to a performer playing a black person. The practice gained popularity during the nineteenth century and contributed to the spread of racial stereotypes. It is widely considered offensive.

Blocks   Scheduled time slots for specific content during programming.

Blogosphere   All of the blogs or bloggers on the internet regarded collectively.

Boatlift   An act of transporting people or supplies by boat; especially an act of transporting refugees in small boats when official modes of transport are blocked.

Bodegas   Small stores located in Spanish-speaking communities that offer groceries, beer and wine, etc.

Body Art   A sub-category of performance art in which artists use their own bodies to make their particular statements.

Bolero   Lyrical song genre accompanied by guitar that originated in Cuba at the turn of the twentieth century. The bolero quickly spread throughout Latin American and the Caribbean, becoming the basis for an international pan-Latin American style.

Border Protection, Antiterrorism and Illegal Immigration Control Act (H.R. 4437)   Known as the Sensenbrenner Act, this legislation directed the Secretary of Homeland Security (Secretary) to take actions to maintain operational control over the U.S. international land and maritime borders, including: (1) systematic surveillance using unmanned aerial vehicles (UAVs), ground-based sensors, satellites, radar coverage, and cameras; (2) physical infrastructure enhancements to prevent unlawful U.S. entry and facilitate United States Customs and Border Protection border access; (3) hiring and training additional Border Patrol agents; and (4) increasing deployment of United States Customs and Border Protection personnel to border areas with high levels of unlawful entry.

Bracero Program   A program from 1948 to 1964 that allowed Mexicans to do farm work in the U.S. as temporary guest workers.

Bric a Brac   Miscellaneous objects and ornaments of little value.

Brokers   Individuals who rented time on radio stations and developed programming to fill the time as well as sold sponsorships or advertising to be aired on and to support the programs.

Button Accordion   An accordion with a keyboard in the form of series of buttons.

Buying Power   The ability of a person, group, or company to buy things, or the amount of money they have available to spend.

Chicano(a)   Mexican-American.

Chinese Exclusion Act   An act from 1882 that prohibited labor by Chinese immigrants in the U.S.

Circulation   The number of copies of a newspaper distributed on an average day.

Code-Switching   The practice of alternating between two or more languages or varieties of language in conversation.

Collectivism   The practice or principle of giving a group priority over each individual in it.

Commonwealth   Refers to the relationship between Puerto Rico and the United States that was approved by Congress in 1952.

Conjunto   Type of ensemble centered around the button accordion and the twelve-string guitar known as the bajo sexto. It developed in Texas and is largely associated with the working class. Conjunto has a counterpart genre with similar instrumentation on the Northern Mexico side of the border known as norteño, which is closely associated with immigrant identity.

Conquistador   One that conquers; specifically, a leader in the Spanish conquest of America and especially of Mexico and Peru in the sixteenth century.

Corrido   Narrative ballad that has flourished in Mexico and the American Southwest at least since the early part of the nineteenth century. The *corrido* has been an important vehicle for social commentary and activism among Mexican-Americans.

Cuban Adjustment Act   An act designed to allow Cuban refugees to become lawful residents of the U.S. after living in the country for one year and a day.

Cuban Refugee Program   A welfare assistance program provided by the U.S. government to Cuban refugees.

Cuban Thaw   A term used to describe the effort to restore diplomatic ties with Cuba by the Obama administration in 2014.

Cumbia   A music and dance genre originally from Colombia. Starting in the 1950s, cumbia quickly spread through South America, Central America, and Mexico. A style of cumbia that developed in the 1970s became an important part of the repertoire of conjunto and norteño bands of Northern Mexico, Texas, and other parts of the Southwest.

Democratization   The establishment or transition to a democratic political regime where the whole population participates in national decisions, typically through elected representatives.

Deregulation (Media)   A process in which a government removes controls and rules about how newspapers, television channels, etc. are owned and controlled.

Diaspora   The movement, migration, or scattering of a people away from an established or ancestral homeland.

Dichotomy   A division or contrast between two things that are or are represented as being opposed or entirely different.

Dictatorship   A government in which absolute power is exercised by a dictator.

Differentiation   The process of maintaining distinguishing or distinct traditions, practices, and customs associated with Hispanic/Latino culture.

Digital Divide   The economic, educational, and social inequalities between those who have computers and online access and those who do not.

Direct-to-Home (DTH)   This technology enables a broadcasting company to directly beam the signal to your TV set through a receiver that is installed in the house. There is no need for a separate cable connection.

Diversification   The action of making or becoming more diverse or varied.

Doobie   This wrapping of the hair with bobby pins is common in Puerto Rico and Dominican Republic that is used after the hair is placed in rollers to make it straight.

DREAMers Movement   A movement to support undocumented youth in the U.S. and rally for amnesty.

Editorial   A statement in a newspaper or magazine, or on radio or television, that expresses the opinion of the editors or owners on a subject of particular interest.

Edutainment   Programming content that is intended to be entertainment but has been developed or adapted to convey a message of social importance.

Embargo   Official ban on trade or other commercial activity with a particular country.

Executive Order 8802   In June of 1941, President Roosevelt issued Executive Order 8802, banning discriminatory employment practices by Federal agencies and all unions and companies engaged in war-related work. The order also established the Fair Employment Practices Commission to enforce the new policy.

Federal Communication Commission (FCC)   A U.S. independent regulatory agency responsible for implementing and enforcing laws and regulations governing communication services such as radio, television, telephone, satellite, and cable.

First-Generation   Designating the first of a generation to become the citizen of a new country.

Format   A description of the overall sound of a radio station. The format is used to help market a station to a particular audience that research suggests has an affinity for the style of music or discussion.

Gendered   Relating or specific to people of one particular gender.

Genre   A category of artistic works characterized by similarities in form, style, or subject matter.

Good Neighbor Policy   A policy implemented by President Franklin Roosevelt during World War II to improve relationships and create economic opportunities with Latin American countries due to rising friction with Germany and Japan.

Greasers   A derogatory term, which has its roots in the early 1900s, that was applied to a person of Mexican descent. The slang word was used to describe the Mexican workers who toiled in the tannery industry and wagon wheel construction, in which grease was used by the workers.

Great Recession   A period of economic downturn experienced by the United States beginning in December 2007. The downturn is not described as depression since the severity has not encompassed the levels of the Great Depression in the 1930s. The U.S. market housing decline is pointed out to be one of the causes of the Great Recession.

Habanera   A Cuban salon dance that gained international popularity during that time, made a strong impact in the musical life of that city, through music arriving not only from Cuba, but also Mexico and other parts of Latin America, where the habanera rhythm had also taken root.

Hart–Celler Act Also known as the Immigration Act of 1965, the act eliminated some of the per-country quotas established before and allowed immigrants from South and Eastern Europe, Asia, and Africa to come to the U.S. It also put restrictions on the number of visas granted to Western Hemisphere countries.

Hashtags A word or phrase preceded by the symbol # that classifies or categorizes the accompanying text (such as a tweet).

High-Context Communication Believed to happen mostly in Asian, Arab, and Hispanic cultures—it is posited that individuals place most of their communicational meaning within context—this means that the communication form can be either explicit or implicit, and that it is mostly hard to decode or interpret by the non-members of the community.

Hispanic Refers to language. If your ancestry is from a Spanish-speaking country, you can be considered Hispanic.

Hispanic Marketing Refers to the planning, development, and practice of marketing programs geared to connect with Hispanic markets by means of consumer insights. These insights are tied to their socio-psychographics and Hispanic cultural heritage—which includes social norms, manners, customs, myths, religion, interpersonal communication forms, social structures, and language.

Hollywood Blacklist In 1947, the House Committee on Un-American Activities (HUAC) headed by anti-communist Senator Joseph McCarthy (R-WI), accusing certain Hollywood entertainment professionals, including some of Hollywood's then leading directors, actors, and writers, as being communist-sympathizers. Many of those named on the Blacklist were prevented from being hired in the film industry, and a number of them were jailed for refusing to cooperate with McCarthy's red-baiting tactics.

Iconography The visual images and symbols used in a work of art or the study or interpretation of these.

Installation An artistic genre of three-dimensional works that can be site-specific and designed to transform a space.

Internal-Localization Approach that deals with the idea of localization within markets, particularly among multi-diversified markets such as the U.S. The idea that any standardized campaign can produce the same results across all market segments is inconceivable. That is akin to saying that an English-language ad can simply be aired on Univision, a Spanish- language TV network, and produce similar results as those received by the same ad aired in the general market.

Jones-Shafroth Act Signed into law in 1917, this act made Puerto Rico a U.S. territory and granted U.S. citizenship to the residents of the island.

Latin Not to be confused with the language of Latin, this term can also be used in relation to the peoples or countries where Romance languages are spoken; specifically: of or relating to the peoples or countries of Latin America.

Latin Jazz   An umbrella term used to refer to two sub-styles of jazz influenced by Afro-Cuban music and Brazilian bossa nova during the 1960s.

Latino   Refers to geography. If a person's ancestry is from parts of the Caribbean (Puerto Rico, Cuba, Dominican Republic), Central or South America, they can be considered Latin. Includes Brazil.

Lector   Someone who reads out loud to other people.

Linear Segmentation   Approach utilized by marketers based on the language of preference and works by identifying consumers as Spanish-dominant, transitional, and English-dominant.

Low-Context Communication   Form of communication that is clear, either verbally or in writing, and non-members of the community can easily understand the message.

Lucha Libre   Wrestling characterized by exaggerated gestures, costumes, and masked characters.

Mainstream   A prevailing current or direction of activity or influence.

Mambo   A ballroom dance of Cuban origin that resembles the rumba and the cha-cha; *also*: the music for this dance.

Market Share   The percentage of an industry or market's total sales that is earned by a particular company over a specified time period.

Masculine   Having qualities appropriate to or usually associated with a man.

Memes   An amusing or interesting item (such as a captioned picture or video) or genre of items that is spread widely online especially through social media.

Merengue   Popular dance form originally from the Dominican Republic that in the 1980s and 1990s rivaled salsa's popularity in New York.

"*México de Afuera*" Ideology   Social movement created and promoted by Mexican intellectuals and entrepreneurs—living in exile to preserve Mexican identity in the U.S. during the 1920s.

Monopoly   Market situation where one producer (or a group of producers acting in concert) controls supply of a good or service, and where the entry of new producers is prevented or highly restricted.

MOS   Film term meaning "without sound," named so due to the accents of early Eastern Europeans filmmakers for their pronunciation of "without" as "mit-out."

Mural   Large-scale painting painted directly on a wall.

Mutual Aid Societies   Organizations that provide benefits or other help to members when they are affected by things such as death, sickness, disability, old age, or unemployment.

National Origins Act   A 1924 act that established immigration quotas from Europe and Asia and the creation of the Border Patrol.

Neutral   Not supporting or helping either side in a conflict, disagreement, etc.; impartial.

New Wave   A genre of rock music popular in late 1970s and the 1980s with ties to mid-1970s punk rock.

Nuyorican   A person of Puerto Rican birth or descent who is a current or former resident of New York City.

Oeuvre   The works of an artist regarded collectively.

Operation Bootstrap   Operation put in place to industrialize Puerto Rico but displaced thousands of rural workers to urban areas.

Operation Peter Pan   An exodus of unaccompanied Cuban children to the U.S. between 1960 and 1962.

Orquesta   A large ensemble featuring brass and reed instruments, electric guitar, bass, and drumset that developed in Texas and was influential throughout the Southwest.

Panamsat   The first private satellite service with global reach emerged.

Performance   Presented to an audience within a fine art context, which can be either scripted or unscripted with or without audience participation.

Periodical   Published with a fixed interval between the issues or numbers.

Platt Amendment   Passed on March 2, 1901, this amendment set conditions on withdrawal of U.S. troops from Cuba, restricted Cuba's authority to negotiate treaties and land transfers to non-U.S. countries and it allowed the U.S. to build a naval base in Guantanamo Bay.

POV   Point of view. In film, the POV is how the story is told; from whose point of view.

Power Distance   Published with a fixed interval between the issues or numbers.

Primetime   The regularly occurring time at which a television or radio audience is expected to be greatest, typically the hours between 8 and 11 p.m.

Prohibition Era   A nationwide constitutional ban in the United States on the production, importation, transportation, and sale of alcoholic beverages that remained in place from 1920 to 1933.

Pull Factors   Conditions that incentivize people to migrate to places where there is a need for labor, offer a better quality of life, and offer other favorable social and economic conditions.

Push Factors   Social and economic conditions that push groups of people to migrate in response to events such as war, economic downfalls, and degrading environmental conditions.

Racializing   To impose a racial interpretation on; place in a racial context.

Ranchera   A type of Mexican country music typically played with guitars and horns.

Readership   Estimates of how many people read a publication, often calculated from surveys, interviews, or using circulation data.

Reggaetón   A form of dance music of Puerto Rican origin, characterized by a fusion of Latin rhythms, dancehall, and hip-hop or rap.

Reggaetonero   Spanish word for reggaetón singer.

Repatriation   To restore or return to the country of origin, allegiance, or citizenship.

Representation   An essential part of the process by which a meaning is produced and exchanged between members of a culture.

Revolving Door Period   A circulation of people from the U.S. and Puerto Rico between 1965 and 1980.

Salsa   A musical genre developed mainly by Puerto Rican musicians living in New York during the late 1960s and 1970s. Salsa quickly became popular throughout Latin America becoming an important symbol of pan-Latin American identity.

Second-Generation   Denoting the offspring of parents who were born to immigrants in a particular country.

Sexualization   To make sexual; endow with a sexual character or quality.

Snaps   On the popular social media application Snapchat, users post brief video clips called snaps, which expire after 24 hours.

Social Integration   A way in which members of a minority community engage in dialog and activities that help them access the resources and opportunities afforded to members of mainstream communities.

Sound Bites   Short sentences or phrases that are easy to remember, often included in speeches made by politicians or celebrities and repeated in newspapers and on television and radio.

Spanglish   Spanish that includes the use of English words.

Spanish Harlem   Also called East Harlem, and El Barrio, is a neighborhood of Upper Manhattan, New York City, that is known for being one of the largest predominantly Latino communities in New York City, mostly made up of Puerto Ricans, as well as a rising number of Dominican, Salvadoran, and Mexican immigrants.

Spot   A TV or radio advertisement, typically lasting 15 or 30 seconds.

Stereotype   A widely held but fixed and oversimplified image or idea of a particular type of person or thing.

Strategic Marketing Communication   Technique meant to create customized campaigns that can facilitate the connection between brands and customers on an emotional level.

Sweeps   One-month ratings measurement periods in television, happening in November, February, May, and July, and used for program scheduling and advertising decisions.

Syndication   The sale or licensing of material for publication or broadcasting by a number of television stations, periodicals, etc.

Talkies   A cinema film with speech and sound made during the period when most films were silent.

Tango   Dance genre originally from Buenos Aires, Argentina that found its way to the United States via Paris during the 1910s and 1920s, marking one of the first waves of exotic fascination that mainstream American audiences developed with Latin American music.

Tech Bubble   A pronounced and unsustainable market rise attributed to increased speculation in technology stocks. A tech bubble is highlighted by rapid share price growth and high valuations based on standard metrics like price/earnings ratio or price/sales.

Tejanos   Texan of Hispanic descent.

Telecommunications Act of 1996   The first major change in telecommunications law since the Communications Act of 1934. The legislation relaxed rules and regulations to influence greater competition among telephone, cable, and broadcast companies. Changes in broadcast ownership regulations allowed companies to own more stations in a community and nationally.

Telenovela   A soap opera produced in and televised in or from many Latin American countries.

Torcedores **and** *Tabaqueros*   Highly skilled tobacco workers who worked at Tampa's cigar factories in the early 1900s.

Treaty of Guadalupe Hidalgo   A treaty that ended the Mexican-American war that lasted from 1846 to 1848. The treaty gave the U.S. Mexican territories of what is now Arizona, California, Colorado, Nevada, New Mexico, Utah, and Wyoming. It also established the Río Grande as the border between Mexico and the U.S.

Ultra High Frequency (UHF) Stations   A radio frequency between super high frequency and very high frequency.

Underrepresented   To give inadequate representation to; represent in numbers that are disproportionately low.

Viewership   Estimates of how many people watch a TV program or network during an average specified time period.

Vlogger   A person who creates content for a blog that contains video material.

Weblogs   Also known as blogs, a website that contains online personal reflections, comments, and often hyperlinks, videos, and photographs provided by the writer.

Wepa Woman   NuyoRican superhero character, who is charged with cultural preservation among her beloved NuyoRicans.

Whitney Biennial   The longest running survey of contemporary art in the United States, with a history of exhibiting the most promising and influential artists and provoking lively debate. The exhibitions were initiated by Gertrude Vanderbilt Whitney in 1932.

Index